OBSERVING AND UNDERSTANDING CHILD DEVELOPMENT

A CHILD STUDY MANUAL

Join us on the web at

EarlyChildEd.delmar.com

OBSERVING AND UNDERSTANDING CHILD DEVELOPMENT

A CHILD STUDY MANUAL

DEB AHOLA

ABBE KOVACIK

DELMAR
CENGAGE Learning™

Australia • Brazil • Japan • Korea • Mexico • Singapore • Spain • United Kingdom • United States

DELMAR
CENGAGE Learning

Observing and Understanding Child Development: A Child Study Manual
Deb Ahola, Abbe Kovacik

Vice President, Career Education SBU:
Dawn Gerrain

Director of Learning Solutions:
Sherry Dickinson

Managing Editor: Robert L. Serenka, Jr.

Senior Acquisitions Editor: Erin O'Connor

Product Manager: Philip Mandl

Editorial Assistant: Stephanie Kelly

Director of Production: Wendy A.
Troeger

Production Manager: J. P. Henkel

Production Editor: Amber Leith

Technology Project Manager:
Sandy Charette

Director of Marketing: Wendy E.
Mapstone

Channel Manager: Kristin McNary

Cover Design: Joseph Villanova

Composition: ICC Macmillan Inc.

For product information and technology assistance, contact us at
Cengage Learning Customer & Sales Support, 1-800-354-9706

For permission to use material from this text or product,
submit all requests online at **www.cengage.com/permissions**
Further permissions questions can be emailed to
permissionrequest@cengage.com

Library of Congress Cataloging-in-Publication Data
Ahola, Deb.
  Observing and understanding child development: a child study manual /
Deb Ahola, Abbe Kovacik.
    p. cm.
  Includes bibliographical references and index.
  ISBN-13: 978-1-4180-1536-7
  ISBN-10: 1-4180-1536-9
  1. Child development—Handbooks, manuals, etc. I. Kovacik,
Abbe. II. Title.
  HQ772.A33 2007
  305.231—dc22
                                        2006000358

Delmar
10 Davis Drive
Belmont, CA 94002-3098
USA

Cengage Learning is a leading provider of customized learning solutions with office locations around the globe, including Singapore, the United Kingdom, Australia, Mexico, Brazil, and Japan. Locate your local office at: **international.cengage.com/region**

Cengage Learning products are represented in Canada by Nelson Education, Ltd.

For your lifelong learning solutions, visit **delmar.cengage.com**
Visit our corporate website at **cengage.com**

Join us on the Web at **EarlyChildEd.delmar.cengage.com**

Printed in the United States of America
6 7 8 11

Table of Contents

CHAPTER 14
SOCIAL, EMOTIONAL, AND CREATIVITY THEORY 270

Preface

From the child itself, she (the teacher) will learn to perfect herself as an educator.
—*Maria Montessori*

INTRODUCTION

Observing and Understanding Child Development is a simple, straightforward manual for examining the growth and development of individual children, yet it is comprehensive in nature. The book serves as a blueprint for looking at the child's unique development within the context of universal trends, cultural experience, and individual growth. One of our main goals in writing this book is to free the teacher or student from placing children into tiny boxes, facilitating a view of them instead as truly marvelous wonders.

This book emphasizes the interrelatedness of all the domains of development and gives the reader an authentic view of the whole child. Although not a great deal of time is spent on child development theorists, the book integrates many of them into the focus and interpretation of observation.

This observation manual was written with teacher preparation students in mind. Skills in observation and documentation are the cornerstone for planning for and interacting with young children. Teacher candidates, child development associate (CDA) candidates, and new teachers at the start of their careers will find this book immensely useful. Throughout our careers we have come to understand that an in-depth knowledge of child development is critical in order to function successfully as an educator of young children. In addition, many teacher preparation programs now require students to complete an in-depth assessment of one child before they can begin to assess the development of all the children in a given class. We sincerely believe that in order for a new teacher to fully understand how development affects the learning of an entire class, you must understand the individual child first.

We decided to write this book when we could not find one that was comprehensive enough to cover all the methods of observations, what to look for while observing, and then how to interpret the observations. Each semester we would hand out the child study project guidelines and be met with blank "deer in the headlights" looks from students. We quickly realized that in order for students to complete this type of project they needed step-by-step directions. For the past two years we have used the material in this book, and the results have been spectacular. We know that students now understand this process much better, and many students tell us that this project is more beneficial to them than anything else assigned to them in college. We hope you will feel the same upon completion of the child study project.

ORGANIZATION OF THE TEXT

The book is divided into four sections.

Part I, "Unlocking the Door: The Keys to Observation," gives an overview of the techniques used to observe children. Each chapter focuses on one particular method and includes examples of each. More importantly, you learn how to carry out the methods. This section is designed to give students the tools necessary to observe children from many different perspectives.

Part II, "Understanding Child Development: Developmental Concepts and Sequences," provides the student with multiple examples, anecdotal records, and tables of the prevalent concepts of development within the domains. The chapters are comprehensive, in that they include the major domains of development as well as creativity, artistic development, and literacy. This section is designed to give students the tools necessary to identify how the child is developing on the inside by observing outward behaviors.

Part III, "Interpreting Observations: Theoretical Perspectives," links the observations that are made with a recognized theory. We took the approach of supplying the concepts before the theory because we have found that without an understanding of what development really looks like, theories are irrelevant. So the student learns about object permanence and observes it before we talk about Piaget's theory of cognitive development. This section is designed to give the student the tools to be able to apply theory to observations.

Part IV, "Putting It All Together," gives the student step-by-step directions on how to write the reports of development and how to put all the pieces of the child study together in order to present it. Writing a comprehensive yet concise developmental domain report is a skill that many of us work on throughout our careers, yet it is imperative that we learn to communicate our findings to parents, colleagues, and other professionals. This section is designed to give the student the tools to write a complete and objective developmental report and present a comprehensive child study.

The chapters contain the following components:

- **Chapter Objectives** set the stage before reading so that concepts can be organized easily for note taking and the student knows the focus of the chapter.
- **Child Study Objectives** direct the student to what needs to be done at the conclusion of the chapter in order to keep up on the child study project.
- An **Introduction** to the major concept of the chapter is provided.
- Brain development sections are located in Part II of the book, providing the student with an understanding of how brain development affects the concepts presented in each chapter.

- The main concept of the chapter is broken down into components and each is explained using examples, tables, anecdotal records, and various diagrams and photos.
- The chapters in Parts II and III of the book have a **What to Look For** section that gives concrete examples of what to look for in a child's behavior when trying to identify concepts and theories.
- Parts I and II contain an **Of Special Interest** section that focuses on the development of children with special needs.
- **Questions to Consider** are found at the end of each chapter and are designed to promote in-depth discussions about the material within the chapter.

FEATURES OF THE TEXT

- Headings and subheadings reinforce chapter content and serve as pegs on which the reader can hang ideas, arrange notes, or build understanding.
- The running glossary calls out unfamiliar words and defines them immediately. Reading the glossary before the text helps to strengthen understanding of concepts during reading.
- Icons in the margin signify various components of content.

  The icon with arrows in a circle signifies that the information relates to cultural variations in the developmental concept or sequence being discussed.

  The star icon refers to topics of special interest, including developmental differences among children. Services and support for children and families with unique needs are included in the discussion.

  The CD icon indicates that related information, exercises, activities, or resources are available on the CD that accompanies this book.

SUPPLEMENT PACKAGE

This book is accompanied by a back-of-book CD-ROM with the following features:

- **Video Streams** that exemplify developmental concepts.
- **Exercises** that strengthen understanding of each chapter's concepts, including practice in writing anecdotal records, filling out checklists, identifying developmental concepts from children's samples, and more.
- **Child Study Activities** that relate directly to the objectives of completing the child study.
- **Resources** that will be useful in completing the child study, including checklists, Web sites, books, and videos.
- **Forms** you will need, such as consent to study, permission to take pictures, and assessment forms.
- **Child Study Outlines, Timelines,** and **Grading Rubrics.**

- Explanations of how the child study project relates to **National Standards** in the area of teacher education.
- **Structured Observation** exercises are provided for each concept of development.

ABOUT THE AUTHORS

Deb Ahola is currently an Associate Professor of Psychology and Early Childhood Education at Schenectady County Community College in New York. She holds an AAS in music from Illinois Valley Community College, a BS in Psychology from University of Illinois, and an MS in Special Education from Illinois State University. She is a certified special education teacher in New York and Illinois, and a certified Montessori directress. She has taught young children for the past 20 years in early childhood education settings, public schools, private schools, and early intervention agencies.

Abbe Kovacik is the mother of two wonderful sons who have influenced her understanding of child development. She is the education director at the Capital District Child Care Coordinating Council, Inc. in Albany, New York, where she serves as an instructor for a Child Development Associate (CDA) credential preparation program. Abbe also serves as adjunct faculty at Schenectady County Community College, teaching child development. She holds a BS in Psychology from Messiah College in Grantham, Pennsylvania, and a Master of Education in Educational Psychology from The College of Saint Rose in Albany, New York.

Mark Ahola, MM, MT-BC, LCAT, wrote Chapter 12—Creativity and Arts. He is currently a music therapist at Wildwood School in Schenectady, New York, serving children with neurological disabilities, autism, and other developmental disorders. He also teaches Creative Arts in Therapy at Russell Sage College, Troy, New York, and maintains a small private practice. Mark has a BA in LAS-Music from University of Illinois and an MM in Music Therapy from Illinois State University. He is a licensed creative arts therapist in New York State and a board certified music therapist. Mark has over 20 years of experience teaching and performing music.

ACKNOWLEDGMENTS

Thanks to all of those who helped with the success of this undertaking.

From Both of Us

Thanks to all of those at Delmar Cengage Learning who helped us through this challenging endeavor. This was a first for both of us and we could not have accomplished this without the support of Erin O'Connor, the guidance of Stephanie Kelly, and most of all the perseverance, patience, and understanding of our developmental editor, Philip Mandl.

From Abbe

Thanks to my husband Steve for pitching in and handling all the things I left undone while busy typing away. A great big thanks to my sons Aaron and Adin for their energy and good ideas. Aaron's computer savvy helped save time and reduced frustration—even when I managed to "lose" documents. Adin's careful editing as he scrutinized each anecdotal record and offered insight for jokes and activities was enormously helpful. I'd also like to thank colleagues at the Capital District Child Care Coordinating Council for their support and encouragement. Finally, I extend a special thanks to Deb for inviting me to join her in this interesting and exciting endeavor.

From Deb

To my colleagues at the college who had to continually hear me say, "I can't get to that right now," and to those who gave me consideration when it came to deadlines and committee work, I would like to say thank you over and over again. A special thanks goes to my husband, who pitched in and wrote a whole chapter to make this book exceptional, and to my son, who continually challenges me to rethink principles of development. I would like to thank the families of the Gateway Preschool for allowing me to share their children and their children's work with everyone who reads this book. Finally, I want to say how grateful I am that Abbe agreed to work on this with me. Without her insights and sense of serenity this would not have happened.

OVERVIEW OF THE CHILD STUDY PROJECT

This book is designed to give you, the student, the tools and the experience to complete an in-depth child study. The following is an overview of the project.

First, you will choose a child to study. In order to do this you will need to

- secure permission from the classroom teacher and the school principal to conduct the child study with the selected child.
- secure the parents' consent to work with and record information about the child.

Note: Explain that you are doing this research for a course in child development, that the child's name will not be used in the report, and that the main purpose of the report is to help you see the relationship between textbook knowledge of child development and real children. Also explain that you are not making a psychological evaluation of the child, nor do you plan to use the information as a classroom evaluation tool.

You will collect the information for your child study by using the research methods outlined below. All of these are explained in more depth in the chapters that follow.

Observe with Anecdotal Records

Observe the child on *five occasions* for an hour during an active play or learning time. You should try to be as unobtrusive as possible; you are not there to play with, or care for, the child. If the child wants to play, explain that you must sit and write for now and that you will play later.

Write down, minute by minute, everything the child does and that others do with the child. Be objective, focusing on behavior rather than interpretation. Thus, instead of writing "Jennifer was delighted when her father came home, and he dotes on her," you should write "5:33: Her father opened the door, Jennifer looked up, smiled, said 'dada,' and ran to him. He bent down, stretched out his arms, picked her up, and said, 'How's my little angel?'"

After your observation, *color code* your notes by developmental domain: Motor (Physical), Social, Emotional, Language/Literacy, Creative, and Cognitive. For example, observation notes regarding cognitive development could be coded red, notes demonstrating social development could be blue, etc.

Create and Acquire Assessment Instruments, Such As Checklists

Based on the criteria found in Chapter 3, "Checklists and Rating Scales," you will create a developmental assessment tool or checklist (with no fewer than 20 items per area of development). The assessment tool should be appropriate to the age and development of the child you have selected for the child study. Remember to create a base (several months below the child's chronological age) and a ceiling (several months above the child's chronological age). Create one tool each for: Cognitive Development, Social Development, Emotional Development, Language and Literacy Development, Physical (Fine and Gross Motor) Development, and Creative Development—six tools in all.

After you **submit** the created tool to the instructor and obtain approval, **administer** the checklist. Include the date the assessment was conducted and the child's exact age (e.g., 6.5 years) at the time of the assessment. Do not include the child's real name or other identifying information.

You will also find an existing checklist appropriate to the child you have selected for your child study. Select tools published by an educational organization for the purposes of developmental assessment. You will need to find one tool to assess each of the following areas: Cognitive Development, Social Development, Emotional Development, Language and Literacy Development, Physical (Fine and Gross Motor) Development, and Creative Development—six tools total. Submit the acquired tools to the instructor for approval prior to administration. Administer the checklists. Include the date the assessment was conducted and the child's exact age at the time of the assessment. Do not include the child's real name or other identifying information.

Create and Administer Structured Observations

Based on the child's age, developmental level, and interests, you will design a structured observation in order to delve into a developmental concept more closely. First, identify the concept you wish to look at more closely. Choose one for each of the six developmental domains listed previously. Then, identify the goals and objectives of the observation, conduct the observation, and assess the development.

Gather Visual Documentation

Throughout the study, you will collect pieces of visual documentation. Take pictures of the child engaging in activities that demonstrate concepts of development. Gather children's drawings, writing attempts, and so on, in order to demonstrate concepts of development.

Interview Families

You will create a parent questionnaire. Your goals are to learn the child's history, especially any illnesses, stresses, or problems that might affect development; the child's daily routine, including play patterns; current problems that might affect the child; and a description of the child's character and personality, including special strengths and weaknesses. Submit the questionnaire for instructor approval and then conduct the questionnaire.

When the child study is complete, it will be time to write the summary reports. Begin by reporting relevant background information, including the child's birth date, gender, age, siblings, economic and ethnic background of the family, and information about the parents or guardians. Describe the child's cognitive, social, emotional, language, and physical development (gross and fine motor), citing supporting data from your research to substantiate any conclusions you have reached. Predict the child's development in the next year. Support your ideas with theory and concepts from the text. List the strengths in the child, the family, and the community that you think will foster optimal development. Also, note whatever potential problems you see (either in the child's current behavior or in the family and community support system) that may lead to future difficulties for the child. Include a discussion of the reasons, either methodological or theoretical, that your predictions may not be completely accurate.

The summary report must be typed and include all areas of development. Remember to address how the child's religion, culture, and family traditions influence development.

I

UNLOCKING THE DOOR
The Keys to Observation

One can draw no specific rules for all this.
It depends on close observation in the particular case.

— William James, *Talks to Teachers on Psychology;*
and to Students on Some of Life's Ideals

1

Observation

CHAPTER OBJECTIVES

- To understand the difference between watching and observing
- To recognize the importance of observation
- To identify the steps to systematic observation
- To understand the nature of observation

CHILD STUDY OBJECTIVES

Upon conclusion of this chapter the student will:

- secure a binder or file folder that will be used to contain and organize observations, samples of development (pictures, children's works), and final reports
- identify a child who will be the subject of a study for the remainder of the semester
- obtain a consent form signed by the parent or legal guardian (a sample is found on the CD-ROM under forms)
- communicate with schools, child care centers, and families in order to set up a schedule of observations

INTRODUCTION TO OBSERVATION

This chapter focuses on the nature and value of observation. Concrete ways to begin observation are presented, and explanations about why we observe are emphasized. However, the primary objective of this chapter is to convince you, the student, that watching children is not the same as observing them, and that only by observing the developing child can we truly understand him. As one becomes proficient at observing children, each experience becomes pleasant and rewarding: pleasant because you have a bird's eye view of nature unfolding right before your eyes, and rewarding because by systematically observing you unlock the secrets of reaching and teaching children. Observing has been likened to an art form—it takes time to perfect but is well worth the effort.

WATCHING VS. OBSERVING

Many students who are studying psychology or sociology like to engage in an activity called "people watching." The steps of the New York City Public Library are a great place to watch people. You simply sit as unobtrusively as possible and watch hundreds or thousands (depending on how long you sit) of people walking, running, or strolling by. As people move past him or her, the devout people watcher will put a label on each person, such as "in a hurry," "upset with significant other," "definitely a tourist." If you have engaged in people watching, you know that quickly and without much reflection you will have made some sort of inference about each person you watch. Although you know absolutely nothing about the person, you think you have pegged him.

In reality, however, the person you thought was in a hurry may simply be someone who likes to move fast, the "upset with significant other" could very well be reflecting on a conversation she had with someone recently, and the "definitely a tourist" could be a city dweller who decided to take some pictures of one of the most magnificent cities in the world. The point is, you don't know! You have been watching, not observing.

In fact, what you will find is that the more intensely you focus on the object of your interest the less you will presume to know. As you watch the person more closely you find other characteristics that do not fit in with your original inference. Whereas your initial assessment of the person was an easy, one-dimensional view, you now have more information, which reveals the real complexity and multidimensionality of the person—the individual. Now you can no longer label them with a word or a phrase and you realize that in order to really know them you would need to systematically study them in a variety of settings and under many conditions. This is observation.

WHY OBSERVE?

The answer to this question is very basic. We observe a child in order to understand the true nature of the child. Once we understand the nature of the individual child in front of us we will be able to reach and teach that particular child. Observing the child

> ➤ *helps us understand who the child is.* Each child has her own temperament, motivations, fears, likes, dislikes, etc. It is important to become familiar with the whole child.

➤ *helps us to develop a relationship with the child.* Consider the people in your life that you trust most. Very likely they are people who know you and your individual needs. They understand why you do what you do. Relationships are built on trust, and children come to trust when their individual needs are met. Study after study (Brazelton & Cramer, 2001; Honig, 2001; Szewczyk-Sokolowski, Bost, & Wainwright, 2005) has found that the relationship between the teacher/caregiver and the child greatly impacts the child's learning, sense of self, motivation, and **emotional regulation.** The development of a strong, trusting, and respectful relationship is the foundation for all teaching.

➤ *helps us prepare and plan for the child.* A child goes through what Montessori (1964) termed "**sensitive periods.**" During these times the child is more apt to learn something new than at another later or earlier time. In order to know when a child is in a sensitive period, perhaps ready to learn to tie their shoes, say the sounds of the alphabet, or engage in conflict resolution, we must carefully observe the child and look for the signs that tell us the child is ready. Although some theories will tell us when a child is supposed to be learning certain skills and understanding specific concepts, we know that each child is on his own timetable. *Development is predictable as far as the sequence goes, but flexible as far as the timing goes.* Some children walk at 12 months, some at 8 months, and others at 15 months. We must know the signs so that our teaching occurs at the most opportune moments.

➤ *allows us to be* **action researchers** *or to practice* **pedagogics.** In order to know if what we are doing is working in any environment we must utilize the experimental method. Parsons and Brown (2002) call it becoming "Action Researchers."

➤ *alerts us to a child's special needs.* Working with young children requires a basic knowledge of possible disabling conditions and delays in development. Only through careful observation can we distinguish what is developmentally appropriate and what is in fact something to be concerned about.

SYSTEMATIC OBSERVATION

When planning a career that will involve working with children, the importance of **systematic observation** cannot be overstated. When we simply look at or watch the child, we interpret what we see from our own personal perspectives. One's own perspective is subjective and shaded primarily by one's own experiences. Thus, instead of

----

Emotional regulation.   The ability to control the expression and experience of emotions.

Sensitive periods.   Time frames during which the child is particularly sensitive to certain types of stimuli or interactions.

Action researcher.   One who uses a strategy of observation for planning purposes.

Pedagogics.   The science or profession of teaching.

Systematic observation.   Carrying out observations in a methodical and organized manner.

FIGURE 1–1 **Steps to systematic observation.**   ● ● ●

1. Identify the information you want to collect.
2. Identify the method(s) you are going to use to collect it.
3. Create a system to organize the information.
4. Create a schedule for observation.
5. Follow an observation schedule.

seeing the child in terms of what is really happening, we see what we expect to see. We must change our interpretation style from subjective to objective, or as Simpson and Tuson (2003) state, "we must 'make the familiar strange'—that is, to try to detach yourself from your own personal automatic interpretation of what is going on, and to try to see events from different perspectives" (p. 11). One of the most effective ways to do this is by engaging in systematic observation.

Systematic observation is habitually observing in a methodical and organized manner. In other words, you develop, organize, and follow a plan to observe. Figure 1–1 outlines the steps to systematic observation.

Applying Systematic Observation

This text is intended for application, so let's see how these steps to systematic observation can be applied to your child study project.

Steps to Systematic Observation

1. *Identify the information you want to collect.* You want to collect information that will provide a developmental profile of a particular child.

2. *Identify the method(s) you are going to use to collect it.* The methods that you will use are found in the remaining chapters of Part I of this text. You will use anecdotal records, checklists and rating scales, structured play observation procedures, and, finally, visual documentation to complete the profile.

3. *Create a system to organize the information.* You will use a binder or file folder in order to organize the information and materials and keep them secure.

4. *Create a schedule for observation.* One of your assignments for this chapter is to develop a schedule for observation with the parents, teachers, and other caregivers of the child. We recommend that you schedule at least six observations for 60–90 minutes each, in as many settings as possible.

5. *Follow an observation schedule.* Follow your schedule of observations. Make sure to carry out your observations as planned. If you are going to miss the observation for any reason, it is imperative that you contact the responsible person to let him or her know and to reschedule.

Now that we have identified the importance and method of systematic observation, it is necessary to discuss your role and responsibilities as an observer of young children.

THE NATURE OF OBSERVATION

Picture this: You are shopping at your favorite department store. As you are looking through the clothes, you glance up and notice a video camera (in fact, they are everywhere nowadays). Does your behavior change? Do you become more self-conscious about what you are doing? Even if you are not doing anything wrong, once you notice that someone might be watching you, the natural instinct is to check your behavior and possibly change it. No more talking to yourself—someone watching might think you're crazy!

This phenomenon is termed the **Hawthorne effect** and it means that once people know they are being watched they will change their behavior—perhaps subconsciously as well as consciously. How the person changes varies greatly, but nonetheless, change will take place. When we observe, we must remember that simply by observing a person, we have changed his or her normal behavior.

When entering an environment to observe a child, you, as an unknown person, will not only change the behavior of the one being observed, but all of those in the environment who know someone is watching, too. A chain reaction of changes is put into motion. Therefore, when you start to observe you must be as unobtrusive as possible. You must try to blend in as best you can; certainly do not call attention to yourself.

At this point many students of child development will ask, "Should I interact with the child if he wants me to?" The answer is "No." In fact, you should not interact with any of the children that are in the environment. Initially, you will want to observe the child in his natural environment engaging in typical activities without any interference, and you will want to put all your energies into observing the child. Even the most skilled observer finds it difficult to focus on the child if he or she is interacting and reacting to him. Later in this book we will be discussing methods of observation that require us to interact with the child and even manipulate the environment to view specific behaviors, but you must remember that by doing so you will have altered the natural response pattern of the child.

OBSERVATION ETIQUETTE

As an observer you must remember this: You are a guest. No matter where the observation is taking place, you are entering into this child's environment and you must behave professionally. Figure 1–2 gives the steps to practicing proper observation etiquette.

Confidentiality

It is a great privilege to be allowed into the life of a child and her family. You must respect that and take responsibility for what it means to practice confidentiality. The parent or caregivers trust that you will not share any information about their child with *anyone*. This point cannot be emphasized enough. When referring to the child in your study, use a fictitious name; when referring to the other children, use notations such as

---

Hawthorne Effect.   A change in someone's behavior due to that person's knowledge of being watched or studied.

FIGURE 1–2   Observation etiquette.

1. Seek permission in writing from parent/family, school administrator, and child.
2. Sign in and out. Provide proper identification. All visitors to schools, child care centers and group family homes should sign in and out on a log provided for that purpose. Additionally, observers should wear a badge with proper identification so that others know that they are visiting the program with permission.
3. Conduct yourself in a professional manner. Arrive to observations on time, fully prepared, and appropriately dressed.
4. Respect the role of other adults present during the observation. The observer should avoid "tampering" with the natural setting by spending undue time discussing the child with the teacher or parent/family during observation. Avoid offering teaching or guidance instruction. Avoid judging the teacher, family, or program.
5. Respect the child. Understand that the child may feel unsure about your presence in their environment. Never enter play without being invited by the child. Never take the child out of the setting.
6. Keep all information about children and families confidential.
7. If you believe that practices may be harmful to children, take those concerns directly to your instructor and do not discuss them with anyone else.

Boy A and Girl B. Never discuss the parents or caregivers with other families, students, teachers, or professors. Remember, you are a guest—don't abuse the privilege.

TAKE THE FIRST STEP

Some of you may be well-versed in doing observations or have been around children a great deal and will be able to go right into a child's environment and begin the process without any sort of preliminary preparation. However, if you are not a person with some observation under your belt or you are not yet used to being around children, it would be a good idea to go into a child's environment and do some informal observing. In Chapter 2 you will be given your first formal observation task of writing anecdotal records, and you may need to get acclimated to a child's environment before you perform that task.

Of Special Interest—Assessing Children with Special Needs

A United States law called the Individuals with Disabilities Education Act (IDEA) ensures that children with special needs will receive the necessary services to help them reach their full potential, free to the family. Originally, these services were limited to children ages 5–18 (school-age) and to the area of education. So a seven-year-old child with mental retardation would be placed in a classroom with other children with special needs, and the special education teacher would teach things like basic math and reading.

FIGURE 1–3   **Basic service goals for early intervention.**

- To support families in achieving their own goals
- To promote child engagement, independence, and mastery
- To promote development in all domains
- To build and support children's social competence
- To promote the generalized use of skills
- To provide and prepare for normalized life experiences
- To prevent the emergence of future problems or disabilities

Source: Bailey and Wolery (1992)

Things began changing, however, when the law was expanded. Now children from birth to five years of age are also covered, and the services range from physical therapy to family support. Essentially, the law says that public health agencies and local school districts need to work together to

➤ *identify* children with special needs early.

➤ design and carry out *individualized* programs for the identified child.

➤ *monitor* the child's progress and modify the program if necessary.

Of course the law is much more complex than this and has many other provisions, but these three directives involve **evaluation** and **assessment**—which are the focus of this manual.

Public health organizations and local school districts must identify children with special needs as early as possible. This provision of IDEA is called **Child Find.** It is very important to identify a child as early as possible, because a child with a disability has a much better chance of leading a typical life if he and his family participate in **early intervention.** Figure 1–3 presents the basic service goals for early intervention. A child suspected of having a disability, or who is at risk for developing one, will be referred to an agency that will evaluate the child in order to establish **eligibility.** If the child has a

Evaluation.   In the context of services supported by the Individuals with Disabilities Education Act (IDEA), evaluation refers to a procedure that is used to determine a child's eligibility for early intervention services.

Assessment.   The ongoing process by which qualified professionals, together with families, look at all areas of a child's development through standardized tests and observation. Both areas of strength and those requiring support and intervention are identified.

Child Find.   Under IDEA, a program intended to identify, locate, and evaluate/assess preschool children with potential developmental delays or disabilities. In some areas it may be called screening.

Early intervention.   Refers to the range of services designed to enhance the development of infants, toddlers, and preschool children with disabilities or at risk of developmental delay.

Eligibility.   Under IDEA this means that a child is entitled to, or qualifies for, receiving early intervention/educational services.

diagnosed physical or mental condition or is experiencing a **developmental delay** he is considered eligible for free services such as special education, physical or occupational therapy, speech therapy, music therapy, and more. In addition, some states provide services for children who may be "**at risk**" for developmental delay. *At risk* means that the child has a condition, or is in an environment that increases the chances of developing a disability.

After eligibility has been established, agencies and local school districts must now assess the child in order to develop a plan for intervention. In other words, they must determine what kind of program would work best for the child, and they must establish goals and objectives for the child.

For children from birth to three years of age, an **Individualized Family Service Plan (IFSP)** will be designed. For children older than three, an **Individualized Education Plan (IEP)** will be designed.* In order to develop these plans, members of a **multidisciplinary team** will test and observe the child to determine her strengths and needs; in the case of the IFSP, they determine the needs of the family as well. The speech/language therapist working with a four-year-old boy might find that he needs speech therapy three times a week and that the therapy should be given in his preschool classroom. In addition, the therapist would write goals to help her acquire the skills and abilities necessary to reach appropriate developmental levels in the area of communication. The social worker might determine that the family of the 18-month-old boy she is

---

*In some areas the Individualized Family Service Plan will be developed for children ages three to five as well as from birth to three.

....

Developmental delay.   A term used when a child has not achieved skills and abilities that children of the same age are expected to master. It can also mean a diagnosed physical or mental condition that has a high probability of resulting in a developmental delay. Some examples include chromosomal abnormalities like Down syndrome, sensory impairments like deafness, and disorders caused by exposure to toxic substances like fetal alcohol syndrome (FAS).

At risk.   A term used for a child when a physical or mental condition is present or when the child is in an environment that increases the chances of developing a disability.

Individualized Family Service Plan (IFSP).   A contract-like document outlining the plan for infants and toddlers with special needs and their families. The plan generally covers the young child's development in the five domains, the goals and objectives for the family and child, and the services that will be used in order to reach those goals and objectives.

Individualized Education Plan (IEP).   A contract-like document outlining the educational program for a child with special needs. The plan generally includes the goals and objectives for the child, the special services that will be given, the plan for monitoring the child's progress, and specific accommodations that will be given to the child in the general education classroom.

Multidisciplinary team.   A group of people with different kinds of training and experience who work together, usually on an ongoing basis. A multidisciplinary team might include a pediatrician, an occupational therapist, a speech therapist, a social worker, and an early childhood special education teacher.

TABLE 1-1   Goals set as part of a child's intervention plan.

Developmental Domain	Possible Goals
Social Competence	Interact with peers Participate in group activities Establish attachments
Communication Skills	Initiate conversations Participate in conversations Express wants and needs Produce understandable speech
Prosocial Behaviors	Respond appropriately to adults Manage emotions appropriately Develop empathy
Motor Development	Coordinate movements Develop balance Grasp writing utensils
Self-Help Skills	Toilet independently Feed independently Dress independently
Cognitive/Readiness Skills	Use problem-solving techniques Identify numbers and letters Acquire pre-reading skills

working with needs to learn an alternative type of communication system so they can enhance his language development. Table 1–1 presents some of the common areas for which goals are written.

Finally, after the plan has been put in motion, progress needs to be monitored. To that end, teachers, doctors, and therapists will conduct more tests and observations to see if the child is in fact reaching the goals put forth in the IEP or the IFSP. If proper progress has been made, new goals are formulated that reflect that progress. If the anticipated progress has not been made, then the team must reassess the situation and determine what should be changed in order for the goals to be reached.

The Limitations of Standardized Testing

As you can see, children with special needs are subject to a great deal of evaluation and assessment. Many tests used to identify children with special needs are **standardized tests.** For example, the Bayley Scales of Infant Development, Second Edition (BSID-II;

Standardized tests.   Norm-referenced sets of criteria designed to assess development.

Bayley, 1993) is a standardized test commonly used to determine the cognitive level of young children. By using this type of test a child's cognitive ability can be compared with other children the same age. If she tests very low, it might be said that she is below average and possibly eligible for services.

Although standardized tests are still used for determining eligibility, there has been much criticism about using them for designing interventions and monitoring progress. Criticisms include:

- The test is given to the child in an unfamiliar and unappealing environment.
- To the examiner giving the test to the child is a stranger, unfamiliar to him.
- There are specific instructions on how to play with unfamiliar toys.
- The test is usually a question-and-answer format with which the child may have minimal experience or ability.
- Examiners (those giving the tests) cannot deviate from the administration procedures dictated in the test manual. Thus, they cannot accommodate the potentially different needs of children with disabilities.
- The tests may be biased against children with disabilities, as they require use of language and motor skills that these children may not possess at the time of the evaluation.
- Children with communication or physical impairments may not be adequately assessed for other strengths they possess, because they cannot demonstrate these skills in a test-taking environment.
- Although standardized tests are generally used in determining eligibility, they were not developed to define intervention needs or monitor progress and, therefore, should not be used for these purposes.

Play-Based Assessment As Best Practice

The limitations of standardized tests have prompted professionals in the field to identify better ways to assess all children, but particularly those with special needs. One method that has been shown to be very valuable is called *play-based assessment*. An organization called Zero to Three defines play-based assessment as:

> A form of developmental assessment that involves observation of how a child plays alone, with peers, or with parents or other familiar caregivers, in free play or in special games. This type of assessment can be helpful because play is a natural way for children to show what they can do, how they feel, how they learn new things, and how they behave with familiar people (Zero to Three, 2005).

Play-based assessment is considered a much more valid method to assess children with special needs. Figure 1–4 gives the reasons why play-based assessment is a preferred method for choosing interventions and monitoring the progress of children with special needs.

The following scenario exemplifies how the problems with standardized testing are solved with play-based assessment.

Twenty-two-month-old Jaime has been receiving early intervention services for the past six months and is due for a formal assessment before the next team meeting. He

FIGURE 1-4   **Benefits of play-based assessment.**   ● ● ●

➢ Play observations provide an opportunity to assess the functional behavior of a young child who either cannot or will not perform in a formal testing situation. Many children "freeze up" when taken out of their natural environments and away from trusted adults and thus do not show what they really know or feel.

➢ Because of the flexibility and spontaneity of a play situation, infants and toddlers may achieve a level of object or symbolic play that they did not demonstrate on standardized assessments. Because play is the "window into the child's learning" much more can be seen from simply watching them rather than asking them to perform.

➢ Play observations can provide important insights into temperamental variables. The child's real self is displayed during play.

➢ Play observation can reveal aspects of the parent-child relationship that help explain the behavior of the child. Play-based assessment brings in the parents as team members.

➢ Play observation can provide insights into all developmental domains of the child. As a child is playing she demonstrates language/communication, social, emotional, physical, creative, and cognitive skills, all at the same time.

➢ Play observations can be used for play-based interventions. These assessments automatically dictate interventions.

Taken in part from Segal and Webber (1996)

has been labeled developmentally delayed and goes to a preschool five days a week for three hours a day in an **inclusive classroom.** A speech therapist and an occupational therapist both work with Jaime about three hours per week, sometimes in his home and sometimes in his classroom. A **speech pathologist** from the county health department has been assigned to do the formal assessment of Jaime. The speech pathologist goes to Jaime's preschool classroom and asks his teacher if there is anywhere quiet they can go in order to do the testing. The classroom teacher directs them to a small corner of the classroom away from the other children. After the speech pathologist sets up her testing, she goes to Jaime to bring him over to her table. Jaime does not want to go—he is playing with his friends. He cries a bit but his classroom teacher convinces him to go over and "play" with this person. When Jaime gets over to the testing area he begins picking up every toy the speech pathologist has set out. After about ten minutes Jaime sits down in the chair. The speech pathologist pulls out a cup and asks Jaime, "What is this?" Jaime looks at her, takes the cup, and throws it across the room. The speech pathologist marks something down on her paper and moves to the next question.

Because the speech pathologist cannot give any kinds of prompts, she had to write down that Jaime did not know *cup.* Furthermore, he did not know what it was used for; his score on intelligence and language development will reflect this.

....

Inclusive classroom.   Education term used to describe learning environments in which students demonstrate a wide range of ability and developmental levels. These classrooms contain children of typical development as well as those with identified developmental concerns.

Speech pathologist.   A professional therapist who evaluates and treats speech and language concerns, including expressive language skills, auditory skills, reading, writing, and cognitive comprehension.

The classroom teacher, having read the report, could not believe that Jaime did not know what *cup* was and what it was used for. So she decided to observe Jaime playing in the housekeeping section of the classroom. It only took about three minutes before she observed Jaime sitting down at the table with the cups and other utensils and using them appropriately. In addition, when Jaime wanted a new cup, he pointed to a cup across the table and said, "Me cup."

Obviously Jaime knew what a cup was and how to use it, but he could not show this on a standardized test. If the classroom teacher had not done her own play-based assessment, knowing the word *cup* and what it was used for might have become a goal for the therapists to work on, thus wasting a great deal of time.

How Play-Based Assessments Are Conducted

There are basically three types of play-based assessments:

- Nonstructured
- Structured
- Transdisciplinary

The purpose of *nonstructured assessments* is to identify all behaviors that occur during a play session. So the assessor, possibly with one other person, observes the child during a play session and notes all that is seen. In many cases, the assessors will watch a parent playing with the child. A *structured assessment,* however, focuses on a previously designed set of play behaviors, using specific play items and eliciting specific behaviors. *Transdisciplinary assessment* involves a team of assessors observing the child at the same time. In most cases, the observations are structured because each team member is looking for specific information. For example, the speech/language therapist would be looking for how the child communicates during play and might have to initiate some type of interaction or set up a certain play scenario.

Summing Up Play-Based Assessment

When assessing children with special needs, play-based assessment has become the method of choice, because it tends to give us a more accurate picture of the child. In addition, play-based assessment drives intervention. One of the main goals of early intervention is to give the child the tools she will need to function in a typical environment. It only makes sense, then, to watch how she functions in her natural environment and then work on what she needs. We certainly do not want to waste precious time on skills a child has already attained or that are not meaningful to her particular culture.

QUESTIONS TO CONSIDER   ○ ○ ○

1. What are the barriers to conducting ongoing, objective observations of children? How can they be overcome?
2. As a teacher of young children, what percentage of time in the classroom should be spent observing: ten percent, twenty percent, more, less? Why?

REFERENCES ○ ○ ○

Bailey, D. B., & Wolery, M. (1992). *Teaching infants and preschoolers with disabilities* (2nd ed.). Upper Saddle River, NJ: Prentice Hall.

Bayley, N. (1993). *Bayley scales of infant development* (2nd ed.). San Antonio, TX: Harcourt Assessment, Inc.

San Antonio, TX: Harcourt Assessment.

Brazelton, T. B., & Cramer, B. G. (2001). *Earliest relationship: Parents, infants, and the drama of early attachment.* New York: Perseus.

Honig, A. S. (2001). *Secure relationships: Nurturing infant/toddler attachment in early care settings.* Washington, DC: National Association for the Education of Young Children.

Montessori, M. (1964). *The Montessori method.* New York: Schocken Books.

Parsons, R. D., & Brown, K. (2002). *Teachers as reflective practitioners and action researchers.* Belmont, CA: Wadsworth.

Segal, M., & Webber, N. T. (1996). Nonstructured play observations: Guidelines, benefits, and caveats. In S. J. Meisels & E. Fenichel (Eds.), *New visions for the developmental assessment of infants and young children* (pp. 207–230). Washington, DC: Zero to Three National Center for Infants, Toddlers and Families.

Simpson, M. & Tuson, J. (2003). *Using observations in small-scale research: A beginner's guide* (Rev. ed.). Glasgow Scotland: University of Glasgow, SCRE Centre.

Szewczyk-Sokolowski, M., Bost, K. K., & Wainwright, A. B. (2005). Attachment, temperament, and preschool children's peer acceptance. *Social Development, 14*(13), 379–397.

Zero to Three National Center for Infants, Toddlers and Families. Retrieved August 1, 2005, from http://www.zerotothree.com

Anecdotal Records

CHAPTER OBJECTIVES

- To understand the nature of anecdotal records

- To distinguish between objective and subjective recordings

- To understand the importance of objective recording

- To write objective and informative anecdotal recordings

CHILD STUDY OBJECTIVES

Upon conclusion of this chapter the student will:

- observe the child for one complete session

- write two or three running records of the child

- write two or three anecdotal records of the child

INTRODUCTION TO ANECDOTAL RECORDING

In this chapter we will explore the first of the recording methods that you will utilize in this child study. Because this method allows the nature of the child to unfold in front of you, it is probably one of the most, if not *the* most effective tool you will use in your study of children.

An **anecdotal record** is used to develop an understanding of a child's behavior, perhaps for the purpose of understanding a developmental concern, or to communicate aspects of a child's development to a parent. Observations recorded as anecdotal records can guide a teacher's capacity to learn how a child acts, reacts, and interacts, casting light on the mysterious workings of the child. The most direct and obvious way to find out what children know and understand is to listen and observe closely as they play.

THE NATURE OF AN ANECDOTAL RECORD

The anecdotal record has been likened to a short story. As Billman and Sherman (2003) state, "Anecdotes tell stories. Stories are inherently interesting, and all cultures use them to communicate information. . . . Anecdotes have a beginning, middle, and an end" (pp. 22–23).

ANECDOTAL RECORD 2–1

Child's Name: Brianna

Date: October 15

Time: 9:48 a.m.

Observer: D. Ahola

Location: Gateway Montessori Classroom

Brianna is playing with the natural wood blocks on her rug in the middle of the classroom. She takes all the blocks off the shelf one at a time, placing the rectangular blocks together, the triangle blocks together, the square blocks together, and two different sized arches together. As she begins to stack the rectangular blocks on top of each other she glances over at the picture of the Sears Tower, which is right next to the block shelf. After looking at the picture for about 10 seconds she looks back at her rug and takes apart her block creation. She then begins to rebuild the structure, this time making a sort of foundation using the square blocks on the bottom and then turning the rectangular blocks on their sides to make them taller. After placing six blocks for the foundation and four blocks for the tower she looks up and makes eye contact with the nearby adult and says, "Lut, I made that" (pointing to the picture).

....

Anecdotal record.   A brief, factual, objective narrative, written after an event. When viewed sequentially, anecdotal records should reveal insights into a child's developmental progress.

Building the Sears Tower

The anecdote, then, is a brief account of what the child is doing, saying, and how she is reacting. It is a snapshot of the child's development that can tell us a great deal about her development in all areas.

An anecdotal record contains

- identifying information: child's name, date of observation, time of observation, name of observer, and the setting.
- description of the child's actions.
- direct quotes from the child (notice Brianna pronounced *look* as "lut").
- nonevaluative language to describe the child's actions.

THE ADVANTAGES OF USING ANECDOTAL RECORDS

> *The anecdotal record allows us to view the child's behavior within the context in which it is happening.* All behavior must be interpreted within the realm of its context. For example, many of us have had the experience of seeing a block fly across the classroom. We know that in order to interpret the child's behavior we need to see what was happening before, during, and after that event. Was the child experimenting? Problem solving? Imitating? Modeling?

> *The anecdotal record allows us to view what are the most important and significant events without any preconceived ideas about what we "should" be seeing* (see Figure 2–1). When we use checklists and other kinds of rating scales, or when we conduct various tests or screening tools, we are focused on a specific behavior. Many other behaviors that may be much more significant are lost to us. That particular snapshot of the child is gone, maybe forever. In order for us to really

FIGURE 2-1 "Hey Frankie, do you see that amazing dodo bird?"
"No way, I'm looking for a finch!"

understand the nature of each individual child, we must be able to observe without little boxes that inhibit our thinking and understanding of the child.

➤ *The anecdotal record allows us to view actual development of the child, and in the case of children with special needs this is especially helpful.* Children with special needs are typically not going to fit into our tests, checklists, or rating scales. Because their development in certain areas is atypical, we are not going to be able to correctly interpret the behaviors of children with special needs, because they cannot be held to the same norms as children with typical development. This does not mean, however, that we can ignore their progress. In fact, it becomes more imperative for us to continually monitor the progress they do make. We must choose methods and particular interventions that tend to enhance their development.

The nuts and bolts of anecdotal recording

1. Anecdotal recording is conducted in the natural setting. Avoid the temptation to manipulate the environment or play situation in order to "capture" what you hope to see.
2. Always identify the child by name or initials, date of birth, and date of the observation. Note: If the anecdotal data are going to be shared with others—for example in a child study—use a fictitious name. Record the time of day, setting, and partners (again, use fictitious names). Write down exactly what other children say to the child being observed. Attending to the context will ensure that behavior is not isolated from the events that have influenced it.
3. Beginning observers may find it helpful to create criteria or questions as a guide for their notes (Mindes, 2003). The High/Scope curriculum uses a framework of "key experiences" from which the teacher can observe children. The key experiences guide

observation, helping the teacher to uncover specific components of development, such as initiative, motor skills, language, and creative representation. Observers may choose to select questions pertaining to the child's mood, problem-solving style, arrival rituals, etc.

4. Attend to detail so that you can later recreate the entire "story" for interpretation. For example, "Meghan ate three slices of toast for breakfast" is a bit too sketchy. All you can glean from such a brief note is that Meghan may have a good appetite. Details describing how she selected the breakfast item, if she spread butter or jelly with a knife, or whether she cut the toast or shared it with a friend provide much more information for later interpretation.

5. Anecdotal notes should be exact. Record events in the order they occur. For example, if Adam arrived at the classroom with a tear-stained face, it is important to note the obvious crying in the correct order, rather than writing "Adam cried this morning when he arrived."

6. Be aware of your own bias. Avoid reporting an event in a manner that colors how it appears. For example: "Bob demonstrated aggression. He pushed Joe while standing in line and stepped on his feet. He laughed as he bumped Joe with his shoulder." Although Bob's behavior is socially associated with aggression, the observer cannot be sure that the intent of the bumping, pushing, and stepping is aggression and not perhaps unsophisticated attempts at friendship, instead.

7. Inferences and interpretations made by the observer are kept separate so as not to create bias. Use objective language and avoid subjective terms such as disruptive, argumentative, cute, lovable, or mischievous, to name a few.

8. Keep notepads or large mailing labels and pens readily available for convenient note-taking. Post-it notes are great for taking anecdotal notes. Develop a system for taking notes that works for you. It may be helpful to create a guide or template with questions or concepts you plan to observe.

9. Be unobtrusive during observations. Avoid disturbing children's play or work.

10. Keep information about children confidential. Information about the child should never be shared with any unauthorized individual.

WRITING THE ANECDOTAL RECORD: JUST THE FACTS

When writing anecdotal records, there are two key words to remember: *objective* and *detailed*. In order to write the anecdotal record with these two concepts in mind, remember to

- make sure you are only recording what you see and not what you *think* you see.
- use nonjudgmental/nonevaluative language.
- record *what* you see, not what you don't see.
- record as many details as possible.

I tell my students when they are embarking on the task of writing their first anecdotal record to keep it simple and record just the facts. Remember the discussion from Chapter 1 regarding the unfolding of the child. The task of the observer is not to judge

| FIGURE 2-2 | Examples of judgmental language. | ● ● ● |

BAD	SMART	BRIGHT	
SLOW (unless used as an adjective for movement)			
DELAYED	BEHIND (unless used as a preposition)		
SAD	FRUSTRATED	CHAOTIC	DELIBERATE
GOOD	INTELLIGENT		
NORMAL			
RIGHT (unless it is used as opposed to left)		WRONG	

or to evaluate, but simply to represent an event as it occurred. This is the overriding premise of writing down anecdotal data. This is not the time or place to make inferences about what you see—simply record your observations. Avoid the temptation to analyze or evaluate events. Doing so can result in a misunderstanding of the child's development. Reflection and evaluation will come later, once the anecdotal data have provided the framework for understanding how the unique child's development unfolds.

Judgmental and Evaluative Language

One way to begin this process is to become aware of judgmental or evaluative language that you may be using. Figure 2–2 presents examples of words or phrases that are judgmental or evaluative.

Labeling Emotions   Another thing to be aware of is labeling an overt sign, such as a smile or frown, with an emotion. When a child smiles it does not necessarily mean she is happy. Likewise, if she frowns, it could mean something else besides being mad or sad. You must record what you see from the child, not what you think you see. Anecdotal records are an accurate account of a particular event, not your overall impression of the event.

Think of an anecdotal record in terms of describing a picture to someone who is unable to see it. In a sense, you are doing just that. Everyone who reads your anecdotal record should have the same picture in their heads after they read it; then each person can interpret it in his or her own way. You must create a picture that is clear and free of ambiguity. Using judgmental or evaluative language clouds the picture. Compare the photo on this page and the photo on the following page. In which photo can you tell what is

really happening and in which do you have to infer what is happening?

When judgmental or evaluative language is used in an anecdotal record, the person reading it will have a distorted picture of the event—a picture created by someone else. It is like asking your friend to read using your glasses. The use of judgmental or evaluative language clouds reality and presents the event with the observer's impressions, biases, or values.

The following is an example of an anecdotal record that used evaluative language.

ANECDOTAL RECORD 2–2

Child's name: Madeline

Date: November 10

Time: 10:17 a.m.

Observer: D. Ahola

Location: Gateway Montessori Preschool

Madeline runs over to the art area—she is really happy. She likes to draw with the markers but she scribbles instead of draws. She can't make anything recognizable yet. She is very secretive about her drawing. She might feel self-conscious about it because some of the other children are already drawing houses and flowers. When the teacher passes by her, she whines to her and says she can't draw her mommy.

A better, nonevaluative anecdotal record would read more like Anecdotal Record 2-3.

ANECDOTAL RECORD 2–3

Madeline moves quickly over toward the art area. While she is gathering her five markers—all different colors—she is smiling and bobbing her head up and down. She sits down at the table and begins using the markers with a tripod-like grasp, in which her fingertips touch the edge of the marker. As she is drawing with the red marker, then the blue, several children stop by her table and she turns away from them and continues to draw. After the children move away from her table she turns back around in her chair and continues drawing. The teacher begins to walk past her and she says to the teacher, "Miss Deb will draw my mommy for me?" The teacher says, "I can help you draw her."

Details, Details, Details

As stated earlier, anecdotal notes are prompt and accurate. Documenting an observation promptly aids recall and preserves important details. As you are writing the anecdotal record, reenact the scenario in your mind and record every movement you remember and everything the child said, word for word. Think of it like a forensics team trying to solve a case. The typical investigation involves uncovering clue after clue until one specific detail is uncovered. That detail then completes the entire picture, thus allowing the team to solve the case. We want to create an entire picture of the child and every detail matters.

THE RUNNING RECORD

Another type of recording method useful in the study of children is the *running record*. Whereas an anecdotal record is produced after the fact, a running record is written at the same time the behavior is occurring. First-time observers may find it helpful to practice with the running record technique in order to develop their skills in anecdotal recording. The running record is beneficial because it allows us to record minute details, but it is not considered practical when trying to collect a great deal of information about a child. Nonetheless, it is a good tool for you to begin to hone your observational abilities.

The running record can focus on the behavior of one child or the events of an entire group. Noting action and interaction for short periods of time allows the observer to gather more specific information. Observations made over a much longer period of time are generally broader in scope. The short "clips" of the running record may uncover developmental concerns, program issues, or environmental concerns. The following example demonstrates a running record.

RUNNING RECORD 2–1

Child's Name: Billy

Date: November 2

Time: 11 a.m.

Observer: D. Ahola

Location: Pumpkin Patch Child Care Center, four-year-olds' classroom

Billy is in the block area with Tanner, Emily, and Nyisha. B. empties a medium-sized, clear toy storage container filled with small cars onto the floor of the block area. He picks up a blue car and turns it over. He examines the tires. E. says, "It has a flat." B. puts the car down as E. hands him a silver car. E. says, "Another flat." B. examines the flat tire. He pushes the silver car with the flat along the rug. "It's a Chevy," he reports. N. clears a path with her hands separating the cars into two piles. N. says, "Let's make a road." B. moves to the low storage shelf of wooden unit blocks. He takes two long, rectangular blocks off the shelf. With a block in each hand B. crawls on his knees to the car pile. "I have the road—let's start," he says looking at N. B. places the blocks on the carpet. N. moves the blocks that B. placed on the rug slightly to the left. T. takes two cars from the pile—one black and one white. He places the black car into his mouth, still holding the end with his left hand. E. quickly steps forward and places her hand on the black car. She says, "No, Tanner, you are too little to play with the car." She takes the white and black cars from T. and turns her back to him. 11: 07 a.m.

As you can see, this is very detailed and difficult to do for long periods of time. However, the running record does capture everything the child is doing and does it objectively.

Of Special Interest—Using Anecdotal Records to Assess Children with Special Needs and Identify Appropriate Interventions

As discussed in Chapter 1, the use of play-based assessment has grown in popularity for children with special needs, because it can give us a much more accurate view of the child's development and general functional abilities. Specifically, the use of anecdotal records can also give us a great deal of information about how to enhance a child's development. We can observe the child in a variety of settings, engaging in a variety of activities, and therefore determine where, when, and how to intervene most effectively. Consider the following example.

Kevin was a four-year-old boy with mental retardation in my inclusive preschool classroom. Kevin appeared to have no verbal expressive communication skills. When asked questions, he would smile, nod his head, or point to something that might have a relationship to what someone had just said. We never heard him speak, however. We began to do anecdotal recordings of him. One day while observing him at the doll washing (one of his favorite activities), I saw his mouth move a bit. Getting as close as I could without interfering with his work, I heard soft sounds coming from him.

Each day we would watch Kevin closely and each of us would take anecdotal records. After one week we came together with our anecdotal records and discovered that a pattern had emerged. One of us had a record that showed Kevin was speaking while he was playing next to another child at the sink-and-float table, another one caught Kevin making soft sounds while he was washing his favorite outside toy (the tractor), and still another heard Kevin repeating words other children were saying while he was at the water table. Of course, it was right in front of us; when he was working in water he would use expressive language—he would talk.

From that point on we offered more water play to Kevin, during which we tried to get more language from him, and sure enough, it came. Without careful anecdotal observation we may never have seen this pattern.

This is but one example of how anecdotal recording can help to determine a child's actual development (before this, many thought Kevin would be incapable of producing functional speech) and, more importantly, help to capitalize on the child's interests, in order to enhance his or her development.

 Now that you have finished this instruction on anecdotal recording, go to the CD-ROM and view the Anecdotal Record as an example.

QUESTIONS TO CONSIDER ○ ○ ○

1. Compare and contrast anecdotal records with running records. In what cases would the running record be more appropriate than the anecdotal record? When would anecdotal records be more useful?

2. Describe practical applications of anecdotal records, such as in the area of planning or monitoring progress.

REFERENCES ○ ○ ○

Billman, J., & Sherman, J. (2003). *Observation and participation in early childhood settings: A practicum guide* (2nd ed.). Boston: Allyn & Bacon.

Mindes, G. (2003). *Assessing young children* (2nd ed.). Upper Saddle River, NJ: Prentice Hall.

Checklists and Rating Scales

CHAPTER OBJECTIVES

- To identify the purposes of checklists and rating scales

- To analyze the appropriateness of different rating scales and checklists

- To understand the uses and misuses of checklists and rating scales

- To identify sources of valid and reliable checklists and rating scales

- To create an appropriate checklist or rating scale

CHILD STUDY OBJECTIVES

Upon conclusion of this chapter the student will:

- identify and obtain one checklist for each domain of development (physical, gross motor, fine motor, cognitive, social, emotional, creative art, and language and literacy)

OVERVIEW OF CHECKLISTS AND RATING SCALES

Checklists and rating scales are additional means for gathering information about a child's development. These formal assessments typically measure the child's developmental performance against a set of predetermined criteria.

The Nature of Checklists and Rating Scales

Unlike anecdotal records, checklists and rating scales have a defined scope. In other words, we look at specific skills and abilities.

Checklists are generally used when there are many behaviors or skills to be observed. They may include:

- descriptive characteristics such as developmental traits
- social/emotional behaviors or skills
- the child's interests
- specific academic skills
- specific knowledge of concepts

The observer marks the child's performance on each criterion on a list. These are called items or, in some cases, **descriptors.** Checklists generally allow the rater no more than two choices for each item, such as met or unmet.

Rating scales are used to describe the degree to which behaviors or traits are believed to be present. Since the rating scale measures degrees of performance, it is appropriately used to understand conduct, motivation, and effort. Administration of rating scales can be by observation, interview, or direct administration. Unlike a checklist, a rating scale offers the observer more than two choices and often uses a graduated scale to express level of performance. Tables 3–1 and 3–2 give example excerpts of a checklist and a rating scale.

Checklists and rating scales provide a quick way to record developmental information. They are relatively easy to learn to use and provide a method of observing an individual child. Keep in mind that both checklists and rating scales describe behaviors or skills without addressing the possible causes. Therefore, it is important that the administrator is familiar with the criteria and that they are clearly observable. Additionally, checklists and rating scales should be relevant to the population. When working with a toddler, it is ineffective to use a list or scale that was designed with the criteria for an older child's developmental sequence.

Purposes of Checklists and Rating Scales

Checklists that are well designed and appropriately used can be useful in understanding children's development and in developing curriculum. Teachers in nursery schools,

---

Descriptors.   In checklists or rating scales, used to identify specific behaviors that a child might exhibit.

TABLE 3–1 Checklist Excerpt: Gross Motor Skills, Ages 2–3

Item	Yes	No	Comments
Jumps in place			
Walks approximately on line			
Jumps from bottom step			
Balances on one foot			
Walks up and down stairs, alternating feet			

TABLE 3–2 Rating Scale Excerpt: Social Skills, Ages 3–5

Item	Occurs Frequently	Occurs Sometimes	Seldom Occurs	Does Not Occur	Comments
Initiates play with peers					
Chooses to join a group of peers					
Takes turns in play situations					

early child care settings, and kindergartens use checklists to determine a child's mastery of "readiness" skills as a means of determining placement recommendations. Teachers use both commercially developed forms and informal tools they have created themselves. For instance, teachers of four-year-olds may meet with district kindergarten teachers to gain an understanding of the curriculum expectations that the preschool children will be expected to meet the following year. With this knowledge they can create and administer a **readiness checklist** that is appropriate to the curricular goals of the kindergarten program in order to inform preschool curriculum and tell the kindergarten teacher of the needs of the children for the next class. Many teachers of first and second grade students use checklists to report an individual child's mastery or progress on stated curricular goals, or specific knowledge and skills in academic and social areas. Teacher comments often support checklists and rating scales. Table 3–3 gives an example of possible items on a kindergarten readiness checklist.

Readiness checklist.   A checklist that identifies specific skills necessary to move on to the next level of learning.

TABLE 3-3 **Kindergarten Readiness Checklist**

Item	Yes	No	Comments
Cuts with scissors			
Traces basic shapes			
Independently uses self-help skills such as toileting, getting dressed, and eating			
Identifies some alphabet letters			
Counts to 10			

Teachers working with children with identified special needs often use developmental checklists or rating scales that are **criterion referenced** to assess development and to establish educational goals to be recorded for the child's Individual Educational Plan (IEP) or the family's Individualized Family Service Plan (IFSP). Such scales or checklists are generally **norm referenced** and have supporting data on **validity** and **reliability.** These checklists are much more detailed in the descriptors for specific skills and sub-skills than are the teacher-made checklists typically used in preschool settings.

Checklists and rating scales can be used with families as a means of conveying information regarding child achievement or the child's progress, as in the case of report cards. Checklists can also be administered by families and used in conjunction with an educator, therapist, or physician as a way to assess development or to diagnose a learning problem. For example, some rating scales are designed for parents and teachers to use in order to detect possible attention deficit/hyperactivity disorder. Table 3–4 gives an example of typical descriptors that can be found on such a rating scale.

Older children may use checklists or rating scales to evaluate their own learning. For example, children may check off facts they know about the rotation of the moon prior to the learning unit and then again after the unit is complete. Table 3–5 gives an example of such a checklist. Students may even comment on information they still want to gain regarding the unit. This technique can be especially successful when students are discouraged about acquiring skills that are difficult, such as in reading or mathematics. Through this process the child gains knowledge of past learning and current

---

Criterion referenced.   A test with items relating to what the child is being taught at a specific time.

Norm referenced.   A test with items that are considered appropriate for an average developing child.

Validity.   Whether a test measures what it is supposed to measure.

Reliability.   Whether a test will give consistent results when given appropriately.

TABLE 3–4   Examples of Questions for Parents and Teachers to Determine ADHD

Item	Never	Sometimes	Often	Frequently
Excitable, impulsive				
Disturbs other children				
Short attention span; fails to finish things				
Constantly fidgeting				
Cries often and easily				

TABLE 3–5   A Checklist to Monitor One's Own Learning

My Facts about the Sun and Moon		
Facts	09/14/05 Did I know it?	09/28/05 Do I know it now?
The distance between the sun and the moon		
The distance between the moon and the earth		
The distance between the sun and the earth		
How much I weigh on the moon		
How much I weigh on the sun		

accomplishments, and can plan for future learning. When done with the assistance of an adult, this use of checklists or rating scales is closely related to the concept of "scaffolding" put forward by Lev Vygotsky (more on Vygotsky in Chapter 13).

Disadvantages to Using Checklists and Rating Scales

Unfortunately, rating scales can be subjective, since developmental terms can have ambiguous references. Take, for example, an item that states, "The child plays well with others." This could mean that the child initiates social interactions, that the child is able to resolve conflict appropriately, or a combination of both. Checklists and rating scales rely heavily on the interpretation of the observer.

Another disadvantage is that checklists and rating scales are limited to observable milestones and do not focus on the specifics of an event. An item that states "Claps hands"does not give any other information. Perhaps the child claps hands in appreciation for another child's accomplishments (social) or claps in rhythm to a beat (creative) or claps in time with a march (motor). Simply checking that a child claps her hands provides only part of the developmental picture.

Because checklists are not open ended, there is no documentation to support the administrator's determination. The parent or teacher reviewing the checklist has little idea of why or how the rater determined the child's performance on any given item. What does it mean to "engage in play cooperatively"? Without the support of recorded comments, the checklist item seems vague and less meaningful to the individual child's actual development.

Because of these limitations it is imperative that checklists and rating scales are used as merely one piece in the puzzle of the child's development. They should never be used alone for evaluation or diagnosis.

Overcoming the Limitations

Although there are disadvantages to the usage of checklists and rating scales, there are several measures that one can take to increase their validity and reliability.

> ➤ First, have more than one individual administer the checklist or rating scale. **Inter-rater reliability,** or agreement among two or more observers, helps to reduce the likelihood of error or bias.

> ➤ Second, always have room on the checklist or rating scale for a section called "Comments."A comment area allows the administrator to give a bit of an explanation as to why she rated an item a certain way. A comment area can also give more information as to the context in which the behavior or skill occurs, and/or any special considerations that need to be taken.

> ➤ Finally, make sure the checklist is valid and reliable. Make sure the list is measuring what needs to be measured in terms of content and developmental level. You wouldn't want to use a checklist for adolescent development on a two-year-old. Information regarding most manufactured checklists and rating scales is available in the *Mental Measurements Yearbook* (Spies & Plake, 2005), located at most college libraries or from http://www.unl.edu/buros. Figure 3–1 presents tips for choosing checklists and rating scales.

Locating Checklists and Rating Scales

Checklists and rating scales can be located by many means. Many child development books have examples of checklists included in the content. Students may use the *Mental Measurements Yearbook* (MMY) to locate the title, author, publisher, and cost of checklists and assessments. The MMY provides reviews of tests, checklists, questionnaires, and rating scales published within a certain time period. The test reviewer gives a general description of the instrument, explaining its purposes, target population, and intended

---

Inter-rater reliability.   Agreement among two or more observers.

FIGURE 3–1 Tips for selecting checklists and rating scales. ● ● ●

Ask yourself these questions when selecting a checklist:

1. Does this checklist match my curricular goals?
2. Does the checklist reflect the interests of the child?
3. Are the developmental criteria appropriate for the child?
4. Will the checklist measure more than one goal?
5. How is the checklist administered?
6. What materials will I need?
7. How much time will the checklist take to administer?
8. Are the criteria clear and objective?
9. Is there a place for teacher comments?
10. Is the checklist brief to fill out?
11. Is the checklist easy to tabulate?
12. How much does it cost?
13. Is the checklist standardized?
14. Are the items objective?

uses. In addition, the reviewer summarizes information about administering the instrument and the scores and scoring procedures. A reviewer may also compare the current edition of the assessment instrument with the content of previous editions.

The Internet is another tool that is easily used to locate checklists and rating scales. A simple search using phrases such as "developmental checklists," "developmental milestones," and "child development scale" will yield countless items. It is always important to carefully evaluate assessment tools found online. Use the tips for selecting a checklist in Figure 3–1.

Community agencies that provide services for children and families may have examples of checklists and rating scales that you could review. School districts, providers of speech and hearing services, special educators, Head Start programs, child care centers and doctors' offices may be places to locate developmental checklists. Your instructor may also have several examples of checklists and rating scales that are likely available for loan or on reserve at the school library. Lists of commercially available checklists, rating scales, and questionnaires can be found on the accompanying CD-ROM.

HOW TO USE CHECKLISTS AND RATING SCALES

Developmental checklists and rating scales can be administered by a variety of professionals in a number of settings and for a number of reasons. Some assessment forms require specialized training; you should seek the guidance of a professional.

Setting the Stage

In order to assure quality and consistency, checklists and rating scales should be performed after the child becomes familiar with the rater. All procedures should be carefully documented to allow reproduction of the results by others. For example, if the child was encouraged to play with or manipulate toys during the assessment, this should be noted. If much of the assessment was conducted through observation but some items were directly administered in a one-on-one session, such items should be noted. Methods that are appropriate to the child's age, development, and temperament should be employed. Typically, checklists and rating scales are not a one-time snapshot of the child's development but part of an ongoing process that follows the child over time.

Remember, checklists should be used in an unobtrusive manner and children should not be removed from settings that are familiar and comfortable.

Steps to Filling Out a Checklist or Rating Scale

After you have chosen the checklist to be used, it is now time to begin filling out the checklist.

1. *Complete identifying information.* The first step is to record all of the identifying information. For each observation, include:
   - child's name
   - child's date of birth
   - the date of the observation
   - the setting in which the observations are being done
   - the name of the rater
2. *Analyze the items on the checklist.* Begin reading each item and determine what types of behaviors you might see that could define that item. Table 3–6 presents several social-emotional criteria on a checklist for ages birth to three years. For each of these items you would need to think about what the statement means. Most importantly, if there are words, phrases, or concepts in the item that you do not know, ask your instructor or consult child development texts to find out what it means.

   For this particular checklist we would need to determine the following:
   ➤ *Focuses on face.* How long does the infant look at the face? Is there anything that can distract from the face? Do the infant's eyes stay fixed?

TABLE 3–6   **Analyzing Items on a Checklist**

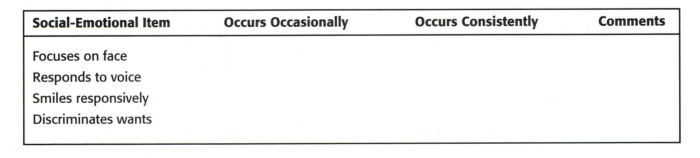

Social-Emotional Item	Occurs Occasionally	Occurs Consistently	Comments
Focuses on face			
Responds to voice			
Smiles responsively			
Discriminates wants			

> *Responds to voice.* How does the infant respond? By turning his head? By moving his body? Are there particular voices that he responds more or less to?

> *Smiles responsively.* First, you would have to decide what is meant by *responsively*. After you have asked your instructor or consulted your child development text, you find that it means that the infant smiles when some type of stimulus is presented—in other words, the infant is not just smiling out of nowhere—it is in reaction to something or someone. Next, you would observe to find out what kinds of stimuli make the baby smile. How often does this happen?

> *Discriminates wants.* How does the infant tell the caregiver what he wants and doesn't want? Does he have preferences for the way he is held, changed, or fed?

It is very important to know what you are going to be assessing. When it comes time to share your results with parents or colleagues you need to be able to explain why you marked an item the way you did.

3. *Rate the items.* Now you can begin to rate the items on the checklist or rating scale according to your notes or your on-the-spot observations. Look at the items in the checklist in Table 3–7. You will see that some items could best be responded to by taking on-the-spot observations.

   Some of the items for on-the-spot observations are the following:

- initiates social contacts with peers in play
- imitates another child or children at play
- plays independently in company of peers
- plays alongside another child

Other items could be completed by consulting your notes or talking with others who know the child. Items to rate via notes or other correspondence:

- has special friend/friends
- chooses his/her own friends

Either way, you must note under comments how you came to this conclusion. Giving specific examples of the behavior in action or identifying the source are probably the best ways to explain your rating.

A checklist typically will have only two choices for ratings, such as:

- met/not met
- yes/no
- occurs often/occurs never
- +/−

A rating scale will have a continuum on which to signify the item. Here are some typical scales:

- 1   2   3   4   5   (1 = never, 5 = always)
- Excellent   Very Good   Good   Fair   Poor

TABLE 3–7   **Social Development Checklist**

Approximate Age in Months	Item	Circle One: Y = yes N = no N/A = not sure			Comments
12–17	1. Initiates social contacts with peers in play	Y	N	N/A	
12–17	2. Imitates another child or children at play	Y	N	N/A	
18–23	3. Plays independently in company of peers	Y	N	N/A	
18–23	4. Plays alongside another child	Y	N	N/A	
24–35	5. Participates in group play	Y	N	N/A	
24–35	6. Shares property with others	Y	N	N/A	
36–47	7. Interacts with peers	Y	N	N/A	
48–59	8. Has special friend/friends				
48–59	9. Chooses his/her own friends	Y	N	N/A	
48–59	10. Plays cooperatively with peers	Y	N	N/A	
48–59	11. Participates in group activities	Y	N	N/A	
48–59	12. Takes turns and shares	Y	N	N/A	
60–71	13. Initiates social contacts and interactions with peers	Y	N	N/A	
60–71	14. Participates in competitive play activities	Y	N	N/A	
60–71	15. Uses peers as resources	Y	N	N/A	
60–71	16. Gives ideas to other children as well as going along with their ideas	Y	N	N/A	
72–83	17. Serves as leader in peer relationships	Y	N	N/A	

Source: Modified from the *Battelle Developmental Inventory* (Newborg, Stock, Wnek, Guidubaldi, & Svinicki, 1984)

- Never   Occasionally   Sometimes   Often   Always
- 2   1   0   (2 = solid in the skill, 0 = never seen)
- Never   Rarely   Occasionally   Frequently   Very Frequently

As you can see, a rating scale leaves a great deal to the interpretation of the rater. It is difficult to distinguish with reliability the difference between *sometimes* and *often* or even *frequently* and *very frequently*. This is why comments and qualifiers are so important when filling out the checklist or rating scale.

4. *Determine general developmental level of the child.* Determining the general developmental level of the child can be done after all the items on the checklist or rating scale have been completed. Consider the example in Table 3–7. This checklist identifying peer interaction is used for children ages one through eight. The column on the left gives the approximate age in months we should see a behavior developing, the second column gives the item, the third column identifies the rating, and finally the important comments column is included. Let's say you were observing a 26-month-old (two years and two months). You would assume that because the child is 26 months she would have shown the behaviors in items 1–6. However, unless you have seen these behaviors or consulted with someone who has, you cannot take them for granted. So during your observations you look for these specific skills and abilities. After you have been assured that all these skills and abilities are present, you begin looking for behaviors that signify the remainder of the items.

After you have filled out all the items, you can now determine the approximate level of development in that particular area. For example, if you have marked *yes* for the child for items 1–5 and again for items 7, 8, and 10, but you observed some questionable behaviors related to items 6 and 9, it would be said that the child is typically developing in the area of peer interaction. It could be noted later that sharing is not fully developed yet, and specifics, such as under what conditions she shares and does not share, could be recorded.

CREATING A CHECKLIST OR RATING SCALE

As a future educator, psychologist, or therapist, there will be times when you will need to create your own checklists.

When to Create Your Own

While premade checklists and rating scales can be very useful in identifying general milestones that each child should be reaching, there are times when a more pinpointed approach is necessary. For example, if you are observing a child that tends to display behaviors that do not quite match other children's behaviors at that same age, you may need to create a checklist that breaks down that particular area of concern into more precise pieces. Consider the example in Figure 3–2.

You might want to create your own checklist because you need one that covers

- a new innovative teaching method.
- a new method for behavior management.
- a particular teaching unit you have developed.
- a specific concern you have for a child.

FIGURE 3–2 Situation that requires a pinpointed checklist.

A Specialized Checklist for Social Interaction

Rashad is a four-year-old boy in an inclusive preschool classroom. Rashad has been diagnosed with Asperger's syndrome (see Of Special Interest in Chapter 8) and does not interact socially with other children at all. The multidisciplinary team that is working with Rashad would like to design some interventions that will meet his specific needs. In order to do this, they decide to create a checklist that will target those behaviors that lead to or discourage social interaction. They begin by observing Rashad using a standard checklist such as the one shown in Table 3–7. Because Rashad scored a *No* on the items 8 and 9 under the 48–59 month mark ("has special friend/friends" and "chooses his/her own friends") they need to go back and determine his **basal**. After doing some observations, they determined that Rashad's basal level was around 24–35 months. He had gotten *Yes* on both of the 18–23 month test items ("plays independently in the company of peers" and "plays alongside another child") but was marked *No* in "participates in group play" and "shares property with others," the 24–35 month markers. They determined they needed to focus on those behaviors related to participating in group play, sharing property with others, and interacting with peers. So they created a checklist with those three items and the specific behaviors under each of them. This is what they came up with:

Participates in group play

❑ Shows interest in what the group is playing
❑ Enters play situations
❑ Resists attempts to be included in group play
❑ Observes group play

Shares property with others

❑ Acknowledges another person's interest in property
❑ Attempts to let another look at property
❑ Allows another to touch property
❑ Shows interest in another person's property

Interacts with peers

❑ Shows interest in peer activities
❑ Shows interest in wanting to interact with peers
❑ Attempts to enter into peer play
❑ Attempts to initiate interaction with peers
❑ In interaction, makes eye contact
❑ In interaction, appropriately responds to others
❑ Uses other forms of interaction, such as gestures

When the team does their observations now, they will be looking specifically at these skills. Then they can design appropriate interventions that target specific behaviors.

Basal.   When administering a test, the starting place for further evaluation.

How to Create Your Own

There are many reasons to create your own checklists and rating scales. Generally the purpose will dictate how you actually create it. For simplicity, this section will provide you with one way to create the checklist.

Steps to creating a checklist

1. *Identify the domain.* In order to create your own checklist or rating scale, you must first identify the domain of development to be studied. For the child study, you will need to create a checklist or rating scale for the following domains of development: cognitive, social, emotional, gross motor, and fine motor, language or literacy (typically use language for children under the age of three and literacy for those older than three), and art or music.

2. *Determine descriptors that will be used to write the items.* In order to complete this step of creating the checklist, ask yourself this question: "What do I want to find out about this child?" Generally, the answers will go something like this:

   - I want to find out how this child is developing socially, emotionally, physically, and cognitively.

   - I want to find out how this child communicates with peers and adults.

   - I want to find out if this child is developing at the same pace as his same-age peers.

   - I want to find out what this child's strengths might be.

   For instance, I want to answer the question, "How is this child developing in relationship to his same-age peers?" In order to do this I must find descriptions of what development looks like for most children at this age, in this particular area of development. One way to gain this information is to use the Internet; the other is to use a developmental text.

   Choose a search engine Web site and type in a term such as "developmental checklists." Many hits will result; you can click on many different ones to hunt for items for your own checklist. Some sites may give descriptions and some may have the actual checklists. Make sure you can identify the domain of development, and choose the right descriptors for your child's age and cultural background.

   A great source for creating a checklist is *Developmental Profiles* by Allen and Marotz (2002). This book outlines developmental milestones for children from birth through age 12. From these, you can create items for your checklist.

3. *Write the identifying information, the items, and the rating system.* Now that you know which descriptors you will be using, you can write the items. It is recommended for the purpose of the child study to have 10–12 items for each domain of development. After each item, you will need to signify the rating in two possible ways:

   ➤ Assign a yes or no rating. After each item, create a column for *yes*, meaning that the child demonstrates the behavior or *no*, the child has not demonstrated that yet.

> ➤ Assign a continuum-type scale. After each item, create several columns that rate the child's demonstration of the behavior. For example, *not present, emerging, mastered;* or *never, sometimes, frequently, always.*

4. *Create the checklist.*

Start with identifying information, including:

- domain of development
- name of the child
- date of birth (DOB) of the child
- date or time span of the observations

Remember, no matter what kind of rating system you use, include a comment section in order to provide more clarification and examples.

Step by step: Creating a checklist

Now let's go through the step-by-step process of creating a gross motor checklist for a 26-month-old child. *The example includes the use of the Internet to gain developmental information. It is important to use Web sites that are reputable and provide accurate information regarding developmental milestones.*

1. *Identify the domain.*

I have decided to create a checklist for gross motor development.

2. *Determine descriptors that will be used to write the items.*

At a popular search engine on the Internet I typed in "developmental checklists" and clicked on one of the top results, the Early Childhood Direction Center (ECDC) site, which has five or six different checklists. I click on one, *"How I Grow: A Guidebook for Parents,"* and then I click on 24–30 months, because the child I want to study is a 26-month-old. The behaviors on the list include the following:

- Jumps, runs, kicks a ball, walks up and down stairs
- Hand skills: Turns pages one at a time, can help to dress and undress herself, turns doorknob and unscrews lids, can feed herself well with a spoon
- Language skills: Can speak in short sentences, begins to name objects in books, uses many new words, able to express needs, relies less on gestures
- Understanding: Can pay attention to activities for longer periods of time, knows some colors, points to four or five parts of the body, can say first name

Then I go back to the ECDC site, click on another checklist, which is called *"Checklist for Growing Children,"* and go to the section on two and three years of age. The behaviors on the list include the following:

- uses two-to-three-word sentences
- says about 50 words
- recognizes familiar pictures
- kicks a ball forward
- feeds oneself with a spoon
- demands a lot of your attention
- turns two to three pages at a time

TABLE 3–8 Checklist Created for the Gross Motor Development of a 26-month-old

Kayla DOB: 01/03	Gross Motor Checklist			Observation: Spring '05
Items	*Never*	*Sometimes*	*Often*	*Comments*
Jumps with two feet				
Likes to run				
Kicks a ball				
Kicks a ball forward				
Walks up and down stairs				

- likes to imitate parent
- identifies hair, eyes, ears, and nose by pointing
- can build a tower of four blocks
- shows affection

The first site I looked at organized the skills into domains. The first set of skills, "jumps, runs, kicks . . ." and so on, all belong in the gross motor domain. I then look at the second list and find that the only gross motor skill on that list is "kicks a ball forward." Combining the two lists, I have five items so far for the gross motor checklist. I continue identifying the items and where they belong.

3. *Write the identifying information, the items, and the rating system.*

   I have decided to use a continuum-type rating system, and I will use *never*, *sometimes*, and *often*.

4. *Create the checklist.*

   Make sure your checklist includes identifying information, items, a rating system, and a comment section. Table 3–8 shows what the checklist looks like so far.

I would now need to go back to the Web sites to find at least five more descriptors in order to write the items.

Remember, when you begin to look for items for your checklist you can also go into specific domains right from the start. For example, instead of using the terms "developmental checklists" in your search, maybe start right off with "gross motor developmental checklists." This will bring up only those in the gross motor domain.

Conclusion

The use of checklists and rating scales in early childhood and early childhood special education is an extremely valuable practice. When you have mastered finding them and using them, you will be able to narrow in on individual development and thus understand the whole child.

Of Special Interest—Checklists and Rating Scales for Children with Special Needs

Checklists and rating scales are primarily used in three ways for children with special needs.

The first purpose is to screen for special needs or to identify a possible condition that will need further evaluation. A checklist could never in and of itself diagnose a developmental disability such as autism. However, a checklist can call attention to the warning signs or "red flags." Throughout the text, as we discuss children with special needs, checklists will be presented that may serve as signs of a possible disabling condition or of giftedness.

A second use of checklists for children with special needs is to identify the child's specific deficits that may make inclusion difficult. These items become the focus of intervention, so that the child can be successful in a general education environment and a social setting. In Chapter 8, "Cognitive Development," the Of Special Interest section delves into play deficits for children with developmental delays. By looking at the table for typical play behavior development, one can identify the specific deficits a child might have. That then becomes the focus of intervention.

Finally, checklists are very helpful for the families of children with special needs in identifying what their needs are. Remember that young children with special needs will be under an IFSP. The needs of the child are considered within the context of the family and their needs, as well. So, when a family is initially being served, it is a must to gain their input (in fact, by law the family must be involved in the planning of the child's program). Checklists are a good way to do this. More on this and examples of a family checklist can be found in the Of Special Interest section of chapter 6, "Parent Interview."

View the Anecdotal Record on the CD-ROM. From that, identify one possible checklist item for each of the following developmental domains: Cognitive, Social, Gross Motor, and Language.

QUESTIONS TO CONSIDER ○ ○ ○

1. What kinds of behaviors and/or development would be best studied via the use of checklists and rating scales? What kinds of development would be difficult to assess using rating scales and checklists? Why?

2. How would you determine if an existing checklist or rating scale is appropriate for children of various cultures?

3. How does qualifying information (written comments) influence understanding of the child's development?

REFERENCES ○ ○ ○

Allen, K. E. & Marotz, L. R. (2002). *Developmental profiles: Pre-birth through twelve* (4th ed.) Clifton Park, NY: Thomson Delmar Learning.

New York State Department of Health. (2005, July 15). *Checklist for growing children.* Retrieved December 20, 2005, from http://www.health.state.ny.us/community/ infants_children/early_intervention/docs/0527_early_help_brochure.pdf

Newborg, J., Stock, J. R., Wnek, L., Guidubaldi, J., & Svinicki, J. (1984). *Battelle Developmental Inventory.* Itasca, IL: Riverside Publishing.

Spies, R. A. & Plake, B. S. (Eds.). (2005). *The Sixteenth Mental Measurements Yearbook.* Lincoln, NE: Buros Institute of Mental Measurements.

The Central New York Early Childhood Direction Center, Syracuse University (2004, April). *Developmental checklists.* Retrieved May 15, 2005, from http://thechp.syr.edu/ Developmental_Checklists.html

University of the State of New York, & New York State Education Department, Office of Vocational and Educational Services for Individuals with Disabilities. (1996, October). *How I grow: Birth through five. A Guidebook for parents.* Retrieved May 15, 2005, from http://www.vesid.nysed.gov/lsn/HowIGrow/intro.htm

4

Structured Observation

CHAPTER OBJECTIVES

- To explain the need for structured observation

- To select a form of structured observation that fits a specific observational purpose

- To design a plan for conducting a structured observation

- To describe ways in which to build rapport with children

- To describe the purpose and method of Functional Behavioral Analysis

CHILD STUDY OBJECTIVES

Upon conclusion of this chapter the student will:

- begin to build a rapport with the child being studied

- identify several concepts of development to be assessed using structured observations

INTRODUCTION TO STRUCTURED OBSERVATION

A very important piece to completing a child study is the use of structured observations. Structured observation differs from other types of assessment such as anecdotal records and checklists in two ways. First, the role of the observer goes from passive to active. When taking anecdotal records and filling out checklists, the observer simply watches for behaviors and records them. When conducting a **structured observation,** however, the observer sets up a situation in order to elicit specific behaviors. The behavior of the observer is the second difference. The observer actually interacts with the child when doing structured observations. This interaction can take the form of questioning, extending play, or reacting to the child's behaviors.

Why Conduct Structured Observations

Although the majority of information on the child's development will come from observing children engaging in typical activities in their natural environment, sometimes we as the observers need to set up situations in order to get specific information. For example, if we want to determine a child's level of cognitive development in the area of **conservation,** we could set up the classic conservation experiment (see Figure 4–1). If we are working with an infant we might want to find out about her sense of **object permanence,** so we might play a game with the keys to find out if the infant looks for the keys once they are out of sight (see Figure 4–1). And if we wanted to know about a seven-year-old's **moral development,** we might ask her to tell us how certain moral dilemmas should be handled (see Figure 4–1). Basically, when we need to know something about the child's development that is not being observed naturally, we need to set up a specific situation, possibly in the form of a test, experiment, or game, in order to give us insight.

Let's say that while we are observing a nine-month-old we see that while her caregiver is walking away she is watching her and the toy that they were playing with together. We note that she keeps her eye on the toy and the caregiver and then when both are out of sight she begins mouthing the next closest toy. We assume then that she has some sense of object permanence because she watches as they both move out of sight. However, there is a developmental continuum of object permanence; it is unknown where she is on that scale. Now would be a good time to do the experiment with object permanence in order to understand where the child is at this stage of development. Remember that "still waters run deep." Many children will not show you everything they can do or everything they understand. We must work to uncover their true emotions, thoughts, and talents.

Structured observation.   A research assessment technique in which the examiner defines developmental goals and objectives that are tested through structured experiences such as games, interviews, experiments, dramatic play, and activities.

FIGURE 4–1   **Explanation of object permanence, conservation, and moral development.**

Cognitive Development Terms

Object permanence is a developmental term that refers to a child's ability to understand that objects still exist even after they are no longer in sight. Infants eight months old or younger tend not to have this ability. It is not until they become more cognitively developed that they understand to search for an object even though it has been hidden from view. The first signs of the recognition of object permanence emerge between two and four months of age, when the infant will look in the direction of an object that has been hidden. Between four and eight months of age, the infant searches for an object partially hidden, and by 12 months of age the child will search for a completely hidden object. One sign that cognition of object permanence has been reached is when the caregiver and child can play a game of peekaboo.

Conservation is a term made famous by Jean Piaget to describe a child's developmental ability to understand how substances or objects change in form. Young children experience difficulty in understanding the concept of conservation. In one of Piaget's famous experiments, children were asked to judge the amount of liquid in two identical glasses. After the children agreed that the amount of liquid in each glass was the same, Piaget poured liquid from one of the glasses into a shorter glass. Although the glasses accommodated the liquid equally, the young children reported that the taller glass held more liquid. Similar reasoning errors made by young children (those in the stage of preoperational thinking) include conservation of mass, generally demonstrated with equal balls of clay. Young children verify that the clay balls are the same size but reason that when one of the clay balls is rolled out into a long "snake" it contains more clay. Piaget proposed that children gain understanding of concepts such as conservation through experience, maturation, and a problem-solving process he called *disequilibrium*.

As children grow and develop, they gain more of an understanding of what is right and what is wrong. For example, most two-year-olds don't understand that it is wrong to take something that is not yours. However, by the time the child reaches school age, she knows that stealing is wrong. This process is *moral development.* One of the classic examinations of moral development involves the dilemma situation. The child is asked to give her thoughts on how a situation involving moral decision-making should be handled.

For example: Is it right or wrong for a mother to steal bread for her starving children? Why or why not?

What is noted is the reasoning behind the child's answer.

Forms of Structured Observation

The type of structured observation you conduct will primarily depend on what particular concept of development you wish to delve into more thoroughly, as well as the age of the child. Table 4–1 identifies several kinds of structured observation and the concepts that lend themselves best to that method.

TABLE 4-1   **Examples of Structured Observations**

Type of structured observation	Concepts to be explored	Examples of specific methods
Interviews	1) Cognitive domain: moral development	1) Present the child with a moral dilemma and ask him or her what the right way to handle it is and why (age: 5–8)
	2) Language development: **articulation**	2) Have a conversation with a child (preferably record it), listening for sounds that the child is saying correctly and sounds that the child might be omitting, adding, or substituting
Games	1) Cognitive domain: memory development	1) Play the "What's Missing?" game. Show the child several objects. Then, after she closes her eyes, you take one away and see if she can remember what is missing (age: 3–5)
	2) Social development: turn-taking, compromising, cooperating	2) Play any board game with the child, looking for the ability to wait for a turn and to work with other children
Set Up Dramatic Play	1) Social development: play skill development	1) Set up a dramatic play that you know the child you are observing wants to get into and play a specific role (e.g., a child obsessed with horses would want to be a horse on a farm). Observe how the child enters the play and negotiates to get the role he wants (age: 4–6)
Experiments	1) Cognitive development: **theory of mind**	Conduct the classic "What's in the Juice Box?" experiment. While the child is watching, show her that inside a juice box you have placed ribbons. Next, ask the child what someone coming in and looking at the outside of the juice box would think was inside. If the child thinks that the person would say "juice," she has developed some theory of mind; if she thinks the person would say that ribbons were inside, she has not yet developed this (age: 3–6)
Activities	1) Gross motor: any locomotive skill or balance skills	1) Set up an obstacle course and observe how the child crawls, jumps, hops, alternates feet, throws, catches, etc. (age: 2–8; depends on the tasks involved)
	2) Fine motor: eye-hand coordination, hand strength, grasp of tools	2) any cutting, drawing, painting, stringing, puzzles, peg boards

Articulation.   The production of speech sounds.

Theory of mind.   Individuals who have developed a theory of mind are able to understand how another person is thinking, thus being able to predict how others will react and their motivations for behavior. Children typically begin to develop a theory of mind around the age of four.

You may think that it will be difficult to identify a particular test to conduct on the child you are studying. No worries—a list of tests related to structured observations for domain-specific concepts are provided on the accompanying CD-ROM.

CONDUCTING A STRUCTURED OBSERVATION

For your child study you are required to prepare and conduct one structured observation for each domain of development. That is, you will do one for each of the following domains: cognitive, social, emotional, gross motor, fine motor, art or music, and literacy and language development.

Doing a structured observation requires planning. You must know exactly what you are looking for and how to set up the situation in order to obtain relevant and useful information. Finally, before you actually carry out the plan, it is wise to try it out on your peers.

Steps to Conducting a Structured Observation

Step 1: Identify the goal and an objective

The first task you must do is identify the goal and the objective of the test you are going to conduct. In other words, what are you going to be looking at? What do you want to find out more about?

Within each of the domains of development are certain concepts of development, which will be presented in detail in Part II. For instance, if you look at Chapter 8, "Cognitive Development," you will see that the concepts are memory, problem solving, logical thinking, and theory of mind. These concepts of development are what you will want to investigate more closely. Within each of these concepts are developmental progressions that signal where the child is developmentally in that particular domain. For instance, if you look closely at the progression of memory development there are signals such as what the child attends to, how long she attends, whether she searches for objects out of view, whether she can hold a visual in her head in order to use it later, and so on.

The goal of the structured observation will relate directly to the concepts within each domain of development, and the objective will directly relate to the specifics or the signals of the concepts. For example, within the cognitive domain a goal might be to investigate memory development in the child. A related objective might be to identify what stage of object permanence the child has mastered. Of course, this would mean that the child being observed is between the ages of 5 and 24 months and that some type of object permanence has already been demonstrated. When deciding on the goal and the objective of the structured observation, keep in mind a couple of considerations:

> ➤ *The test needs to be appropriate for the age of the child.* You wouldn't test object permanence on a preschool child because that is not relevant; you are looking for the highest expression of the concept that the child can possibly demonstrate. A preschool child (unless there is a special need involved) has mastered object permanence long ago. Likewise, you wouldn't test a three-year-old

(again, assuming that the child has not been identified as gifted) for theory of mind because it is unlikely that it would have emerged yet.

➤ *The chosen test must relate directly to your previous observations of the child and should reflect a "need to know more about this" perspective.* For example, you may observe that Talia, the 30-month-old girl in your class, does not use **expressive language** (does not talk) but clearly understands when playing with other children or when in a group situation. All of your anecdotal records and checklists suggest that she does not have expressive language and this is a concern. So, you decide to test this further—maybe Talia is not confident enough to speak to other children, maybe she has a very quiet voice and cannot be heard, maybe she needs more **wait time** between a question and giving an answer, or maybe she really does not have expressive language. So the goal of the test would be to investigate Talia's expressive language development, and the objective would be to identify in what situations (if any) she uses expressive language.

Step 2: Carry out the test

After the goal and the objective have been identified, the next step is to plan the testing procedure. The procedure involves four major components:

➤ *Introduction.* How will you introduce this activity, experiment, or game to the child? Remember, some children will be slow to warm up. Your introduction will either pull them in or push them away. It's a good idea to find out what really interests the child and use that to pull in the child, if your goal, for instance, is to investigate a child's expressive language and your objective is to identify the child's use and understanding of **prepositions** (i.e., *next to, behind, in front of*, and so forth). If you are going to play a game with him in order to gain this information, you will want to pull the child into the game using something that interests him. So, if you find that a child likes dinosaurs you could find several different dinosaur models, pictures, or cards and show them to him, saying, "Would you like to play with the dinosaurs with me?" Or maybe you would have developed some kind of game to play and in that case you would ask, "Would you like to play a game using these dinosaurs with me?" If the child likes dinosaurs your work is almost complete! Always invite the child into your game or activity. Never use coercion.

Expressive language.   Expressive language is the part of language that allows us to communicate to others our thoughts, feelings, and needs. Receptive language allows us to understand what others are trying to tell us.

Wait time.   When interacting with someone, this is the time between one person's question or comment and the other person's answer or response. When children are first developing expressive language, or when the child has a special need, wait time may need to be longer.

Prepositions.   Small words we use with nouns to indicate time, location, movement, and manner. Examples include *in, on, under, on top of*, etc.

➤ *Creation of a Plan and Gathering Materials.* Once you have determined how you will entice the child, you must consider how to carry out the test and which materials to gather together. For example, now that you have figured out that you are going to use dinosaurs to attract the child, you need to develop a plan for how you will have him demonstrate his knowledge of prepositions while playing with the dinosaurs. Perhaps you decide to play a game in which you will hide the dinosaurs while his eyes are closed (make sure the child is comfortable with closing his eyes), and when he opens his eyes you will give him clues as to where the dinosaurs are hidden by saying, "The brontosaurus is *under* the table," or "The tyrannosaurus is *next to* the plant." You would carefully observe whether the child goes to the dinosaur by listening and comprehending the clue or if he continues to look and simply finds it by searching. If the child has no trouble using the clue to find the dinosaurs then you could go to the next level to see if he can use the prepositions to give the clues himself. So you would say, "Now I'll cover my eyes and you hide the dinosaurs." Then *he* would have to give you clues using the prepositions. Of course, both versions of this game assume that the child knows the names of the dinosaurs (something you would know from previous observations).

➤ *Questions.* While you are engaging the child in the activity, you need to ask questions that will help you determine the child's developmental level. These questions need to be developed before you actually start the test, and they should relate directly to the identified objective. Using the example above (the dinosaur game) consider the questions you could ask in order to better understand the child's comprehension and use of prepositions. For example, you might place three dinosaurs next to each other and ask the child, "Which dinosaur is the brachiosaurus *next to?*" or "Can you put the pterodactyl *below* the block shelf?" No matter what type of structured observation you are conducting, you need to think of questions before you begin. You will think of some as you are working with the child, but make sure you have some to start the process.

➤ *Documenting the results.* Create an assessment sheet before you begin the observation that reflects the identified goal and objective of the observation. Table 4–2 gives an example of the assessment sheet that could be used for preposition comprehension and usage. A blank assessment sheet can be found on the accompanying CD-ROM.

Step 3: Interpret the observation

Finally, after you have conducted the observation, you will interpret the results. The interpretation will summarize the observation and provide a very general evaluation of the child's development in that particular area.

For example, the interpretation for Louis's observation might read like this:

Louis is 3.5 years of age. He demonstrates appropriate use and comprehension of prepositions. He is able to find objects given prepositional clues and he is able to give prepositional clues to another person. He demonstrated an understanding of and correctly used *in, on, under, behind, next to, in front of,* and *on top of.* Louis demonstrates age-appropriate use of prepositions.

TABLE 4–2 **Assessment Form for Structured Observation**

Child's Name: Louis DOB: 06/13/02 Date of Test: 11/05/05	Goal: To investigate language development Objective: To determine use and comprehension of prepositions	Procedure: Play a game with the dinosaurs. Ask child to find dinosaurs using prepositions as clue. Ask child to give clues using prepositions.
Indicator of Objective	**Yes/No**	**Comments**
Looks for objects by using the clues *in, on, under, behind, out of*	All are yes except *out of*	Louis found objects easily using these words. However, he looked inside the sensory box rather than out of it several times before he found the dinosaur.
Looks for objects using the clues *next to, in front of, on top of, beside*	All except *beside*	Louis would take several seconds to think about the words used before he looked.
Gives clues using *in, on, under, behind, out of*	Could use *in* ("inside") and *under*	After several times of saying "the T-rex is by the table" I would ask him to clarify—by pretending I didn't know where to find it. After several tries he used *inside* and *under*.
Gives clues using *next to, in front of, on top of, beside*	Used all of these	Possibly because he now knew how to play the game he was able to use these very well.

BUILDING RAPPORT WITH CHILDREN

In order to conduct some types of structured observations on children, your first task is to connect with the child and establish **rapport**. Before you can ask the child to play a game with you or answer some questions, she has to be familiar with you, and most importantly, she has to trust you. Once a sense of trust has developed you can conduct your structured observations. Figure 4–2 summarizes ways in which to build rapport and trust with children.

ETHICS OF CONDUCTING STRUCTURED OBSERVATIONS

Because you will now be interacting with the child it is extremely important to consider how your intrusion will affect the child. Basic rules of thumb are as follows:

➤ *Never coerce the child into interacting with you.* Invite the child, spark the child's interest so she wants to work with you, show interest in what she is doing first.

....

Rapport. Relation of mutual understanding or trust and agreement between people. It is being "in sync," being on the same wavelength as the person you are talking to.

FIGURE 4–2 Building rapport and trust with children.

Building Trust with Infants

Building trust with infants requires that you read their signals. When they want interaction they will let you know by smiling, looking at you, and reaching in your direction. When they are overstimulated and do not want any more interaction they may turn their heads away, flap their arms and legs, or close their eyes. Watch them and take the hint when to continue interacting and when to leave them alone for a time. Also, make sure parents or trusted caregivers are within the infant's visual range.

Building Trust with Toddlers

The toddler will be much more difficult to build trust with because the typical age for a heightened level of stranger fear is anywhere from 12 months to 25 months. If the child is in a stage in which anxiety is high around strangers, hang back for a longer period of time.

Let the toddler see you talking pleasantly with her caregiver—she will take cues from those she trusts as to whether or not you should be in that circle. In addition, practice the following:

- Use a very soft voice.
- Let the toddler come to you first.
- Stay down on her level—make eye contact.
- Move slowly.
- Be calm.

Building Rapport with Preschoolers

In order to build rapport with a preschooler, practice the following:

- Have the caregiver introduce you to her. Then, go to the side to watch.
- Observe what she is doing.
- Stay down on her level.
- When she makes eye contact, smile.
- Answer questions any of the children in the environment might have for you and make sure to give them time to respond to any questions you might have for them.
- Show interest in the preschooler's activity.
- After several observations, ask to join in an activity. Do not monopolize it; let her run it.
- When she is not engaged in another activity, ask her to join you.

When a child is particularly anxious about strange adults and does not seem to be responding, you may have to ask the caregiver to conduct the structured observation.

➤ *Never take the child out of her natural environment in order to conduct the observation.* Unless you are functioning as the classroom teacher, in which case the child knows you very well, always conduct the observation in the environment that the child knows and trusts. Not only does this lower the level of anxiety, it also affects the child's responses.

➤ *Never sacrifice the child's physical, emotional, or psychological health or well-being in order to conduct the observation.* This may appear to be a no-brainer but sometimes we don't realize how emotionally detrimental some of our observations can be. For example, we may want to find out about the child's level of attachment, but we could not ethically conduct an attachment test in which we have mom leave the room while the child is left with a stranger, just to see how she reacts!

There are far too many examples of structured observations to avoid. Just keep in mind how it would make the child feel. If the child is going to feel anxious, sad, angry, or afraid, do not conduct that particular structured observation. Bottom line: Always respect the child and do no harm.

Of Special Interest—Functional Behavior Assessment

Have you ever observed a child or worked with a child whose inappropriate behaviors are not affected or changed by traditional management techniques, such as ignoring, redirection, or the dreaded "time out"? When this occurs it might be time to conduct a **functional behavior assessment** of the child's behavior. A functional behavior assessment is a special type of assessment that looks very closely at a behavior that may be causing harm to others or to the child himself. It is called *functional* behavior analysis because the purpose of the assessment is to identify *why* the child is behaving in a certain way, and the function that the behavior serves.

A functional behavior assessment is conducted when a child is exhibiting **maladaptive behaviors** that are interfering with learning, initiating, and/or maintaining positive social relationships or else causing harm to herself or others. Many times children with autism or sensory integration disorder* will engage in behaviors that are aggressive, inappropriate, or self-injurious, because those behaviors are serving some sort of need for the child. In other words, these behaviors have a function. Consequently, traditional methods of trying to change the behavior do not work. The objective of conducting a functional behavior assessment is to determine the need that the behavior serves. For instance, why does a child regularly verbalize a string of profanity during story time? This behavior might function as a release from boredom, an expression of frustration, an opportunity for securing attention, or in rare cases, a result of a biological dysfunction such as a **tic disorder** (Dieterich & Villani, 2000).

Autism will be discussed further in chapters 8 and 9, in the Of Special Interest section. *Sensory integration disorder* is discussed in the Of Special Interest section of chapter 7.

Functional behavior assessment.   A plan designed to identify the reasons why a child behaves in a certain manner—often referred to as identifying the *function* of the behavior.

Maladaptive behaviors.   Behaviors that get in the way of the child's ability to function within the typical environment.

Tic disorder.   A disorder characterized by a tic or repeated impulsive action, present in either a vocal or motor form.

In general, functional behavior theory states that maladaptive behaviors are either a means to get something or to avoid something. Wallin (2001) identifies several of the possible purposes maladaptive behaviors can serve:

- To gain attention
- To gain a tangible consequence (toy, candy, token)
- To gain a sensory consequence to increase or decrease stimulation that is tactile, taste, auditory, visual, proprioceptive (sense of body in space), or vestibular (sense of balance)
- To self-regulate emotions: to calm down if agitated or raise arousal level if depressed
- To escape or avoid an undesirable situation. Consider the following example.

Escape behavior   A child with autism often tries to avoid situations in which he is asked to or forced to "come out of his own world," such as playing or communicating. A two-year-old child with autism I began working with would appear to fall asleep just as I started the therapy session. I would stop the therapy and leave. His mother reported that as soon as I left he would wake up immediately. The clinical director at the agency I was working with directed me to continue the therapy even while he was "sleeping." That is, I was to still stay with him, request his interaction, and keep contact. At first I thought, This is crazy! How can I continue the therapy while he is asleep? But I continued, just as the director instructed (she was an expert in the field after all—not to mention my boss). I began the therapy as usual and as usual he fell right to sleep. However, after 10 minutes of my continuing the therapy he woke up and began kicking, shaking his head, and crying—all escape behaviors as well. After several weeks of sticking with the therapy he began to cooperate and eventually he would run to the door when I arrived, take my hand, and lead me to our therapy area. I would never have believed it if I didn't see it.

Although these behaviors are common among children with special needs, escape behaviors can be confused with what is in reality an avoidance behavior, which is a response to an upcoming transition or activity. Consider the following.

Avoidance behavior   When a child becomes agitated and uncooperative every day during circle time, the initial hypothesis may be that she finds the group presentation undesirable, and she is attempting to escape from that situation. However, the child may, in fact, be attempting to avoid the task or event that comes after the circle. If circle time is right before lunch, and the lunchtime routine is typically noisy and over-stimulating, the child may begin to exhibit some behavior as a protest to the thought of having to go into that situation.

How to Conduct a Functional Behavior Assessment

Indirect and direct methods of gathering behavioral data are used in functional assessment. These methods are used to predict the likely future occurrence of a behavior, based on knowledge of present behavior (Dieterich & Villani, 2000). Indirect methods include completing rating scales and checklists such as the *Behavior Assessment System* for Children (BASC; Reynolds & Kamphaus, 1992) and the *Child and Adolescent Functional Assessment Scale* (Hodges, 1994). Another indirect measure involves interviewing those individuals who work with the child, specifically those who are with the child when the behavior(s) in question take(s) place. Ask the following questions:

- In what settings does the behavior occur?
- In what setting does the behavior not occur?
- Who is present when the behavior occurs?
- What is happening just prior to the behavior?
- What happens immediately after the behavior?

Direct methods of gathering data involve careful observation. This precise type of observation is sometimes called identifying the ABCs of a particular behavior. The ABCs are:

A ntecedent

B ehavior

C onsequence

The *antecedent* is what is happening directly before the targeted behavior. The *behavior* is what has been targeted as the maladaptive behavior and the *consequence* is what happens directly after the behavior is exhibited (what the child gets out of it). The child should be observed at various times of the day and across all environments. From that, patterns or trends should emerge that give clues as to what need the behavior serves. At that point a new, appropriate behavior that serves the purpose can be taught to replace the maladaptive behavior. Consider the following example.

Analyzing the behavior in order to intervene David was a six-year-old boy with autism in our inclusive kindergarten class. Although he was relatively high functioning, he would regularly engage in self-injurious behavior, namely biting himself until he broke the skin and began to bleed. We decided to do a functional behavior assessment on David with the targeted behavior being biting himself. We observed David in the classroom, on the playground, during special activities such as music and gym class, and we also interviewed his mother and the speech therapist with whom he worked daily. It only took several days to realize that biting took place in an environment in which the sensory stimulation, namely sound, increased. It was noted that during computer time, while David was wearing headphones, he never engaged in self-biting. On the playground, David would typically wander off by himself and again was never seen biting himself. However, in the classroom when the noise level began to rise slightly we would see David first begin to rock and then start biting himself. We concluded that the increased sound was too stimulating and by rocking and biting himself he would increase other sensory system stimulation, thereby alleviating the stimulation to his ears. We began to teach David to go to a shelf on which there were a pair of headphones (which all the children knew were David's headphones) and put them on. So whenever the noise level began to be too much, he would go and put them on himself. What was really great was that after he would put on the headphones you would see him smiling as he moved around the classroom.

Conclusion

Functional behavior assessment can be an excellent tool to understand why children are behaving the way they do. Too often, teachers and parents rush to use disciplining techniques that are not only harmful to the child's self-esteem but are also ineffective. It is important to realize that children who are identified as developmentally delayed have special needs that they may not be able to tell us about. It is our job to find out what those needs are and to meet them whenever possible.

QUESTIONS TO CONSIDER ○ ○ ○

1. What kinds of techniques would be used when dealing with a child who is uncooperative at best and aggressive at worst?
2. How do structured observations explore concepts differently than other types of observations?
3. Identify ways in which to discover children's interests and motivations in order to do structured observations.

REFERENCES ○ ○ ○

AlleyDog.com. (n.d.). Glossary. Retrieved August 1, 2005, from http://www.alleydog.com/glossary/psychology-glossary.cfm

Dieterich, C. A., & Villani, C. J. (2000). Functional behavior assessment: Process without procedure. *Brigham Young University Education and Law Journal,* Issue 2, 209–217.

Hodges, K. (1994). *Child and adolescent functional assessment scale* (Rev. ed.). Ypsilanti, MI: Eastern Michigan University, Department of Psychology.

Reynolds, C. R., & Kamphaus, R. W. (1992). *Behavior assessment system for children: Manual.* Circle Pines, MN: American Guidance.

Wallin, J. (2001–2004). Functional behavior analysis. Retrieved June 10, 2005, from http://www.polyxo.com/fba

5

Visual Documentation

CHAPTER OBJECTIVES

- To gain understanding of the types and purposes of visual documentation
- To understand how visual documentation is related to developmental domains
- To gain skills in gathering and storing visual documentation
- To understand the influence of art on children about whom we have special concerns

CHILD STUDY OBJECTIVES

At the conclusion of this chapter the student will:

- collect visual documentation related to each developmental domain.
- use visual documentation to reflect on and report aspects of an individual child's development.
- arrange and store visual documentation in a neat and organized manner.

INTRODUCTION TO VISUAL DOCUMENTATION

You have heard the phrase "seeing is believing," haven't you? It means that someone can tell you something over and over again, but until you actually see it with your own eyes you can't really believe it. More importantly, you can't understand it. Visual documentation is a critical piece of a child study because it allows us to delve into the child's development using a concrete and permanent record. Visual documentation is quite simply something that we can look at in order to gain insight into the child's development; it can take many different forms. Figure 5–1 identifies the various types of visual documentation.

FIGURE 5–1 **Forms of visual documentation.**

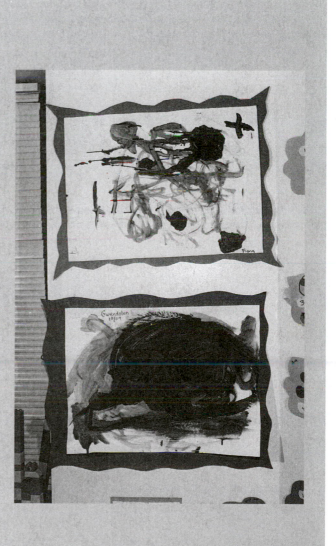

Samples of children's work

- Drawings, paintings, collages
- Writing (from scribbles to numbers and letters)
- Attempts at writing name
- Books dictated or illustrated by children
- Computer printouts: art, writing, and creative experiences
- Graphs of science-related experiments

(Continued on next page)

FIGURE 5–1   **Forms of visual documentation (*Continued*)**

Photographs of children's work and accomplishments
- Artwork
- Dramatic play activities
- Block building
- Accomplishments (sitting up, smiling, walking, eating solid food, rolling over, dressing self, climbing to top of a ladder)

Photographs of children involved in everyday routines and activities
- Self-feeding (using hands or spoon, drinking from a cup)
- Collecting leaves on a nature walk
- Performing personal care routines (brushing teeth)
- Playing peekaboo

Audiovisual records
- Audio recordings
- Children reciting stories they have made up
- Infants babbling
- Children making animal sounds, singing alone or with a group, or engaged in dramatic play

Video recordings
- Children participating in everyday activities and routines
- Field trips or special events
- Accomplishments, routines, and activities as described above

Source: U.S. Department of Health and Human Services, Head Start Bureau

PURPOSE OF VISUAL DOCUMENTATION

The purposes for visual documentation are as numerous and varied as the methods of collecting such documentation. In fact, the type of documentation may be selected with a specific purpose in mind.

Documentation to Record Important Events

Visual documentation often catalogues important life events. Many people photograph birthday and holiday gatherings as a means of assigning significance to the event. Weddings and births are filmed and lives are chronicled in diaries. The documentation of children's work, ideas, and representations can serve a similar purpose. The following story illustrates this.

On one occasion during an observation at an early care and education setting I was approached by a small girl. I had been taking notes on a legal pad. The girl asked: "Are you writing words?""Yes," I replied, as I tilted my pad so that she could view the cursive lines across the page. Without hesitation she pulled a small chair close to mine and commanded: "Write this." She began. "Today is Jackie's last day at school." With a glance in my direction she added, "that's me.""I am moving to Texas and I had to give my dog away. Texas is too far for a dog to go. He will be on a farm here. I won't see my teacher or my friends or the toys at this school anymore. Texas has teachers and toys." Jackie continued her dictation until all the pages of my tablet were filled with her story. She repeated some parts of the story over and over. She stopped often to ask if I could read the story back. She indicated, "that's an important part" as I read and reread her dictation. When finished, I asked if she wanted the story. She answered seriously: "No, you keep it. This is an important story to keep safe." Jackie had a purpose. She documented an important event in her life and shared it with someone who in her eyes must have seemed very official, taking notes in the corner of the classroom.

Visual Documentation to Aid Memory

Collected documentation of events or activities helps us to remember. Mem Fox (1985) alludes to the significance of documentation as a memory aid in her children's story of Wilfred Gordon McDonald Partridge, a small boy who befriends 96-year-old Nancy Allison Delacourt Cooper and helps her to remember events of her own life through a collection of artifacts from his experiences. Simple items such as seashells, a feathered puppet, and a football serve as visual representations of memories significant to their lives separately and then shared.

Documentation and Self-Image

Documentation of children's work sends the message that it is worthy of recording. Once during a visit to a Head Start classroom I observed a teacher sketching children's block buildings as they engaged in construction. Children checked her accuracy as they focused on their own representations. They took pride in the detail of their own work as they assessed and reflected on the block structure and its representation.

Documentation to Include and Inform Families

Visual documentation presented in an organized manner creates a bridge between the parent/family and the classroom. As families note photos of their child or examples of his work, they begin to better understand the learning process and perhaps see the child's development in a new way. Reflecting on children's work can influence our understanding of an individual child's development and serve as a gage for understanding developmental norms. Through the careful examination of visual documentation, teachers can expand the body of research that informs curriculum development and teaching practices. Visual documentation reveals the event as well as offering insight into the goals, interests, and values represented by the documentation.

REGGIO EMILIA EDUCATIONAL APPROACH

The Reggio Emilia educational approach, named for a village in Italy, uses visual documentation as a means of helping children explore ideas, understand more about themselves and others, and reflect on their work. Children engage in inquiry through language activities, problem solving, collaborative efforts, and project work. More than a product resulting from a singular activity, the Reggio Emilia approach uses documentation as an agent as well as a reflection.

For the Reggio Emilia approach, documentation is part of the learning process. This process includes children, their teachers, and their families. Documentation serves as an agent for planning, communicating, and reflecting. Children's experiences, including all of the processes of those experiences, are visually recorded and displayed for others to consider. This display, presented in the form of documentation boards with photos, graphs, and stories, reflects the child's perspective on his or her own learning.

A preschool located at Virginia Polytechnic University used the Reggio Emilia approach to document the community experiences of the duck pond located on campus. Young children at the school showed an abiding interest in the pond, so teachers decided to use this interest as a way to guide children's inquiry. The entire community participated in a study of the duck pond. Students from preschool to college engaged in the study of geography, ecology, entomology, water quality monitoring, poetry, environmental art, and even computer science.

Preschool children studied the growth and habits of the ducks at the pond. They observed fish, worms, salamanders, and tadpoles. They incubated duck eggs in the classroom and documented the hatching. The children documented their experiences with stories, graphs, and sculpture made from trash found at the duck pond.

Middle school children interviewed community members and alumni about their experiences at the duck pond and recorded responses in stories and on video and audiotape. Besides the middle schoolers' project to chronicle the duck pond's impact on the community, seventh and eighth graders engaged in many learning activities, including mapping, creative writing projects, animal studies, and a computer game based on the duck pond.

Art students at the college created environmental art at the duck pond with hanging objects from trees, floating footprints on water leading to a suspended door on shore, and performance art. Students documented their understanding of concepts through language (both written and oral), painting, sculpture, graphics, maps, dance, photography, computer programs, video, or any other media (Broughton, 1998).

ADVANTAGES OF VISUAL DOCUMENTATION

There are several unique advantages to using visual documentation along with other forms of indirect and direct assessments.

Viewing What Cannot Be Documented

Try this simple experiment. With one other person, go to the park or a mall, someplace with many activities going on all at once, and agree to focus on a set of two or three people to do anecdotal recordings on. After about five minutes, get together and compare notes. How many similarities did you find? What things did each of you focus on? Were they the same things? What things did one of you miss that the other recorded? More than likely, your notes will differ significantly. Even when using nonjudgmental and nonevaluative language, each of you will see something different. This is why visual documentation is so important in order to do a valid and complete child study.

All the other methods we talk about in this book for gathering developmental data on children are going to involve on-the-spot interpretation. As much as we try, none of us can be completely objective when recording children's behavior. But in using visual documentation there is no way our own biases can enter into the recording (except, of course, for what we choose to gather) and it naturally preserves varied perspectives on the actual events of a situation. Let's face it, no matter how objective and nonevaluative our language might be when writing an anecdotal record, there will still be a hint of bias because of what we chose to focus on during the observation. For example, an anecdotal record of a toddler climbing on top of a mini-gym might read as on the next page.

This is a very objective account and it does tell us about Alisha's gross motor development and even a bit about her emotional development (she is demonstrating **autonomy** and risk taking). However, if we were to view the videotape of this same scenario we would see much more that would tell us even more about her motor and emotional development. For instance, we would see how Mr. Roberts was right next to her while the whole thing was going on and how she kept looking at him each time she went up another rung. We would see the strength it took for her to pull herself completely up on the platform. And finally, we would see how she wavered back and forth between wanting Mr. Roberts to help her down and wanting to do it herself. After seeing this, our interpretations would be very different.

A Permanent Record

Another enormous advantage to gathering visual documentation is that it is a permanent record of how the child is developing, which can be shared between professionals and, more importantly, with families. Describing development by using a checklist or an anecdotal record is beneficial, but for most people a visual is much more effective. A parent or consulting professional who actually sees the child engaged in an activity or looks at a piece of the child's work understands the child's development much better and perceives the concepts of development more clearly. In addition, visual documentation provides a concrete record of the child's progress.

ANECDOTAL RECORD 5–1

Child's name: Alisha

Date: April 12

Time: 4:00 p.m.

Observer: J. Parker

Location: Mill Road School

18-month-old Alisha placed both hands on the lowest bar of the climbing apparatus and pushed her body weight into the two bars above it. She lifted her right hand to the next highest bar and lifted her right leg up to the first bar. She then lifted her left hand up to the next bar and her left leg to the first bar. She continued this pattern until her right hand was on the top of the platform of the climber. Then she laid down on the platform and slid her whole body onto the platform. She stayed sitting upright on the platform for about one minute, then signaled to Mr. Roberts (the toddler teacher) that she wanted to get down. Mr. Roberts lifted her back down.

DEVELOPMENTAL SIGNIFICANCE OF CHILDREN'S SAMPLES

Taking pictures or videotaping children engaged in activities or interactions gives us a wealth of information that can be used in many different ways. The question now becomes, "What kinds of information can I get from children's samples?" Children's samples are products created by children that can give us a window into their development.

....

Autonomy.   In child development, this means the child's sense of independence or being able to accomplish goals alone.

Information from Children's Drawings

A good amount of information can be gained about how a child is developing in various domains from his or her drawings.

Cognitive development   When young children paint or draw they rely on memories, images, experiences, and perceptions to create the product. The child's concept of a dog will come out in her picture of the dog. Her picture will reflect her experiences with dogs and how she perceives dogs. The objects in children's drawings will be representative of their culture as well. For example, a child living in the Midwest will have limited ability and inclination to create something representative of an ocean (Schirrmacher, 2006). The drawings of children can also tell us the following:

- The amount of detail a child uses gives us an idea of how much the child is discriminating and remembering.
- What a child includes in a picture can tell us something about how the child understands the physical world.
- A child's use of figure versus ground (does it look like some things are in the background?) tells us about his or her use of space.

Social-emotional development   A child's drawing or painting can give us insight into how the child is feeling and what is important to him. Although only trained professionals can really diagnose children's emotional development through art, children do express emotion through their art. As Malchiodi (1998) states: "To deny that children express emotions through art would ignore a significant part of who they are and how they perceive themselves and the world around them. Art is a potent container for their emotional lives and is undeniably an important aspect of understanding children" (p. 111).

Self-portraits and pictures of the family can also give us some insight into a child's sense of self and relationships with family members—especially when it comes to the structural element of size. A figure with a large size can indicate admiration or domination. A small-sized figure can indicate feelings of inadequacy or wanting to hide. More on emotional development and art appears in this chapter's Of Special Interest section.

Creative development   Of course, creative development can be demonstrated through children's paintings and drawings. The use of color and color combinations, the novel uses of art media, the complexity of the objects, and the ability to evoke emotion from the observer are all indications of creative development.

Information from Children's Writing

Another type of visual documentation, children's writings, can also tell us a great deal about fine motor and literacy development.

Fine motor development   Writing attempts go from simple to complex as children develop more control over their writing.

Literacy development   Writing to communicate gives us insight into the child's literacy development. Literacy development can be tracked by noting characteristics of a child's writing. Examples include:

- Children's story-writing attempts
- Name-writing attempts
- Left-to-right progression
- Sound discrimination

Although a great deal of information can be gleaned from looking at children's work, make sure you don't try to psychoanalyze the child. I have heard observers making comments such as, "Look at all the black he used in this picture, he must be depressed" or "Look how big the mom is in this picture and how small the dad is, the mom must be the boss in that family." The reality is, maybe the child likes the color black and maybe the child's mother is larger in stature, thus explaining the picture. Don't jump to conclusions regarding children's art; many interpretations are possible. Consider the following example.

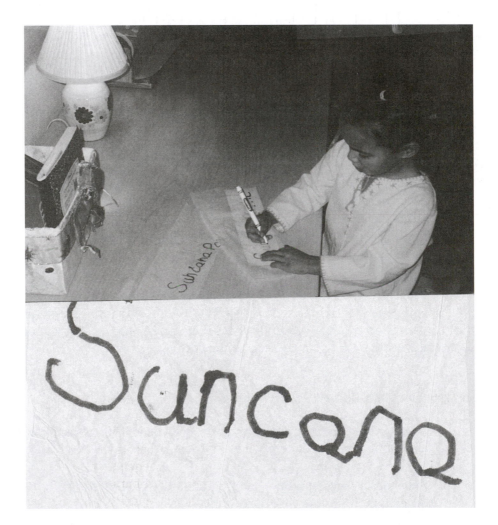

The Opera Story

An experienced early childhood educator tells the following story during parent orientation meetings at the cooperative nursery school where she teaches.

When I was just beginning my career, I was intrigued by the drawings and paintings constructed by children. I had been trained to examine and analyze children's work as reflections of their development as well as possible indicators of emotional well-being. On one occasion during my student teaching rotation, I observed a four-year-old boy at the easel. I watched, mesmerized, as he carefully painted four "people-like" figures on his painting. He added detail and color to each of the figures. I remember thinking that the four figures were likely representations of his family. He painted a smile on the tall figure and earrings on the obvious female figure. After spending an extended period painting, the boy stepped back, reviewed his picture, and turned to me to ask, "May I have two pots of black paint and two paintbrushes?" Black paint? I wondered. I was excited that I might share the work with his parents when they arrived at the day's end. However, it was the practice at that time to refrain from speaking to children about their art so as not to influence it. So without saying a word, I retrieved two pots of black paint and two clean paintbrushes. I handed them to the child.

With a dripping, heavy paintbrush in each hand the boy covered the entire painting in blackness. I held my breath. I could resist no longer. Half hoping that this behavior was not a window into the child's feelings about his family, I approached and in as controlled a tone as I could manage I asked: "I'm wondering why you covered your painting in black paint." The boy looked up into my face and with a smile replied: "The opera is over. The curtain is closed."

Source: Lita Eskin—Mayfair Nursery School, Scotia, New York

GATHERING VISUAL DOCUMENTATION

The best way to start to gather visual and other types of permanent documentation is to develop a system. You will need to obtain permission, decide on methods, label the works, and store the works.

Obtain Consent

The first task is to obtain permission to take pictures or video. Just as a consent-to-study form must be filled out by the families, a release for taking pictures must be signed as well. (A sample release form is on the CD-ROM.)

Identify the Methods To Be Used

Next, you need to identify the methods that you will use to take pictures and/or videos. A highly recommended tool is a digital camera that also has the capability to take movies. The digital camera has become a critical piece of equipment in our lab school because we can take as many pictures as we want and then burn them onto CD-ROMs and even make PowerPoint presentations from them. Digital images can be stored easily and printed, as well. A camera that requires film of any kind can become a costly endeavor and will usually not be used as often because of the expense and the inconvenience.

Having access to a copy machine is also very beneficial because many times children will not want to give up their works—so asking if you may copy them is sometimes a good compromise. Of course, if you only have a black and white copier and the picture you want is full of color, you could always take a digital picture of it, too.

Label the Works

After taking the pictures or getting a copy of a child's work you must date the work and provide a brief anecdote as to its significance. If the child dictated a narrative, include that as well. The photo below shows an example of a piece of visual documentation and the written documentation that goes with it.

ANECDOTAL RECORD 5–2

Child's name: Gabriela and Rebecca

Date: May 04

Time: 11:10 a.m.

Observer: Ms. D

Location: Gateway Montessori

Two girls use wooden unit blocks to construct a structure. The structure has elements of bridging with blocks spanning the space created by other blocks. They place blocks end to end to create an enclosure. Blocks are arranged by laying them flat and by standing them on edge. The girls create balance and symmetry with the blocks and assign the structure an imaginary social label "pool." The girls work together to draw a representation of the structure on a tag board label. The girls tape the label to the structure and announce "pool open."

Reflection:

Cognitive: Girls demonstrate stage four of block building as the structure has elements of enclosures, bridging, vertical and horizontal block orientation and an imaginary label.

Language: The children draw and "read" their drawings as a form of communication.

Social: Children work cooperatively.

Self: Children demonstrate a sense of accomplishment as they examine and document their work.

Creative: Children create a drawing or representation of their work.

Store the Documentation

Finally, you will need something to store the child's work and other visual documentation in. Remember the works will not always be nice and neat 8½" x 11" pieces of paper, so plan accordingly. Perhaps an oversize file folder would work best, or an unused pizza box.

Steps for gathering and presenting visual documentation

1. Obtain permission.
2. Acquire appropriate technology.
3. Take pictures or gather works.
4. Label documentation with anecdotes, dictations, and date.
5. Store documentation.

Of Special Interest—Children At Risk and Art Therapy

Children who experienced a traumatic event are sometimes considered *at risk* for developing emotional difficulties. Traumatic events include:

- Being a victim of violence, such as child abuse or kidnapping
- Witnessing violence, such as a shooting, stabbing, or beating
- Being involved in a shocking accident, such as a car wreck or fire
- Being involved in or witnessing a natural disaster, such as a hurricane, tornado, or tsunami
- Experiencing a loss of a loved one through death, divorce, or separation

The Value of Art for Children At Risk

The value of making art for children at risk is really twofold.

First, insight into how the child is processing the particular trauma can be gained by noting and analyzing how and what the child draws, paints, or molds. A drawing can provide information on developmental, emotional, and cognitive functioning, accelerate expression of hidden traumas, and express confusing or paradoxical feelings and perceptions (Malchiodi, 2001). Consider the example of the five-year-old boy who witnessed his father getting shot and killed by a police officer and now draws himself very small in pictures with adults in uniform. This can reflect a desire to stay hidden or out of sight by staying very small and undetectable. By discovering how the child is processing the trauma, therapists and other professionals can intervene more effectively.

Second, the act of creating the art can be very therapeutic in and of itself. Because drawing evokes a multisensory experience, it allows the child to tap into feelings and emotions that verbal processing alone does not. Drawing and painting provide self-soothing experiences that are particularly helpful in reducing stress and lessening the symptoms of post-traumatic stress syndrome (Malchiodi, 1990; 1997).

Assessment Tasks

Described below are two of the tasks that an art therapist might ask of a child who has been traumatized. **It is very important to remember, however, that these exercises should be done under the supervision of a certified art therapist.** If a child has created a picture and wants to share the experience with you, the best response is to simply listen and document what the child has said. This information can be very helpful to anyone working with the child in a therapeutic manner.

1. *Draw a "what happened" picture.* For this task, the child is simply asked to draw the traumatic event. The art therapist will ask questions regarding what the child is drawing and what is going on in the picture. This task can help alleviate some of the anxiety about the traumatic event.

2. *Draw a picture of yourself when the event happened.* For this task, the child is asked to draw where he was during the event and what he was doing. The basic objective is to find out how the child sees himself in relationship to the event. This can be very helpful in seeing how the child is processing the traumatic event and how he perceives himself.

Drawing and creating art are good methods for assessing how a child who is at risk for emotional difficulties due to trauma perceives the experience. In order to work with the child, the therapist must know how the child understands the event and how she sees herself. So the role of the teacher and observer is to offer multiple opportunities to create art, and more importantly, to note children's narratives concerning their art.

QUESTIONS TO CONSIDER ○ ○ ○

1. How does the collection of and reflection on visual documentation inform understanding of child development differently than other means of documentation such as checklists, anecdotal records, and structured play observations?

2. How does the process of documenting ideas or work influence the child's development?

3. List the strengths and weaknesses of using visual documentation as a means of assessing a child's development.

REFERENCES ○ ○ ○

Broughton, S. (1998). The great duck pond project: Building a community of learners around a campus landmark. Blacksburg, VA: Virginia Polytechnic Institute and State University, University Relations. Retrieved August 1, 2005, from http://www.unirel.vt.edu/vtmag/winter98/feature2.html

Fox, M. (1985). *Wilford Gordon McDonald Partridge.* La Jolla, CA: Kane/Miller.

Malchiodi, C. A. (1990). *Breaking the silence: Art therapy with children from violent homes.* New York: Brunner-Routledge.

Malchiodi, C. A. (1997). *Breaking the silence: Art therapy with children from violent homes* (Rev. ed.). New York: Brunner/Mazel.

Malchiodi, C. A. (1998). *Understanding children's drawings.* New York: Guilford Press.

Malchiodi, C. A. (2001). Using drawing as intervention with traumatized children. *Trauma and loss: Research and interventions, 1*(1). Retrieved May 11, 2005, from http://www.tlcinst.org/drawingintervention.html

Schirrmacher, R. (2006). *Art and creative development for young children* (5th ed.). New York: Thomson Delmar Learning.

U.S. Department of Health and Human Services. (1998). *Head Start training manual.* Alexandria, VA: Head Start Publications Center.

Parent Questionnaire and Background Information

CHAPTER OBJECTIVES

- To understand the importance of gathering developmental information from families
- To understand the components of a good parent questionnaire
- To select and construct questionnaire questions
- To evaluate questionnaires and interviews

CHILD STUDY OBJECTIVES

At the conclusion of this chapter the student will:

- research and construct a parent questionnaire.
- administer the parent questionnaire.
- research and construct a comprehensive background history of the child.

INTRODUCTION TO FAMILY INVOLVEMENT IN THE ASSESSMENT PROCESS

Parents and guardians can contribute considerably to the body of information regarding their child's abilities, strengths, possible difficulties, and educational needs. As first observers of their child, parents have had many opportunities to see the child in various settings. Additionally, families have longitudinal data regarding trends and patterns of development followed by their child that may not be available from any other source. As advocates for their child the family brings a unique perspective to the child study. Their observations, questions, and ideas can benefit the child study and add to the overall understanding of the child.

Lines of communication between parents and teachers should always be open.

Parents are generally eager to share information about their child as well as to gain information from the teacher's perspective regarding their child's developmental progress. Concerns may be pressing but the parent is unsure of how to initiate dialogue regarding questionable behavior. The mother of a nine-month-old recently asked her caregiver, "Have you noticed how his hands tremble?" This gave the provider the opportunity to share some of the concerns she has had regarding the child's developing motor skills. This parent has valuable information about the child's present motor functioning and about the past history of the child's development. This past history can include past experiences, trauma, or hereditary considerations.

Information from parents can include:

- Medical history
- Current symptoms or concerns
- Child's current developmental functioning
- Developmental history
- Personality
- Social-emotional adjustment
- Family information
- Cultural Information

CULTURAL VARIATION

Working with Culturally Diverse Families

Culturally diverse families, like all families, are interested in their child's growth and development. Initiatives in early education and school settings that have been successful in partnering with culturally diverse families include the following strategies:

1. PERSONAL. Interpersonal communication is most effective with culturally diverse families, particularly when that communication is in the parent's native language. Home visits are particularly effective in establishing a trusting relationship.
2. BILINGUAL. Communication, both written and oral, should be available in multiple languages in addition to English. Families may feel more positive about answering questions if they can understand them well.
3. CULTURE. Make an effort to understand key aspects of all cultures and their impact on the child's development. It is your job to seek out cultural information, both global and personal.

Source: Espinosa, 1995

Reliability of Parent/Family Input

It is important to note that all information from families may not be reliable when viewed through scientific lenses. Parents are as unique as their children; therefore, not all parental reports are equal. Some families may not accurately remember details of the child's early life and others may have taken copious notes regarding their child's firsts. Parents and guardians need time to fill out questionnaires or respond to survey questions, so those with limited time may not provide the depth needed for an accurate understanding of the child's history. Additionally, families may have a biased view regarding their child's development. Interestingly, research indicates that parental reports of current behavior *are* reliable, particularly when information is gathered through well designed, structured interviews or inventories (Liechtenstein & Ireton, 1984). Researchers need to be careful, however, about response bias with questionnaires. A bias response known as the halo effect can occur with rating scales, where parents or guardians may rate their child high on all scales, regardless of the child's actual performance or ability.

THE SCOPE OF PARENT QUESTIONNAIRES

Parent questionnaires are designed to obtain accurate information regarding the child's current or past development. Questionnaires are typically broad in their scope, encompassing information about the child's medical history and health, developmental milestones, personal habits, preferences, and family information. Shorter questionnaires may be devised to determine more narrowly the child's present development, learning style, or adjustment to new situations.

Commercially produced questionnaires can be used to gain information regarding a child's development. An example of such a questionnaire is *Infant Development Inventory* (IDI) questionnaire, which asks parents to describe their infant and answer questions about "What's Your Baby Doing?" using an Infant Development Chart (Ireton, 1994). Additionally, parents can report any concerns about their child's health, development, or behavior.

Developing a questionnaire designed for use by families takes more time and consideration than simply selecting and using a commercially published survey. The benefits of designing a parent questionnaire specific to the child or children with whom you are working may outweigh the additional effort. Questions can be constructed to increase your understanding of a child's developmental functioning in an area that has been difficult to observe. Perhaps you are curious about the child's diet or food preferences. I once observed a child who refused all the food served at the child care setting. Upon interviewing the family I learned that the child had severely limited food preferences, some of which were never served at the center! Teachers had spent time and money evaluating this child's social abilities due to her aggressive behavior toward other children late in the day. It was only after speaking with the family that I was able to determine that the catalyst for the aggression was hunger. Additionally, you can construct questions that give families the opportunity to state their goals and values, helping to create a learning environment reflective of the child's own culture. A friend recently shared a story of her volunteer work in an impoverished village in Africa. Volunteers assessed the needs of the community and decided to build a medical facility. After speaking with local villagers they discovered that it was a soccer field that the community most desired. She learned that an individual perspective influences our understanding of quality of life issues. Likewise, the perspective of the family should influence the queries made in your questionnaire.

Developing a Parent Questionnaire

➤ *Determine the purpose and objectives for developing the parent questionnaire.* The purpose of developing a parent questionnaire may be to gather developmental information regarding an individual child's development. The objective may be to uncover past medical and developmental history, such as prenatal development and characteristics at birth. The objective may focus on gathering current health and nutrition information. Formulating an understanding of a child's daily eating, sleeping, and play behaviors can be enormously helpful when conducting a child study. On the other hand, the purpose may be to examine a specific developmental domain that requires more information to fully understand the scope of the child's development. For example, the child may appear unresponsive verbally during observations and interviews. It is important to gain an understanding of how the child's language usage differs, if at all, in the home environment.

➤ *Design specific questions that meet your purpose and objectives.* For example, if you are primarily interested in conditions surrounding the child's prenatal development, the following questions may be appropriate:

- What was the length of your pregnancy?
- What was the child's weight at birth?
- Were there any unusual factors or complications during pregnancy?
- Did your child have any medical problems at birth?

If your primary concern is in gathering information regarding the child's daily routine, the following questions may be appropriate:

- Is your child toilet trained?
- How many hours does your child sleep at night?
- Does your child nap?

➤ *Administer the questionnaire.* The questionnaire could be mailed home or given directly to a parent for him to complete on his own, to be returned at a later time. Interactive questioning of the parent is also appropriate. This interview-type administration allows the student researcher to clarify information or ask additional questions for more information. However, this method does not allow the parent to check documentation such as baby books or medical records in order to give the most accurate answers.

DESIGNING QUALITY QUESTIONNAIRES

The quality of the questionnaire is only as good as the quality of the question. There are two basic types of questions.

Types of Questions

Close-ended questions incorporate answers or response categories that are specified beforehand, such as yes/no, multiple choice, or ranking. In carefully written close-ended questions, the question and responses mean the same thing to nearly all respondents. Close-ended questions are faster to administer and easier to interpret.

However, close-ended questions may prompt the parent to answer in a way she thinks she is expected to respond. Due to the closed nature of this type of question, important information may be unwittingly omitted (Losh, 2002).

The second type of question is known as the *open-ended question*. These questions are generally used to generate ideas, allow flexibility, and reduce the likelihood of researcher bias. Open-ended questions take longer to administer, may produce longer answers, and are subject to your own interpretation.

Types of Questionnaire Items

1. Open-ended question
Describe your child's engagement, over the past 4 weeks, in exercise, sports, or physically active hobbies.

2. Close-ended questions

Attitude Questions
Your child is highly energetic.

Strongly disagree   Disagree   Neutral   Agree   Strongly agree

Rating Questions
How often does your child watch television?

_____Per day

_____Per week

_____Per month

_____Never

_____I'm not sure

During the past week has your child played outside?

Yes

No

I don't know

Close-ended questions should ask about only one topic at a time. Questions that include more than one topic are called *double barreled*. **Double-barreled questions** are easily identified by the use of "and" and "or" connectors (Losh, 2002). It is difficult to interpret a double-barreled question, because it is unclear to which question the parent has responded. A double-barreled question might look like: "Does your child swim and ride her bike?" or "Does your child do household chores and get allowance? If a parent answers in the affirmative, you can't be sure if the child swims and rides a bike or if she engages in only one of the activities. A parent who answers in the negative may have done so because the child swims but does not own a bike.

....

Double-barreled questions.   Questions that address more than one topic and use "and" and "or."

Response Options

Response choices should include all of the possibilities parents may have to the question. "Did your child play outside today?" could elicit a *yes*, a *no*, or perhaps *I don't know*. In order to gather the most accurate information, vary the format of the questionnaire. For example, a popular questionnaire format is the **Likert item,** where people are asked whether they strongly agree, agree, are undecided, disagree, or strongly disagree with an attitude statement. A questionnaire with only Likert items encourages **acquiescence response.** In acquiescence response, people tend to generally agree or disagree with nearly every statement on the questionnaire regardless of how they actually feel (Losh, 2002). Varying the question format keeps the respondent thinking and the answers accurate.

Scope of Questions

Questions that ask about specific locations or time frames are useful in gathering accurate information. Asking parents where their child was born could garner responses such as New York, Ellis Hospital, or in a taxi. It is more helpful to phrase the question with location confines such as: "At what hospital was your child born?" It is generally not a good idea to use hypothetical questions. In other words, do not ask parents to report how they "might feel" or how their child "might respond." The answers to such questions are generally inaccurate because people have not fully considered their responses. Asking a parent, "How do you think your child would respond in the event of a fire?" is nearly impossible to answer, except "scared" (and a survey probably isn't necessary to obtain that information).

Complexity of Questions

Break complex questions down into two or three separate questions. Suppose you were to ask a parent: "What do you do when your child has a temper tantrum? Tell me all the actions you take: (a) time out, (b) spanking, (c) bribery." This question is confusing and will yield inaccurate information. Construct three smaller questions, such as "(1) When your child has a temper tantrum do you use time out? (2) Do you spank your child when she has a temper tantrum? (3) How do you feel about bribing your child?" Avoid the use of professional jargon. If you have questions regarding object permanence, ask questions such as "Does your child play peekaboo?" or "Does your child search for a dropped object?" Use complete sentences so that the parent understands what you are asking. Avoid **hot button words** such as *punishment, fair, bad, immature,* and *delayed,* to mention a few.

Likert item.   Questionnaire item that asks respondents to select from a scale the degree to which they agree or disagree with the test question.

Acquiescence response.   When respondents either agree or disagree with every item on the questionnaire, regardless of their true feelings.

Hot button words.   Words that evoke high emotion.

Questions to Avoid

Avoid including leading and loaded questions in your questionnaire. A leading question is one that leads the parent to choose one response over another by its wording. Leading questions are generally hidden within a statement and are presented as if there is a preferred response, such as "Don't you agree that children should engage in active play daily?" A loaded question is a question that carries an assumption, and is worded in such a way that the respondent who answers the question directly admits to accepting that assumption. For example, it is inappropriate to ask a parent, "Is the child's acting out directly caused by the marital strife in the household?" No matter how the parent answers the question, it is assumed that marital strife exists!

Use the following checklist to help you in choosing the appropriate types of question and to critique the questions once they are written.

Checklist for constructing questions

❏ Which question type will gather the most information?
❏ Will this question type gather accurate information?
❏ Are the questions written in the family's native language?
❏ Is the format easy to understand?
❏ Does the order of questions build from one topic to another?
❏ Questionnaire will not require a long period of time to complete.

GATHERING BACKGROUND INFORMATION

Information regarding the child's medical history, care and education history, and family history can shed light on many aspects of a child's development. The knowledge that a child has had chronic asthma since infancy may contribute to your understanding of the child's overall physical development. Premature birth may have an impact on many areas of a child's development and may influence how you view the child's current level of mastery.

Early Experiences

Gathering information regarding the child's early education or elementary education history can give you some idea of the child's prior experiences. Those experiences may have influenced the child's social or emotional development. Take, for instance, a child who spent the first three years of her life enrolled in a child care setting that experienced high teacher turnover. As a result of the teacher turnover the child experienced multiple broken attachments during periods of critical social development. Consider the developmental implications for a child who was cared for in a kibbutz, an Israeli settlement, in the war-torn West Bank (see Sagi, van IJzendoorn, Aviezer, Donnell, Koren-Karie, Joels, et al., 1995; Sagi, van IJzendoorn, Aviezer, Donnell, & Mayseless, 1994; Oppenheim, Sagi, & Lamb, 1988). Since a child's development does not occur in isolation, the collection of historical information is not just nice but imperative.

One context in which the child develops is the family. Gathering historical information about a child's family can greatly enhance your view of the child's development. Children of farmers may understand categorization or relationships of plants and animals that may influence other cognitive abilities. A child who resides with a large extended family may have communications skills that reflect diverse styles and perhaps multiple languages. Children who struggle in poverty may not have the proper nutrition for the growth of their brains and bodies. The collection of this data contributes to your knowledge of every developmental domain and the child's functioning within that domain.

Information regarding the child's background can be gathered from parents, classroom or center records, and children. Asking parents to share information about the child's birth, infancy, early experiences, and family is a good place to start. Interviewing children and parents should be done privately and on their schedule. Remember to keep all information that you gain confidential.

Methods for Collecting Data

Early childhood centers and schools collect information regarding medical history, growth and development, and family composition. With parent permission you may be able to view these documents to gain a better understanding of how the child's background has influenced her current development. For example, the child may have had ongoing speech and language services. Longitudinal documentation related to the child's language development in the form of the child's Individual Educational Plan (IEP) may be available for your review. Such documents are confidential and require formal releases from parents.

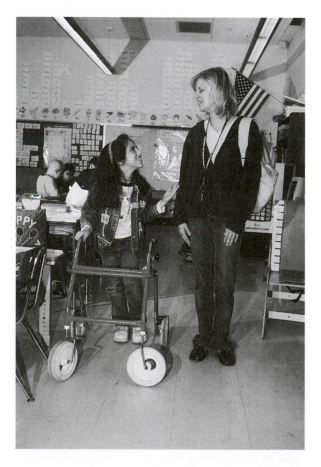

Interviewing children is a common practice in the field of education. Jean Piaget, Albert Bandura, and B. F. Skinner all spent time asking children questions and carefully recording their responses. Informal interviews are likely the most successful with children, as their attention may wane. Questions should be a natural part of the conversation. During daily activities the child may report that while living in Alaska her family went ice fishing as a means of getting food and now they buy fish at the store. Follow-up questions about life in Alaska are appropriate and may be welcomed by the child.

Of Special Interest—Developing Goals and Objectives According to Family Needs

Through individual education planning, those who work closest with the child have the opportunity to collaborate. The terms Individualized Family Service Plan (IFSP) and Individual Education Plan (IEP) are global terms referring to written documents outlining a plan to address the individual learning needs of a child. The team of people who come together to work on the IEP include the child, family, teachers, community advocates, and service providers. Each member of the IFSP and IEP team has different knowledge of and experiences with the child. Collaborative planning enables the team to identify, coordinate, and make use of resources and strategies that will offer the best opportunity for the child's development. This process ensures that each area of the child's development is considered in the plan. IFSP and IEP collaboration takes time and commitment from all those who are involved in the child's life. However, the benefits are well worth the effort.

A key ingredient that has been recognized over the past years in the planning of the IFSP or IEP is the input of the families. In fact, it is now the law that when the IFSP is being created, the parents must take part in the planning of the goals and the objectives for the child. The IFSP and IEP planning process is important because it provides the family with an arena in which to voice their opinions and concerns. The IEP also provides a framework for communicating with the family. Through the IEP process families are able to communicate goals and values, contribute their perspectives, understand and support school plans, and discuss questions (McLean, 2005).

Assessing the Needs of the Family

To begin this process the child's **case worker** will set up meetings in the child's home to talk with the parents on the concerns and challenges they face raising a child with special needs, as well as their hopes and dreams for their child's future. During the interview the case worker will determine what kinds of needs the family has as well as what they believe the child needs. The case worker may also give the parents a questionnaire to fill out that will give more insight into what the needs are. A typical family needs questionnaire would ask questions regarding the following:

❖ Do you need *information* on child development or your child's condition, such as how to play or talk with your child, information regarding types of services available for your child, or how to handle your child's behavior?

❖ Do you have *family or social supports* such as someone to talk to, someone to help with chores, someone to watch the children when you need to be away?

❖ Do you have any *financial* needs? Are you able to pay for shelter, food, transportation and clothing, babysitters, equipment the child may need?

....

Case worker.   In early intervention, this person organizes and oversees a particular child's case. This is the "go to" person in helping the family coordinate services.

❖ Do you need help locating *child care*?

❖ Do you need access to *community support* systems such as support groups, understanding doctors, and dentists who will take your child?

Because the needs of the child are inextricably linked with the needs of the family, a family needs assessment is critical to working with the child with special needs.

View the Anecdotal Record on the CD-ROM. Create three questions you might ask parents concerning the child's development based on the Anecdotal Record.

QUESTIONS TO CONSIDER ○ ○ ○

1. How might you address the concerns of a parent who is concerned about the confidentiality of information gathered in the parent questionnaire or background history?

2. Who might you contact to get a better idea about the child's educational experiences? What steps might you follow to gather such information?

3. List three techniques you might use to develop the parents' or guardians' trust in you and your involvement with their family.

REFERENCES ○ ○ ○

Espinosa, L. M. (1995). *Hispanic parent involvement in early childhood programs*. Urbana, IL: ERIC Clearinghouse on Elementary and Early Childhood Education. (ERIC Digest No. ED382412.)

Ireton, H. (1994). *Infant Development Inventory*. Minneapolis, MN: Behavior Science Systems.

Liechtenstein, R., & Ireton, H. (1984). *Preschool screening*. New York: Grune & Stratton.

Losh, S. C. (2002). *Methods of educational research*. Web-based course, Florida State University. Retrieved January 12, 2006, from http://edf5481-01.fa02.fsu.edu/Questionnaires.html

McLean, L. (2005). *Individual Education Planning: A handbook for developing and implementing IEP*. Manitoba, Canada: Department of Education.

Oppenheim, D., Sagi, A., & Lamb, M. E. (1988). Infant-adult attachments on the kibbutz and their relation to socioemotional development four years later. *Developmental Psychology, 24*(3), 427–433.

Sagi, A., van IJzendoorn, M. H., Aviezer, O., Donnell, F., Koren-Karie, N., Joels, T., et al. (1995). Attachments in a multiple caregiver and multiple infant environment: The case of the Israeli kibbutzim. In E. Waters, B. E. Vaughn, G. Posada, & K. Kondo-Ikemura (Eds.), Constructs, cultures and caregiving: New growing points of attachment theory. *Monographs of the Society for Research in Child Development, 60*(2–3), 71–91.

Sagi, A., van IJzendoorn, M. H., Aviezer, O., Donnell, F., & Mayseless, O. (1994). Sleeping out of home in a kibbutz communal arrangement: It makes a difference for infant-mother attachment. *Child Development, 65*(4), 992–1004.

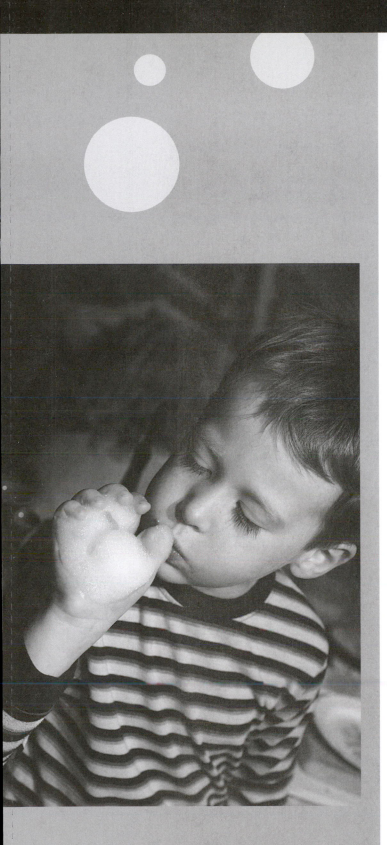

II

UNDERSTANDING CHILD DEVELOPMENT
Developmental Concepts and Sequences

There is in the soul of a child an impenetrable secret that is gradually revealed as it develops.

—Maria Montessori

Physical and Motor Development

CHAPTER OBJECTIVES

- To discuss the principles of brain development that particularly pertain to physical development

- To describe physical development in terms of changes in body size and proportion

- To identify infant states and understand their significance to cognitive development

- To describe sensory and perceptual development

- To discuss the significance of the presence and later absence of reflexive responses

- To identify the developmental milestones of gross and fine motor development

- To recognize possible symptoms of sensory motor integration disorders

CHILD STUDY OBJECTIVES

At the conclusion of this chapter the student will:

- code physical (growth and fine and gross motor) development for each of the existing anecdotal records.

- develop a checklist for gross and fine motor development.

- gather and label visual documentation relating to gross and fine motor development.

- prepare a plan for (identify goal and objective) and conduct a structured observation for gross and fine motor development, interpreting the results (by completing an assessment form and writing a brief summary).

INTRODUCTION TO PHYSICAL AND MOTOR DEVELOPMENT

In this chapter we focus on the development of the child's body. In some circles this is called the biosocial domain of development (Berger, 2002) or the physical domain. Physical development refers to the changes that occur in the body over time, including body size, body proportions, tissue makeup (body mass index), skeletal growth, and hormone production; motor skills both gross and fine; sensory development; and physical health, such as immunities, childhood illness, and disease.

BRAIN DEVELOPMENT

The brain development principles discussed in this chapter relate directly to the timing of the emergence of many skills and abilities seen in infants and young children. The ability to gain control of physical movements and mental activity can be attributed to hierarchical development, lateralization, and differentiation. The capability to react quickly and process information efficiently can be attributed to myelination.

Hierarchical Development

At birth, the entire brain is formed but not yet developed. Brain development occurs from low to high; this is called **hierarchical development.** The **brainstem,** which is the part of the brain that controls basic functions like sucking and swallowing and breathing, is fairly well developed at birth, but the parts that control the neck muscles, arms, legs, etc. are still under development. Also, because the lower part of the brain is basically running the show early on, the infant's reactions are reflexive in nature. Throughout the first year of life a pediatrician tests the infant's reflexes in order to assess neurological development. When an infant demonstrates specific reflexes, it means that certain brain connections are intact and developing at a normal rate. Although it is a good sign to see reflexive responses initially, it is also a good sign when these reflexes begin to disappear and thoughtful action begins to take the place of reflexive action. Reflexive reaction should give way to controlled action. When the infant begins making purposeful, controlled movements, we know that the higher parts of the brain are connecting up and developing.

Lateralization and Differentiation

During the first months of life the brain is also going through the process of **lateralization.** The part of the brain that tells the shoulders to move is separate from the part that tells the

---

Hierarchical development.   Refers to the progression of development in the brain from low to high. The lower parts of the brain link up first, followed by the high parts of the brain.

Brainstem.   Part of the brain that connects to the spinal cord and contains the lower structures of the brain.

Lateralization.   The process of division of the functioning of the human brain into two hemispheres. One side controls things such as language and the other regulates motor skills. This division is relative, since most brain functions require both hemispheres but do so to a lesser degree as children mature.

Cephalocaudal development proceeds from head to toe.

Proximodistal development proceeds from the midline to the extremities.

right thumb to move. The right side of the brain controls the movements on the left side of the body and vice versa. One of the parts of the brain that controls muscle movement is called the "motor strip" and is located in the higher areas of the brain; therefore, it takes time to develop. As the infant's brain is developing from low to high, corresponding motor control emerges from head to toe. This is called **cephalocaudal** development. The typical pattern is for the infant to first gain control of head, shoulders, and neck, then the upper torso, then the hips and pelvis, and finally the legs (see left photo).

Just as control develops from head to toe, it also develops from the center to the peripheral, or from gross to fine. This is called **proximodistal** development and the developmental process in the brain responsible for this is called **differentiation**. As the brain develops, the connections between the neurons become more and more refined. Likewise, we can see that the young child's movements become more refined and precise (see right photo).

....

Cephalocaudal.   Progression of development from head to toe.

Proximodistal.   Progression of development from the inner part of the body (midline) to the outer parts.

Differentiation.   A process by which the structures in the brain become more and more specialized.

Consider this example. Let's say you wanted to call your aunt in Chicago. First the connection has to get to a general area in the Midwest. Next the phone system has to narrow that connection down to Illinois. The system refines the search again to Chicago. Then it has to make the connection to Lake Shore Drive, narrow that down to your aunt's apartment building, and finally make the most precise connection—to your aunt's phone. This is differentiation. The infant first controls gross motor movements, because the brain's connections are global in nature. The connections first control the leg, but to get to specific parts of the leg and finally the toes, the brain will need to do some precise wiring, and this will take some time.

As differentiation and lateralization continue, young children gain more and more control over their movements and their mental actions. Table 7–1 summarizes the progression of development.

TABLE 7–1   **Progression of Development**

Progression of Development	Cephalocaudal	Proximodistal
Earlier	Head	Trunk
	Shoulders	Arms
	Neck	Legs
	Torso	Hands
	Hips/Pelvis	Feet
	Legs	Fingers
Later		Toes

Refined motor tasks

Myelination

The brain is continually striving to become a more efficient information processor. One way this occurs is through the process of **myelination.** At the end of each neuron, or nervous system cell, is a part called the axon. When messages are sent within the brain or from the brain to the body, they travel along the axon. Thus, when you put your hand on a hot stove, the message of VERY HOT goes from your finger to your brain. The message gets to the proper place in the brain (motor area) and quickly sends the message back down to your hand to MOVE IT! If the axon is myelinated, the message will travel faster. As more and more neurons become myelinated, the child can perform tasks much more quickly, move more rapidly, and speak more fluently.

The Progression of Myelination   As with all other kinds of brain development, experience affects the rate of myelination. The emerging abilities seen in infancy and childhood relate to the rate at which different brain structures myelinate. The area that is slowest to fully myelinate is the frontal cortex, which begins myelination at approximately six months of age and continues throughout childhood, adolescence, and adulthood. Spurts in the development of the frontal lobes have been found to occur from birth to two years, seven to nine years, and in the mid teens. The frontal lobes are critical in the executive functions such as organizing and planning. They are central to emotional development and control, as well.

Nutrition and Myelination   Nutrition also plays a part in brain development and specifically myelination. Animal and human studies have shown that severe malnutrition during fetal growth and early infancy retards brain cell division and alters nerve myelination. A vitamin B12 deficiency during the prenatal period has been linked to *demyelination* (prevention of myelination), usually in the spinal cord area (Lovblad, Ramelli, Remonda, Nirkko, Ozdoba, & Schroth, 1997). Malnutrition has been associated with slower **habituation** rates in infants, and later in early childhood with lower IQ scores, poor attention and memory, and lower school achievement (Eysenck & Schoenthaler, 1997; Lozoff, 1989; Ricciuti, 1993).

CONCEPTS OF PHYSICAL GROWTH AND DEVELOPMENT

In order to fully understand the physical growth and development of children, one needs to consider how their bodies grow and change in size and proportion. Growth spurts, nutrition, and health care are all important aspects to explore when documenting the physical well-being of a child. The concepts of physical growth and development go far beyond a child simply getting larger in size. The development of sensory and perceptual systems goes hand in hand with physical development. It is a combination of

....

Myelination.   A process by which axons (nerve endings) become surrounded by myelin (a fatty substance), thereby speeding up transmission of messages between neurons.

Habituation.   Refers to a decrease in responsiveness to a particular stimulus.

the child's physical growth, perceptual and sensory development, and environmental factors that make up the arena we call physical growth and development.

Growth and Changes in the Body

Governed by heredity and greatly influenced by environmental conditions, physical development and growth are highly individualized processes (Allen & Marotz, 2003). Rapid brain and body growth occurs during the prenatal period and within the first year of life. Physical growth is directly linked to progress in other developmental areas and is responsible for increasing muscle strength, coordination, and control. Children's bodies change in size and proportion, and fat, muscle, and skeletal composition. A child's physical development is an important barometer by which to measure the child's general well-being.

Changes in Size   Although children's physical development appears to be steady, it actually occurs in spurts. During infancy, changes are rapid. In the first three months of life infants gain an average of two pounds per month. By five months of age the infant's weight has doubled and by the end of the first year it has tripled. Not only do infants gain weight, but they make great strides in height. By age two the infant's height is 75 percent greater than at birth. In comparison, body growth during the preschool and middle childhood years is slow and steady. The human child experiences great growth spurts again in adolescence.

Changes in Proportion   As the child grows in height and weight, different parts of the body grow at different rates; body proportions change accordingly. In fact, an infant or toddler's head and torso accounts for most of her body length or height. As children's bodies develop, the limbs become proportionally longer. This is clearly evidenced in the toddler's heavy head, large torso, and short legs. There is, however, an exception to the rule. During adolescence the growth of the feet and hands precedes the rapid growth in height and weight.

Changes in Muscular and Skeletal Composition   Major changes in the fat and muscular composition of the body take place with development. Babies and toddlers have more fat in their bodies, but the school-age child is more angular and slender. Girls have slightly more fat than boys and continue to develop fat in their limbs in adolescence, whereas boys reduce limb fat at this time. Unlike fat, muscle tissue grows slowly in infancy and childhood and becomes more rapid in adolescence. Adolescent males experience greater muscle development than do females. Skeletal growth begins in prenatal life in the form of cartilage and continues until the individual's twentieth birthday. In growth plates, located at each end of long bones, cartilage is gradually converted into bone. Besides increasing in length, the bones of the skeleton also grow in width, a process that takes place without the intervention of cartilage. Bone width growth is much like the growth of a tree expanding in girth; new layers are deposited as the result of cell growth.

      More information regarding children's physical growth and National Health Statistics growth charts can be found on the accompanying CD-ROM.

Unhealthy Growth Variations   Although there is a great deal of variation in an individual child's height and weight, there are times when the child's physical size becomes

TABLE 7–2   Potential Physical and Psychological Consequences of Obesity in Children and Youth

Physical Health	Emotional Health	Social Health
• Glucose intolerance and insulin resistance • Type 2 diabetes • Hypertension • Sleep apnea • Menstrual abnormalities • Impaired balance • Orthopedic problems of the knees, ankles, or hips	• Low self-esteem • Negative body image • Depression	• Stigma • Negative stereotyping • Discrimination • Teasing and bullying • Social marginalization

Source: Institute of Medicine of the National Academies

an area of concern. Two conditions that pose a threat to the continued well-being of the young child are obesity and failure-to-thrive syndrome.

CHILDHOOD OBESITY   Childhood obesity is becoming a national health concern. A child who is above the 85th percentile using body mass index (BMI) is considered overweight, and a child that is at or above the 95th percentile is considered obese. The Institute of Medicine of the National Academies has identified various negative consequences of obesity (see Table 7–2).

FAILURE-TO-THRIVE SYNDROME   Failure to thrive is a condition in which an infant is not growing normally. Specifically, it is diagnosed when an infant's or child's weight for age falls below the fifth percentile of the standard NCHS growth chart, or if it crosses two major percentile lines. However, about 25 percent of typically developing infants will shift to a lower growth percentile in the first two years of life and then follow that percentile, and this is not failure to thrive. Also, infants with Down syndrome, **intrauterine growth retardation,** or premature birth follow different growth patterns.

Krugman and Dubowitz (2003) identify some of the possible causes of failure to thrive. In some cases it is that the child cannot eat enough food or absorb enough vitamins and minerals in the food because of some organic cause. It can also be caused by either extreme of parent behavior, neglect or hypervigilance. No matter what the cause, it is very important for a child to get treatment when failure to thrive is diagnosed, because untreated it could lead to a variety of other problems.

Intrauterine growth retardation.   A condition in which the fetus does not grow enough while in the uterus.

Possible Causes of Failure to Thrive

Inadequate caloric intake
- Incorrect preparation of formula (too diluted, too concentrated)
- Unsuitable feeding habits (food fads, excessive juice)
- Behavior problems affecting eating
- Poverty and food shortages
- Neglect
- Disturbed parent-child relationship
- Severe reflux

Inadequate absorption
- Diseases such as liver disease or lung disease
- Genetic abnormalities such as cystic fibrosis or Down syndrome
- Cow's milk protein allergy
- Vitamin or mineral deficiencies
- Chronic infection (e.g., human immunodeficiency virus)
- Metabolic disorders such as increased metabolism or hyperthyroidism

Source: Krugman and Dubowitz (2003).

Infant States

Adults spend a good deal of time observing and reporting what infants spend time doing. Mothers, fathers, and caregivers often remark: "He gave me two hours of sleep," "He didn't sleep through the night for the first year," "He has a fussy period every evening," or "He looks at the shadows on the wall." Like detectives, we search for clues to help us understand the infant's state of sleeping and of being awake. This important work helps us assist the newborn in his capacity to self-regulate. The infant's ability to respond to the environment is influenced by her state of arousal. Infants differ in the amount of time they spend in each state. Time spent in an alert state responding to adults is important to learning and establishing relationships. Aspects of sleep, alertness, and crying are important when considering infant states of arousal (Deiner, 1997).

Hours of Sleep in Infancy The average newborn sleeps much of the day and night; that is, approximately 17 hours. The newborn wakes every few hours for feedings, play, and crying. Although there is no set schedule for infant sleep patterns, newborns generally sleep about eight to nine hours in the daytime and about eight hours at night. Most infants do not begin sleeping through the night (six to eight hours) without waking until about three months of age, or until they weight 12 to 13 pounds. Newborns and infants have a small stomach and wake every few hours to eat (Fogel, 2000).

States of Sleep Infants, like adults, have various stages and degrees or states of sleep (see Table 7–3). Infants may be active or quiet during sleep. Infant sleep patterns are well established when they are born, since they are formed during the last months of gestation. Active sleep or REM (rapid eye movement) sleep is the light sleep when the

TABLE 7–3   **Infant States**

Quiet sleep	Breathing is regular, eyes are closed and not moving, and the infant is primarily motionless.
Active sleep	Muscles are more tense than in quiet sleep, eye movement may be present, breathing is irregular, and spontaneous starts, sucks, and body movements occur in rhythmic bursts.
Drowsiness	The infant opens and closes his or her eyes, increases activity, breathes more rapidly, smiles occasionally.
Quiet alert	Eyes are open, scanning the environment. Infant body is still and breathing is more rapid than in sleep.
Active alert	Active movement of the body and limbs. Infants are less focused on environmental stimuli than in quiet sleep.
Crying	The infant vocalizes, changes facial expressions. Elevated breathing and activity.

Infant states of alert and quiet alert

child dreams. The eyes move rapidly back and forth and the infant may engage in body movements such as sucking or exhibit reflexes. Breathing may be irregular during active sleep. During quiet sleep or non-REM sleep the infant's sleep pattern progresses from drowsiness, with the eyes drooping, opening, and closing with occasional dozing, to light quiet sleep that includes starting or jumping in response to sounds. Finally the infant becomes quiet with regular breathing and no movement. Quiet sleep may occur several times during sleep, with the infant moving between periods of active sleep and waking.

Awake States   Infants also demonstrate differences in how they are when they are awake. When the infant awakens at the end of a sleep cycle there is typically a quiet alert phase. The infant's eyes are open, scanning the environment. During this quiet alert time, infants stare at objects and respond to their environments. This quiet phase is often followed by the active alert phases with movement of the body. Although infants remain attentive during the active awake phase, they focus less on external stimulation. Crying generally follows the active awake phase. Activity and respiration are elevated during crying and are accompanied by vocalizations and facial expressions.

Crying and Shaken Baby Syndrome

The research of Dr. Ronald G. Barr indicates that infants all over the world have inconsolable crying behavior in the first few months. Some infants cry more than others, with about 20 percent of infants experiencing colic. Inconsolable crying bouts occur in the first four months of life, usually peaking during the second month. Increased numbers of hospitalizations for shaken baby syndrome occur at this time. Shaken baby syndrome is a term used to describe the symptoms and consequences resulting from violent shaking or impacting the head of an infant or small child. The consequence is typically severe brain damage. The degree of brain damage depends on the amount and duration of the shaking and the forces involved in impact of the head.

Source: National Center on Shaken Baby Syndrome

Significance of Infant States   Awake or active states are important for the processing of environmental stimuli that leads to the infant's perceptual and cognitive development. Infants respond to their environment by seeking out stimuli such as turning their head toward the sound, or by withdrawing from the stimuli such as in turning away. During the first few months of life infants become increasingly tolerant of stimuli of various degrees of intensity and complexity and are less likely to withdraw from interesting stimulation. Such stimuli could be the source of information for the developing brain. In fact, presentation of moderate stimulation may increase the developing brain's ability to sustain attention. As the infant's caregiver, it is important for you to read the signs and offer the infant the opportunity to sleep or to experience increased stimulation. Below are signs of sleep readiness and awake/activity readiness.

SIGNS OF SLEEP READINESS

- Whimpering
- Facial grimacing, frowning, or pouting
- Back arching and pulling away
- Rubbing eyes

- Yawning
- Looking away
- Fussing
- Pulling on ears

SIGNS OF ACTIVITY READINESS

- Facial alertness, such as widening of the eyes and brightening of the face
- Seeking eye contact
- Hands open with fingers relaxed
- Verbal cues of giggling, babbling, or talking
- Smiling
- Sustained eye contact

Back to Sleep

Research has found a link between sudden infant death syndrome (SIDS) and infants who are placed on their stomachs to sleep. Experts agree that putting a baby to sleep on his or her back is the safest position. Additionally, soft surfaces, loose bedding, and overheating with too many blankets increase the risk of SIDS. Cigarette smoke is also associated with increased risk of SIDS.

Source: National Institute of Child Health and Human Development (2005).

Sensory Development

As the developing child's body is growing, the sensory systems are developing at the same time. A sense, such as seeing, hearing, smelling, tasting, or touching, is a system that perceives information from the infant's environment. Infants are amazingly perceptive, with a diverse repertoire of behavior that helps them to learn about and to adapt to their environment.

The Development of Vision: Seeing Infants' vision is different from adult vision, but it serves their developing needs. Normal vision at birth is about 20/600. Vision rapidly develops between birth and six months of age, with acuity reaching about 20/50. Vision continues to develop more gradually to reach adult levels of 20/20 at about three to five years of age (Haith, 1990). Newborns see best in dim lighting and are most attentive to contrasting colors. Binocular and peripheral vision is not fully developed in the newborn, so it is like looking through two separate tunnels that don't come together. To get an idea of what newborn vision is like, take a piece of wax paper and hold it about eight inches from your eyes. Newborns track the part of an image that has the most contrast, rather than focusing on the entire object. Infants can see some colors at birth, yet not as an adult sees color. This ability develops rapidly, and by about three to four months the infant's color vision is similar to an adult's (Maurer & Maurer, 1988).

Auditory Development: Hearing   The auditory system is among the most developed of the infant's senses. Although the fetus has the ability to hear sounds from outside the uterus, the newborn's auditory cortex, like the visual cortex, is fairly immature. The newborn's brain does not have the ability to sort out the sounds, and therefore hearing is not the same for an infant as it is for the adult. The infant hears a loud noise such as the barking of a dog as well as the continuing reverberations. The adult brain ignores multiple vibrations, hearing only the principal sound, whereas the newborn hears repeated sounds. A newborn is responsive to high frequency sounds such as his or her mother's voice. Although the newborn can hear both parents' voices the male's lower voice tone is harder for the infant to locate (Maurer & Maurer, 1988).

Otitis Media: Chronic Ear Infections

Otitis media, an inflammation of the middle ear (behind the eardrum), is one of the most common illnesses of childhood. An infection of the middle ear can cause a mild hearing loss that will last until the fluid in the ear is gone. Most children will have at least one episode of otitis media by one year of age. And 10–20 percent of children will have otitis media three or more times, with fluid lasting an average of one month each time. Persistent ear fluid is more common in children under two years, but it can be seen in children older than two.

Because this can happen when the child is learning to speak, it is normal to have real concerns. If the child cannot hear the sounds of language, a delay in speech is possible. If there are concerns, a hearing evaluation and/or speech and language evaluation may be appropriate.

Some common signs of an ear infection

- Child pulls on ear
- Child says ear hurts
- Drainage from ear
- Fever (acute otitis media)
- Irritability
- Poor sleep

Possible signs of a hearing loss

- Having difficulty paying attention
- Showing a delayed response or no response when spoken to
- Saying "huh?" often
- Not following directions well
- Turning up sound on radios, TV, CD-ROMs
- Withdrawing from other children
- Being overactive or uncooperative

Olfactory Sense-Smelling   Infants have the ability to discriminate between pleasant and unpleasant odors and they show preference for the smell of their mothers (Porter, 1991). As early as six days a newborn can distinguish between the breast milk of his mother and that of another mother. The developing sense of smell may help the infant come to "know" familiar people and places.

Gustatory Development: Tasting   Newborns have the ability to discriminate among sweet, acidic, salty, and bitter tastes. As anyone who has fed an infant can attest, they prefer sweet tastes and spit out bitter or sour foods.

Tactile Development: Touching   Although the newborn does not detect very light touch many early reflexes, such as rooting, Moro, sucking, and stepping, are stimulated through tactile sensations. It is important to note that tactile stimulation plays an important role in the emotional development of infants. Touch helps to stimulate physical growth, contributes to visual understanding, and strengthens attachment behaviors.

Perceptual Development

Although infants have the ability to see, hear, taste, smell, and feel, their senses are not as finely developed or as discriminating as those of the adult. A **sensation** is simply the stimulation of sensory organs such as the eyes, ears, and skin and the transmission of sensory information to the brain. **Perception** is the process by which sensations are organized and integrated as a means of understanding the world.

The Development of Depth Perception   As with many areas of perception, the infant's ability to perceive depth is not fully functioning at birth. The ability to judge the relative distances between two objects and whether objects are close or far is called **depth perception.** Some aspects of depth perception begin to appear at around four months of age. It is unclear if the development of depth perception is a function of experience or is governed by a biological timetable, or if it is perhaps a combination of both.

In human vision, separate images (one from each eye) are aligned on the retinas so that one image is seen. This is referred to as **binocular vision.** In infants under the age of four months old this fusion of images does not occur. As binocular vision develops in infants, they are more precise in their reaching and depth perception. At around four months of age the infant experiences a transition in the development in depth perception, referred to as **stereopsis.** Simply stated, stereopsis is when each eye captures its own view and the two separate images are sent on to the brain for processing. When the two images arrive simultaneously in the back of the brain, they are united into one picture. The mind combines the two images by matching up the similarities and adding in the small differences. The small differences between the two images create a multi-dimensional image that results in depth perception.

Infants under the age of two months fail to respond or even blink when an object is looming or moving closer as if to crash. Infants older than two months blink or move their heads backward as objects get closer.

Gibson and Walk (1960) studied infants' depth perception by using a small cliff with a drop-off covered by glass. The cliff is a glass-topped table divided in half. On one side

---

Sensation.   Receiving information via one of the sense organs.

Perception.   The process by which we understand sensory information.

Depth perception.   The ability to judge the relative distances between two objects.

Binocular vision.   The simultaneous use of the two eyes.

Stereopsis.   The ability to perceive a three-dimensional depth, which requires adequate fusion (union) of the images from each eye.

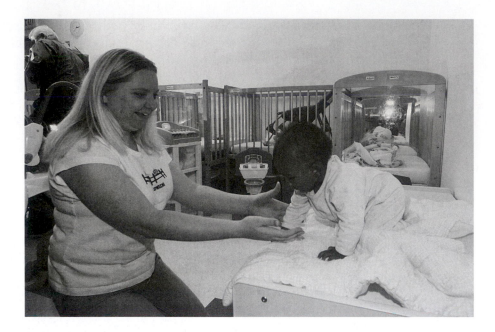

it appears that the surface is directly under the glass and on the other side the surface appears to be several feet below the glass table. The floor under the cliff is typically patterned, so the depth is easy to perceive. The infant is placed on the glass. Crawling infants, about six to nine months, avoid the "deep side" even when encouraged to cross over by a trusted adult. Such refusal indicates that infants understand depth perception by six months old. However, infants at five months of age have no reaction to being placed on the cliff side of the table. The photo above demonstrates the visual cliff.

Parts to Whole Perception   Newborn infants also fail to integrate images that they see. They tend to fixate on parts of the image without creating a whole. For example, the infant tends to fixate on the chin or hairline when looking at a face, on the corner of a triangle or square, or on the external contours of an object. Scanning horizontally requires fewer eye movements and therefore is easier for the young infant.

At two months old scanning patterns change and the child integrates more of the total picture. Scanning of the face will include the interior contours such as the eyes and the mouth. Although the newborn enjoys the contrast of stripes, the two-month-old is more interested in complex patterns such as a checkerboard or picture of a person (Deiner, 1997). Infants who examine the interior contours of a face or object gain better perception of the object.

Finally, infants gain **intermodal perception** by seven months of age as they are able to match the voices of children and adults, respectively. This requires the infant to integrate both visual and auditory cues for perception.

....

Intermodal perception.   The ability to use one sensory modality to identify an object or event that is already familiar to the infant through another sensory modality. For example, there are connections between hearing and vision, such as seeing lips move and hearing speech sounds.

CONCEPTS OF MOTOR DEVELOPMENT

Children's **motor development** is evidenced by their ability to move around and control various parts of their body. Refinements in motor development rely heavily on maturation of the brain, environmental sensory input, healthy physical growth of the body and nervous system, and opportunities to practice. The infant indicates the desire to use the spoon during feeding by an increased number of attempts to secure the spoon from the adult. This behavior is often accompanied with improved eye-hand coordination, a desire to eat the food, and an awareness of feeding oneself. Growth, maturation, coordination, desire, and practice all play a part in the child's eventual success at self-feeding.

The toddler's first attempts at feeding himself involve the use of the whole hand and the spoon.

The ability to feed oneself increases with more controlled movements.

Motor development.   The growth and change in motor behavior that reflect the interaction of maturation and the environment. These behaviors include both gross motor skills such as walking and fine motor skills such as drawing.

TABLE 7–4   **Criteria for the Apgar Score**

Rating	Heartbeat	Reflex Irritability	Muscle Tone	Color	Respiratory Effort
0	Absent	No response	Limp	Blue, pale	Absent
1	Slow (below 100)	Grimace	Weak, inactive	Body pink, extremities blue	Irregular, slow
2	Rapid (over 100)	Coughing, sneezing, crying	Strong, active	Entirely pink	Good: baby is crying

Source: Apgar, 1953.

Reflexes

Motor development during early infancy is reflexive, meaning that it is involuntary. **Reflexes** are not learned or developed through experience. Infant reflexes are the first form of human movement and primarily serve in gathering information or seeking nourishment. Infant reflexes are the foundation of voluntary movement skills that develop later as children gain more control over their motor actions and reactions. Normally developing infants are expected to respond to specific stimuli with a specific, predictable behavior or action. Variation in, or absence of, response may be a sign of abnormality in development. The infant's reflexes serve as a diagnostic tool for the assessment of wellness in infants. You are likely familiar with the Apgar scoring system administered at one minute and again at five minutes after birth. The Apgar score assesses muscle tone, respiration, color, heartbeat, and reflexes with a rating of 0 to 2, for a maximum score of 10. Table 7–4 shows the categories and scoring of the Apgar. A total of 7–10 means the baby is doing well, 4–7 means slight concern, and 0–4 means extreme concern for the health and well-being of the baby.

Categories of Reflexes   Reflexes can be classified into three categories: primitive, postural, and locomotor. *Primitive reflexes* are predominantly used for protection, nutrition, or survival. They include sucking and rooting reflexes, grasp reflexes, and startle reflexes. Primitive reflexes occur within the first few months of life. Later in infancy, reflexes are preadaptive, meaning that the infant begins to gain voluntary control over movements.

Postural reactions begin at around four months of age and help to maintain posture in a changing environment. Initially, these are similar to reflexes; however, later they are incorporated into the general repertoire of movements. Such reflexes include neck and body righting, labyrinthine righting, pull-up, and parachute reflexes.

Locomotor reflexes are related to later voluntary movement. Such reflexes include swimming, crawling, and stepping.

Table 7–5 gives an overview of categories of reflexes and the developmental patterns of each.

....

Reflexes.   Involuntary responses to a stimulus.

TABLE 7–5 **Categories of Reflexes**

Reflex	Stimulation	Infant Response	Developmental Patterns
Primitive Reflexes			
Blink	Flash of light or puff of air	Closes both eyes	Permanent
Moro	Loud noise or being dropped	Arches back and throws out arms and legs, then retracts them	Disappears within three to four months, persists to the sixth month in some infants
Rooting	Cheek stroked or side of mouth touched	Turns head toward stimulus, opens mouth, begins sucking	Disappears within three to four months
Sucking	Object touching mouth	Sucks automatically	Disappears within three to four months
Palmar grasp	Touch to palm of hand with finger or object	Hand closes tightly around finger or object	Disappears at end of fourth month
Palmar mandibular or Babkin	Pressure applied simultaneously to the palm of each hand	Eyes close, mouth opens, head tilts forward	May persist until the sixth month
Plantar grasp	The application of slight pressure with a fingertip to the ball of the foot	All toes flex as if to grasp	Must disappear before the child can stand or walk, usually before three months
Babinski	Stroke sole of foot	Twists foot, fans out toes	Disappears within nine months to one year
Tonic neck	Infant placed on back	Forms fist with hands and makes a "fencer" pose	Disappears within two months
Postural Reflexes			
Landau's reflex	Infant placed on stomach, face down	Raised head and arched back	Appears at three months and persists through first year
Labyrinthine righting	Tilt infant while in an upright position	Head moves to stay upright	Begins at four months and disappears at the end of first year
Pull-up	Place infant in supported standing position and tip in any direction (forward, backward)	Arms extend or flex to maintain an upright position	Begins at three months and disappears around the first birthday
Parachute	Infant in upright position is lowered toward group rapidly	Legs and arms extend	Begins at four months
Neck and body righting	While infant is on back, turn head to one side, or turn legs and pelvis to other side	Infant's body follows head in rotation, or trunk and head follow in rotation	Begins at four months and lasts until eleven months

(Continued on next page)

TABLE 7–5   **Categories of Reflexes (*Continued*)**

Reflex	Stimulation	Infant Response	Developmental Patterns
		Locomotor Reflexes	
Crawling	Alternately stroke the foot soles of an infant who is lying prone on the floor or in a crib	Infant's legs and arms move in a crawl-like action	May appear from birth to three or four months and disappears before voluntary creeping begins
Stepping	Hold infant above surface and lower infant's feet to touch surface	Moves feet as if to walk	Appears during the first month and may persist through the sixth month
Swimming	Place infant face down in or over water	Makes coordinated swimming movements with arms and legs	Appears in first month and persists through sixth month

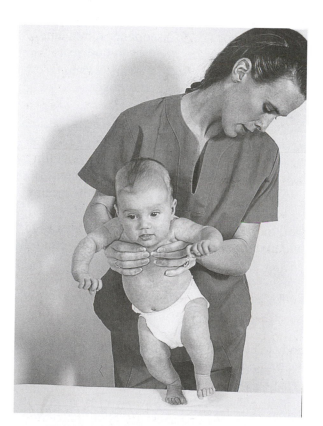
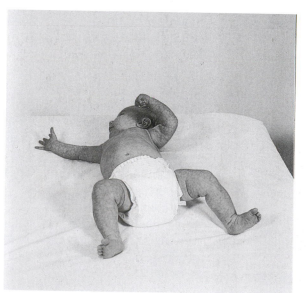

The stepping reflex and the tonic neck reflex

Motor Development

Motor development is continuous. Maturation of motor development goes from gross or large movements to fine or small movements. Complex skills such as skipping build on earlier learned skills of walking and jumping. There is a predictable pattern or sequence that children follow in their motor development.

Demonstrations of gross motor/gross muscle and fine motor development

"Cruisin'": moving from one place to the next

Gross Motor Development

At about one month, infants can lift their heads while lying on their stomachs. Eventually they lift their chests as well as their heads. Infants gain increasing control of their heads and manage to hold their heads up by age six months. Movement from one place to another, or locomotion, occurs in an orderly sequence of activities that includes rolling over, sitting up, crawling, creeping, walking, and running. Although sequential, motor development occurs unevenly from child to child, as each child develops at his own rate. In fact, some children skip a step in the sequence. For example, eight-month-old Jasmine creeps around the classroom on hands and feet without ever crawling. Since the stages of motor development overlap, the child is generally not "expert" in one skill before engaging in another.

Most infants begin to roll over between four and six months of age, and they sit independently at about seven months. Children engage in a variety of crawling and creeping behaviors between eight and nine months old. Crawling behavior may begin with rocking back and forth without actual locomotion. Beginner crawlers may only go in reverse, and ultimately crawlers develop more sophisticated creeping behavior in which they move themselves along on their hands and feet.

Infants engage in many variations of locomotion. Seven-month-old Aaron gets from place to place by rolling over and over. Ten-month-old Jayda gets from place to place by sitting upright and swinging her arms to herself, moving across the floor on her bottom. Six-month-old Michael alternately moves his elbows along the floor, chest up, legs outstretched in a sort of combat crawl.

TABLE 7–6   **Gross Motor Milestones**

Age at Which Behavior Often Emerges	Gross Motor Milestones
3 months	On back: turns head freely from side to side, head centered most of the time On stomach: lifts head strongly, faces straight ahead
5 months	Rolls completely over in any direction On stomach: raises head and chest, supporting self on forearms or arms Sitting, supported: holds head erect and steady
10 months	Sits alone for 30 seconds or more Pulls self to stand by furniture
11 months	Pre-walking progression: creeping on hands and knees or hands and feet Gets from lying to sitting without aid
14 months	Stands alone: 10 seconds or more Walks well alone

Standing occurs simultaneously with crawling and creeping. Most eight- to nine-month-old infants can pull themselves up and stand while holding onto something. They cruise from place to place, using sofas, tables, and shelves as support.

Between 12 and 15 months, infants begin to walk by themselves, earning themselves the name of toddler. Toddlers work hard to perfect their newly developed skills. Top-heavy and inexperienced, these new walkers, runners, and climbers fall often. As children mature, they experience increased strength, coordination, and balance, making locomotion smoother. By age two toddlers can climb, run, walk backward, kick, and jump.

Table 7–6 identifies the age in months at which infants and toddlers reach milestones related to walking. The progression from creeping to crawling to walking follows a classic developmental sequence. Each new stage in locomotion allows children to move more rapidly and involves a qualitative change in the pattern of their behavior.

CULTURAL VARIATION

Native American Hopi children who are strapped to cradle boards during their first year of life make rapid advances in motor development once released from the boards. They learn to walk at about the same time as children who were given the opportunity to experiment with milestones such as sitting up and crawling.

During the preschool years, children greatly advance in their gross motor skills, which employ the use of large muscles for locomotion. The three-year-old can balance on one foot, walk up steps alternating feet, and hop off the ground. Four-year-olds

Activities such as the rings require strength and coordination.

Cooperative games require motor planning ability and coordination.

TABLE 7–7 **Gross Motor Skills Young Children Develop**

Locomotor	Stability	Manipulative
Walking	Turning	Throwing
Running	Twisting	Catching/collecting
Hopping	Bending	Kicking
Skipping	Stopping	Punting
Galloping	Rolling	Dribbling
Sliding	Balancing	Volleying
Climbing	Jumping and landing	Paddling
Crawling	Stretching movements	Pedaling
Swimming		
Skating		
Dancing		

abandon the push trike for the tricycle, which requires coordination and strength to pedal. Although quite accomplished with the tricycle, the preschooler may still rely on pushing the bike much like a push trike when obstacles such as hills or gravel are encountered. Skipping is another new skill to the four-year-old. It seems that this complex skill of balance and coordination is best learned through demonstration. Table 7–7 identifies the categories of gross motor skills and gives examples of each.

What to Look For in Gross Motor Development

- ❑ Does the child walk up stairs, two feet to a step?
- ❑ Does the child kick a large ball?
- ❑ Does the child try to stand on one foot?

❑ Does the child go around obstacles while pushing or pulling a toy?

❑ Does the child throw a ball underhanded?

❑ Does the child pedal a tricycle?

❑ Does the child complete a forward somersault?

❑ Does the child hop three hops with both feet?

❑ Does the child catch a bounced ball?

❑ Does the child push a wagon or doll stroller?

❑ Does the child roller skate?

❑ Does the child skip rope?

❑ Does the child ride a two-wheel bike?

Throwing and catching requires coordination, balance, and reflex control.

 In video stream eight on the accompanying CD-ROM, notice all of the gross motor skills that the children must utilize to perform the tasks.

Fine Motor Development

As the child's movements become more refined and she gains more control of her movements, fine motor development begins. As the young child is able to perform more controlled and precise movements, she is also able to care for herself more effectively.

Reaching, Grasping, and Manipulating   Of all the motor skills, reaching may play the greatest role in infant cognitive development, because it opens up a whole new way of exploring the environment (Berk, 2004). Fine motor development begins with the infant engaging in what might be called pre-reaching, which is basically swiping at an object without making any contact. The baby does not have enough control yet to maneuver the arm or hand to the exact location of an object.

At three to four months, the infant will begin to try to grasp objects with the **ulnar grasp,** in which he uses the whole hand to try to hold on to something. He will also begin to touch the fingers of one hand with the other. At five months, he will begin to transfer toys from one hand to the other. Between six and eight months, his grasp will improve and he will begin to use wrist movements.

Between 8 and 12 months the infant will begin using a **pincer grasp,** a well-coordinated way of picking up small things with the thumb and the index finger. The crawling infant now has the ability to pick up those small pebbles, little pieces of yarn, and dropped crumbs from the floor (and of course they will go right into the mouth).

In video stream three on the accompanying CD-ROM, view fine motor development with pincer grasp.

Use of Tools and Fine Motor Development

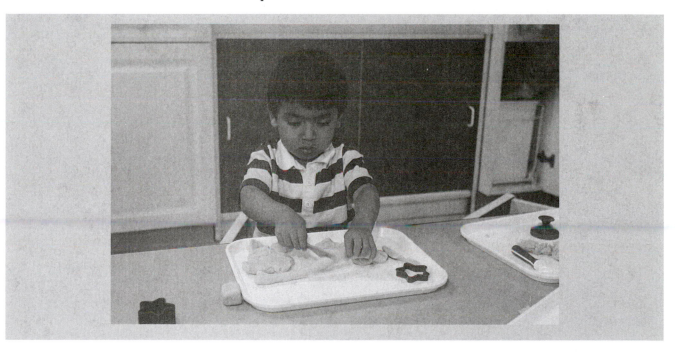

....

Ulnar grasp.   Uncoordinated grasp of a young infant in which the fingers close against the palm.

Pincer grasp.   A well-coordinated grasp involving the oppositional use of the thumb and index finger to pick up objects.

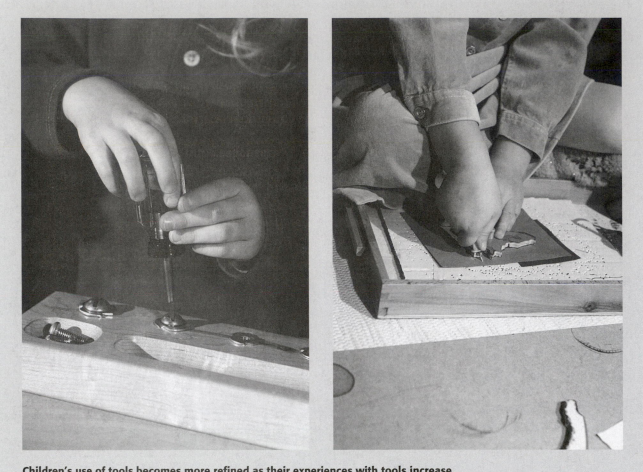

Children's use of tools becomes more refined as their experiences with tools increase.

The toddler will begin to stack blocks. He will also be able to place two or three pegs in a pegboard before he gets tired of it. He has begun to enjoy scribbling. Later in the year, he will be able to make a circular scribble and a vertical line. He will also hold the crayon with his fingers instead of his fist. He has begun to use his finger to point to objects. He will be able to do simple, three-piece, knobbed puzzles. Table 7–8 identifies fine motor skills and the ages at which they typically occur.

During the preschool years the child will experiment with various ways in which to hold a pencil, crayon, and paintbrush. In most cases, it is during this time that **hand dominance** will emerge. Puzzles, bead stringing, using scissors, and building are popular activities for three- and four-year-olds. Most three-year-olds can build a 10-block tower of blocks, cut on a straight line, and copy or trace various shapes. (The development of drawing is discussed in Chapter 12, "The Creative Arts," and the development of writing is covered in Chapter 11, "Language Domain and Literacy Development.")

....

Hand dominance.   The preferred use of one hand over another for tasks such as writing, drawing, cutting, and other motor activities.

| TABLE 7-8 | Fine Motor Development |

Age	Possible Fine Motor Accomplishments
1–2 months	Most actions are reflexive, pre-reaching, opens and closes hands carefully, may hold object for a few moments
3–4 months	May swipe at dangling objects, reaches with arms Clenches rattle and puts it in mouth
5–6 months	May swap object from hand to hand, may hold bottle Reaches out when sitting, often in a raking motion (reaching out and pulling a number of objects in at once)
7–9 months	Clasps hands and enjoys banging objects together; may grab for a toy with one hand; learns to open fingers at will and drop or throw objects; puts objects in containers, then takes them out; may finger holes on a pegboard and enjoy toys with moving parts like wheels or levers
10–12 months	May hold crayon and try to scribble; intrigued by tiny things; likes to turn pages, often not one by one; fascinated by hinges and may swing door back and forth; points with index finger; accurately picks up small objects with thumb and index finger in a pincer grasp
12–18 months	Holds two or three objects in one hand, turns containers over to dump contents, builds small towers of blocks and then knocks them down, puts round peg into correct hole, tries to fit things inside each other, may roll ball to others and pick up objects in motion, drinks regularly from cup, sorts many shapes and drops them in matching holes, takes toy apart and puts it back together, unzips zippers
19–24 months	May stack three or four blocks, may take off socks and shoes, throws ball overhand instead of tossing it, may turn pages one at a time, enjoys finger painting and scribbling with big crayons, loves to inspect tiny objects, shows *hand preference,* may put on shoes but often on the wrong foot, tries to buckle car seat belt, likes to play with clay, may draw a crude circle if shown how
2–3 years	Child learns to coordinate movements of the wrist, fingers, and palm; may unscrew lids, turn knobs, unwrap paper; learns how to hold a pencil in writing position; loves to draw with chalk and crayons; imitates vertical and horizontal strokes, but may have difficulty making a cross with two lines; may use small scissors; rotates jigsaw pieces and completes a simple puzzle
3–4 years	By the age of three, child will have enough muscle coordination to play a simple musical instrument; can zip and button; can copy simple letters and shapes; can use simple tools requiring thumb and forefinger manipulation *Hand dominance* is demonstrated by age four in girls, five in boys

Self-Help Skills   Self-help skills will develop quickly during this time because of the control the child has gained over small muscle movements. Just think of all the tasks that you can only accomplish by using your hands. Imagine how a child feels when she can finally do things for herself—she can button and zip, pour her own juice, spread her own peanut butter, pull her own pants up, scoop her own cereal.

Demonstrations of Self-Help Skills

The development of self-help skills relies heavily on fine motor development.

What to Look For in Fine Motor Development

- ❏ Does the infant swipe at objects in the air?
- ❏ Does the infant make contact with objects?
- ❏ How does the infant/young child pick up objects?
- ❏ Does the young child show any defensiveness when asked to hold a writing utensil?
- ❏ Does the young child coordinate hand-eye movements?
- ❏ Does the young child use writing utensils? If so, how are they held?
- ❏ Can the young child manipulate tools or other objects, such as screwdrivers, scissors, hammers, etc.?
- ❏ Can the child manipulate using his fingers, for example, tear paper, screw in bolts, etc.?
- ❏ Can the child draw simple shapes?
- ❏ Can the child copy shapes, letters, or numbers?

Of Special Interest—Sensory Integration Dysfunction/Sensory Processing Disorder

How an individual child takes in information and processes it is based on her senses. Sensory experiences include touch, movement, body awareness, sight, sound, and the pull of gravity. Taken all together, sensory information gives the child a picture of her world, of herself, and of how she relates to the world around her. The brain processes and organizes the sensory information and then integrates it or puts it all together—this is called sensory integration.

As children grow, this process naturally develops. Motor planning ability is the typical outcome, as well as the ability to adapt to incoming sensations. But for some children, sensory integration does not develop as efficiently as it should. When the process is disordered, a number of problems in learning, development, or behavior may become evident.

Children that are particularly at risk for having a sensory integration (SI) dysfunction include those who were born premature, have autism or another **pervasive developmental disorder** (PDD), or have a learning disability. (Further explanations of PDD appear in the Of Special Interest section of Chapter 9.)

Sensory integration focuses primarily on three basic senses: tactile (touch), vestibular (the sense of balance), and proprioceptive (the sense of the body in space). These three senses are interconnected and are also connected with other systems in the brain. When a child presents with SI, the result is typically an over-responsiveness or an under-responsiveness to the sensory system. The child may avoid certain sensory stimulation or may seek out sensory stimulation.

....

Pervasive developmental disorder.   A diagnosis along the autism spectrum.

Responses within the Tactile System   The tactile system involves the sense of touch. This information includes light touch, pain, temperature, and pressure.

An *over-responsive*, tactilely defensive child may:

- withdraw when being touched.
- show aggression when being touched.
- refuse to eat certain "textured" foods.
- refuse to wear certain types of clothing.
- complain about having his hair or face washed.
- avoid getting his hands dirty (e.g., with glue, sand, mud, finger paint) and use his fingertips rather than whole hands to manipulate objects.

An *under-responsive*, touch-seeking child may:

- crave pressure (typically pressure on the joints).
- crave compression.
- overuse paint, glue, etc. (the child paints himself up his whole arm).
- seek hard touch, which can be misconstrued as being aggressive.

Responses in the Vestibular System   The vestibular system refers to structures within the inner ear (the semicircular canals) that detect movement and changes in the position of the head. For example, the vestibular system tells you whether your head is upright or tilted (even with your eyes closed).

If the child is *over-responsive* or hypersensitive to vestibular stimulation, the following symptoms may be seen:

- Fearful reactions to ordinary movement activities (e.g., swings, slides, ramps, inclines)
- Trouble learning to climb or descend stairs or hills
- Apprehension in walking or crawling on uneven or unstable surfaces
- Appearance of clumsiness

If the child is *under-responsive* or hyposensitive to vestibular stimulation, the following symptoms may be seen:

- Actively seeking very intense sensory experiences, such as excessive body whirling, jumping, and/or spinning
- Appearance of hyperactivity

Responses in the Proprioceptive System   The *proprioceptive system* provides us with an awareness of body position or the body in space. It allows us to sit properly in a chair and to step off a curb smoothly. It also allows us to manipulate objects using fine motor movements, such as writing with a pencil, using a spoon to drink soup, and buttoning one's shirt.

Dysfunction of the proprioceptive sense typically results in the following motor skill problems:

- Very poor fine motor skills, such as handwriting
- Very poor gross motor skills, such as kicking, catching, or throwing a ball
- Difficulty imitating movements, such as when playing Simon Says
- Trouble with balance, sequences of movements, and bilateral coordination

DYSPRAXIA   Another dimension of proprioception is praxis, or motor planning. This is the ability to plan and execute different motor tasks. When a child has difficulty in this area he may be diagnosed with **dyspraxia.** Children with motor planning disorders have particular difficulty with forming a goal or idea or developing new motor skills. These children often are clumsy, awkward, and accident-prone.

Although dyspraxia may be diagnosed at any stage of life, increasing numbers of children are identified as having the condition. When dyspraxia is identified at an early stage, children are less likely to have problems with acceptance by their peers and with lowered self-esteem, so early detection and diagnosis is critical. Table 7–9 shows possible symptoms that may be exhibited by a child presenting with dyspraxia.

TABLE 7–9   **Symptoms that May Indicate Dyspraxia**

From Birth to Three Years	From Three to Five Years	From Five to Seven Years
Irritable from birth	Avoidance of tasks that require good manual dexterity	Difficulties in adapting to a structured school routine
Significant feeding problems	High levels of motor activity, difficulty remaining still	Difficulties in physical education lessons
Slow to achieve expected developmental milestones in the gross and fine motor domains	High levels of excitability	Slow at dressing
	Loud/shrill voice	Unable to tie shoelaces
Failure to go through the crawling stages, preferring to "bottom shuffle" and then walk	Easily distressed and prone to temper tantrums	Barely legible handwriting
	Bumps into objects and falls over	Immature drawing and copying skills
	Hands flap when running	Inability to remember more than two or three instructions at once
	Difficulty with pedaling a tricycle or similar toy	Continued high levels of motor activity
	Lack of any sense of danger (jumping from heights, etc.)	Hand flapping or clapping when excited
	Poor fine motor skills, such as difficulty in holding a pencil or using scissors	
	Drawings may appear immature	

Dyspraxia.   A sensory processing disorder that involves the inability to plan and carry out motor functions.

Interventions for Children with Sensory Integration Disorders

The interventions used for children with SI or sensory processing disorder range from reactive (changing the environment after the responses/symptoms are seen) to proactive (doing exercises in order to avoid the responses).

Recognizing the Responses   The first and most important way to help children with sensory integration disorders is to recognize the child's behaviors as coping mechanisms rather than as "bad" behaviors that must be eliminated. Consider the following scene.

ANECDOTAL RECORD 7–1

Child's Name: Ian

Date: April 14

Time: 9:28 a.m.

Observer: T. Jones

Location: Self-contained classroom at Springfield Elementary

Ian is sitting with the children while they are listening to a story being read by Joan, his preschool teacher. As the story progresses, the children come to recognize and recite (more like yell) the reoccurring phrases in the book. As the noise level increases Ian begins looking away—he looks up at the ceiling and about 30 seconds later looks over to the side of the room. As the children become more vocal and all begin to yell the phrase, Ian begins to make a whirring noise and begins to flap his hands on the sides of his body. This continues until Ian begins biting his forearm.

Ian is a four-year-old boy with what is known as pervasive developmental disorder—not otherwise specified (PDD-NOS). The noise level became unbearable for him, and he began trying various coping mechanisms. In this case we would need to help Ian by prompting him to move away from the group, asking the children to whisper their responses, or showing Ian how to use headphones when he feels the noise level is beginning to be too much for him.

Exercises to Prevent Nonfunctional Behaviors   Occupational therapists (OTs) can help children with sensory integration disorders in myriad ways. After the OT has developed some strategies to help the child cope with his disorder, she can also teach these to parents, classroom teachers, and other caregivers. The interventions are generally designed to help the child organize and calm the senses. Each child requires an individual technique, depending on his sensory integration difficulty. The key to helping children overcome the symptoms related to sensory integration disorder is to watch them and try to understand what makes them feel calm and relaxed and what makes them anxious.

The following are some standard interventions for children with sensory integration disorders. Of course, it is necessary for an OT to evaluate the child and design an appropriate program.

FOR TACTILE SENSE

- Brushing (some children respond well to a brush or brush-like tool going over various parts of the body)
- Stimulation activities, particularly close to defensive parts of the head or body
- Rubbing different parts of the body with different textures
- Sensory stimulation, such as play with Play-Doh, shaving cream, or rice in a bowl

FOR STIMULATION SEEKERS

- Opportunities to move safely
- Swings
- Trampolines

FOR STIMULATION AVOIDERS (CALMING THE SYSTEM)

- Joint compression (applying pressure to certain joints)
- Weighted blankets
- Make a "hot dog" or "burn to" (roll the child in a mat or large blanket)
- Supply tent-making materials

Sensorial experiences help the child with a sensory processing disorder organize the information from their senses.

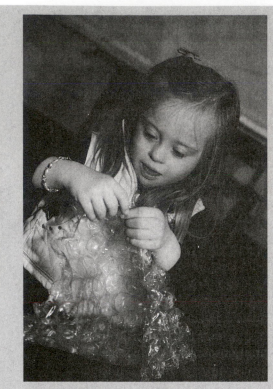

popping bubbles from bubble wrap

covering with blankets

bouncing, jumping on the mini-tramp

exploring with shaving cream

Print the Anecdotal Record from the CD-ROM. Highlight (code) the behavioral indicators of motor (fine and gross) development. Coding can be done best by using highlighters, colored pencils, or thin-tipped markers. Crayons do not work well.

QUESTIONS TO CONSIDER ○ ○ ○

1. How does physical development affect the child's cognitive development? Social development? Emotional development?

2. Describe and discuss how the child's physical health affects development.

3. List examples of appropriate activities for fine and gross motor development.

REFERENCES ○ ○ ○

Allen, K. E., & Marotz, L. R. (2003). *Developmental profiles: Birth through twelve* (4th ed.). Clifton Park, NY: Thomson Delmar Learning.

Apgar, V. (1953). A proposal for a new method of evaluation in the newborn infant. *Current Research in Anesthesia and Analgesia, 32,* 260.

Berger, K. S. (2002). *The developing person through childhood* (3rd ed.). New York: Worth.

Berk, L. (2004). *Developing through the lifespan.* Boston: Pearson Custom Publishing.

National Institute of Medicine of the National Academies (September 2004). Childhood obesity in the United States: Facts and figures. Fact Sheet. Retrieved February 7, 2005, from http://www.iom.edu/Object.File/Master/22/606/FINALfactsandfigures2.pdf

Deiner, P. L. (1997). *Infants and toddlers: Development and program planning.* New York: Harcourt Brace College Publishers.

Eysenck, H. J., & Schoenthaler, S. J. (1997). Raising IQ level by vitamin and mineral supplementation. In R. J. Sternberg & E. G. Grigorenko (Eds.) *Intelligence, heredity and environment* (pp. 363–392). Cambridge, UK: Cambridge University Press.

Fogel, A. (2000). *Infancy: Infant, family, and society* (4th ed.). Belmont, CA: Wadsworth.

Gibson, E. J., & Walk, R. D. (1960). The visual cliff. *Scientific American, 202,* 64–71.

Haith, M. M. (1990). Perceptual and sensory processes in early infancy. *Merrill-Palmer Quarterly, 36,* 1–26.

Krugman, S. D., & Dubowitz, H. (2003). Failure to thrive. *American Family Physician, 68*(5), 1–6.

Lovblad, K., Ramelli, G., Remonda, L., Nirkko, A. C., Ozdoba, C., & Schroth, G. (1977). Retardation of myelination due to dietary vitamin B12 deficiency: Cranial MRI findings. *Pediatric Radiology, 27*(2), 155–158.

Lozoff, B. (1989). Iron and learning potential in childhood. *Academic Medicine, 65*(10), 1050–1066.

Maurer, D., & Maurer, C. (1988). *The world of the newborn.* New York: Basic Books.

National Center on Shaken Baby Syndrome. (n.d.). *Understanding Infant Crying.* Retrieved on July 20, 2005, from http://www.dontshake.com

National Institute of Child Health and Human Development. (January, 2005). *National back to sleep campaign.* Retrieved July 20, 2005, from http://www.nichd.nih.gov

Porter, R. H. (1991). Mutual mother-infant recognition in humans. In P. G. Hepper (Ed.), *Kin recognition* (413–432). Cambridge, UK: Cambridge University Press.

Ricciuti, H. N. (1993). Nutrition and mental development. *Current Directions in Psychological Science, 2,* 43–46.

Cognitive Development

CHAPTER OBJECTIVES

- To describe how information is organized in the mind and how this organization develops

- To explain how the process of synaptic proliferation affects cognitive processing in the brain

- To identify the developmental components of memory, problem solving, and logical thinking in young children

- To recognize demonstrations of memory, problem solving, and logical thinking tasks in young children

- To describe the concept of theory of mind

- To analyze children's symbolic play development

CHILD STUDY OBJECTIVES

Upon conclusion of this chapter the student will:

- code the cognitive development for each of the existing anecdotal records.

- develop a checklist for cognitive development.

- gather and label visual documentation relating to cognitive development.

- prepare a plan for (identify goal and objective) and conduct a structured observation for cognitive development, interpreting the results (by completing an assessment form and writing a brief summary).

INTRODUCTION TO COGNITIVE DEVELOPMENT

Cognition is simply defined as "coming to know," denoting a process. The process of developing cognitively moves from external to internal, from simple to complex, from compartmentalization to **automaticity**. Children collect building blocks of understanding from which they build a solid foundation. Although the processes of mental organization, understanding, and problem solving are internal, the careful observer can pick up cues as to how the child is thinking by studying the child's behavior. There are few moments more satisfying in a teacher's life than watching a child having an "aha" moment, because when a child makes a connection on the outside you can bet that a connection is being made on the inside as well. To understand this phenomenon better, the major components of cognition first must be discussed.

Children can seriate many objects, including shells, rocks, and leaves.

Schemas

All information resides in the mind in the form of **schemas**. From the time of conception, humans form schemas. They are constructed from every sensorial experience the new life encounters. Each sound, taste, smell, touch, and sight adds new information to the developing mind and then deposits it into a schema. Initially the child creates schemas by attending to attributes of concrete objects and experiences. For example, the child creates a schema of a dog with the attributes of hairy, four legs, ears that stand up, long nose, teeth, and tail. The child creates schemas of everything she experiences, from animals to people, from toys to machines, and from plants to planets. The child is also creating schemas for ways of eating, ways of sleeping and, very importantly, for emotions. From these schemas the child is able to **classify**, **categorize**, **seriate** and compare.

....

Automaticity.   Refers to automatic brain functions developing through experience and cognitive operations.

Schemas.   Organizational or conceptual patterns in the mind.

Classify.   To assign things or people to classes or groups.

Categorize.   To group things together because of common characteristics.

Seriate.   To arrange things in order—from smallest to biggest, lightest to darkest, thickest to thinnest, tallest to shortest, etc.

In video stream 4 on the accompanying CD-ROM, view preschool children classifying with clues.

As time goes by and the child develops language, schemas are created by abstractions as well as concrete experiences. Information now deposited into schemas is not necessarily experienced concretely but rather created by the child by manipulating existing schemas in her own mind. From these schemas the child is able to solve problems, invent, and predict.

Schemas then are likened to "anchors in the mind." Each existing piece of information has a secure place to reside, and each new piece of information has a place in which to connect. Although schemas are anchors, it does not mean that they don't change. Schema development is a continual process because each new experience will change the existing schema. Take, for example, the child who creates a schema for *dog*. At first it consists of hairy, ears that stand up, and a long tail. As the child gains more and more experiences with dogs she will come to add into that schema dogs with short hair (some have no hair at all), dogs with floppy ears, and dogs with short, stubby tails. This explains why the young child upon seeing a skunk might say "doggie, doggie," over and over again. But she will learn quickly the difference between a dog and a skunk if she gets too close! In other words, her schema will change dramatically as her experiences change. Think of how your schema of *love* has changed and will continue to change throughout your lifetime due to personal experiences.

Equilibrium

The child is constantly working toward a state of **equilibrium.** When the child has reached a state of equilibrium, he can comprehend all the stimuli presented to him because it has been placed into a schema. When an infant or young child is presented with a new stimulus (new information), he wants to make sense of and understand it—it is instinctual. Understanding the new information comes from connecting it to something he knows, something he has a schema for already.

Assimilation and Accommodation

When the child is presented with a new stimulus (new information) he can search his existing schemas and if it fits into one he can simply place the new information into it and use it again. This is called **assimilation.** When the child is presented with a new stimulus and there does not seem to be an existing schema to fit it into, he must create a new schema. This is called **accommodation.**

Think of the processes of assimilation and accommodation like working on your computer in a word processing application. You write a paper, maybe on the cognitive development of children, and after you have saved it you want to store it in a place where you will be able to find it. So you look at your existing files and ask yourself: Does

----

Equilibrium.   A mental state of calmness and composure; a state of balance.

Assimilation.   The integration of new knowledge or information with what is already known.

Accommodation.   A process by which existing knowledge or schemas must be adjusted to allow the integration of new knowledge.

this fit in with any folder I have? Maybe you have a folder started on cognitive development or even child development and the paper can fit nicely into it. This is assimilation. If, however, you search your existing folders and nothing like this document exists and it just doesn't fit anywhere, then you will need to create a new folder or file in order to fit in this new document. This is accommodation. This is an ongoing process for all humans. But for infants and young children, who are continually confronted with new information, this can be overwhelming at times. Because of this, teachers must remember that new information they introduce to children will be learned much more efficiently if it is linked to existing knowledge.

BRAIN DEVELOPMENT: SYNAPTIC PROLIFERATION

The aspect of brain development to be discussed in this chapter is one that allows the child to learn something new by enabling him to readily attach it to something learned previously. This concept is called **synaptic proliferation**.

The brain is continually "wiring itself up." When a child is born he possesses many neurons that are ready and waiting to connect to each other in order to form networks. The brain wires itself up by the process of one neuron reaching out to another neuron to form a connection, or **synapse**. Each neuron can hook up to literally hundreds of other neurons and ultimately form thousands of networks. The more connections and networks that exist, the more efficiently information can be learned.

Synaptic proliferation occurs when an existing connection within the brain is stimulated and then creates another connection from the original one. This phenomenon has been likened to opening another road from one that has been paved, in the process strengthening the already paved road. By carving out another pathway for information to travel through, the brain has increased the efficiency of its cognitive processing and strengthened the original pathway by making it more resilient to change. In terms of memory, this means that you now have more ways to access previously learned information and the original learning is basically stored permanently.

One way to understand synaptic proliferation is by the analogy of building alternate routes. Consider this: You wake up on Monday morning and begin getting ready to go to work or school. You hear on the news that there is an accident on one of the roads that you would typically travel on to get to your destination, so you decide you will go a different way. On the way, you see that a car is stalled at a light two blocks ahead of you, so you turn and change your course. As you continue, you see the traffic light just ahead of you turning yellow and decide to get around that light by turning. You keep turning and winding around until you get to your destination five minutes ahead of your usual time. The next day you decide to take that same route because it was faster; this time you arrive ten minutes ahead of time because instead of deciding when and where to turn, you do it automatically.

If you had only had one way to get to work or school, you would have been late and in some cases that would spell trouble. Because you had many alternative routes available you were able to make appropriate decisions and solve your way around all

....

Synaptic proliferation.   The rapid growth in the number of synapses within the brain.

Synapse.   The entire junction between two neurons, across which communications flow.

Children's strategies for completing tasks become more automatic with repeated experiences.

the curve balls that were thrown. Now you have a whole new way to get to work or school, and you can get there on autopilot. This is how synaptic proliferation aids us in our cognitive development—by giving us more connections and more opportunities to link up information, and by making new learning experiences become more automatic.

As you are observing children, note when you see this phenomenon occurring. For instance, watch as a child tries to complete a 12-piece puzzle for the first time and how he completes it the second and the third time. You should notice that the speed with which he finished the puzzle changes. His strategy for completing a new 12-piece puzzle changes as well. You will see many examples of this throughout the child study.

CONCEPTS OF COGNITIVE DEVELOPMENT

Although the study of human cognition encompasses numerous principles, this book will focus on four major concepts: memory, problem solving, logical thinking or reasoning, and theory of mind.

Memory

Many of us think of memory as reciting facts and remembering names. This is semantic memory, a significant piece of the remembering brain. However, memory is much more than simply repeating back what one has learned. Rather, it is using what one has learned in order to learn more. David Sousa (1995) says it well: "Memory gives us a past and a record of who we are and is essential to human individuality. Without memory, life would be a series of meaningless encounters that have no link to the past and no use for the future. Memory allows individuals to draw on experience and use the power of prediction to decide how they will respond to future events" (p. 31).

The Developmental Course of Memory   Memory involves three interconnected processes: **encoding, storage,** and **retrieval.** In order for children to encode information

Encoding.   The manner in which information is processed for storage. Encoding information requires one to pay attention to it, elaborate on it, and sometimes produce images of it.

Storage.   The manner in which information is retained in memory. Many times it is classified as short-term or long-term memory.

Retrieval.   The process of taking information out of memory storage.

received through their senses they need to do something with it, transform it in some way that is suitable for memory storage. Storage is simply how memories are maintained or kept over time, and retrieval is the process of fetching the stored memory. For example, one might rehearse an important telephone number, elaborate on a story, or break information down into manageable chunks. Young children may code by images, holding the likeness of their mother or father in their memory visually. A young toddler may encode verbally, using the word, such as mama or dada, as a peg on which to hang a concept (Ellis, 1979). Preschool children may use symbolic memory codes, in which the symbol stands for some event or abstraction. Take for instance 23-month-old Matthew, who, when asked by an adult friend where he is going, sings the familiar advertisement, "Bada ba ba ba, I'm lovin' it" to indicate that he is going to McDonald's for lunch.

In video stream 2 on the accompanying CD-ROM, view memory and retrieval behavior among toddlers.

Consider an infant who, after a short period of time, seeks to "find" a hidden object after seeing it placed in the hiding place. We would say that this infant has developed some concept of *object permanence,* because by looking for the object she shows us she understands that the object still exists, even though she cannot see it. In order to accomplish object permanence the infant must create a mental representation of the original hiding place and the ability to hold that memory during the delay. Ultimately, as the infant develops into a toddler, she uses greater internalization. Toddlers can imitate models that are not present, wave bye-bye, or blow kisses even if no one is blowing kisses back. The toddler can imitate gestures that she cannot see herself make, as when making faces, and can seek an object when it is not in its usual location. The preschool child will be able to retrieve the memory after substantial delay because she has encoded the information in some manner. These are all indications of memory development.

Imitative games like patty-cake are memory practice for the infant.

Although young children can recall information, particularly when it is meaningful, **recognition** is better developed than **recall**. This is partly due to the child's inability to understand the need for the use of memory aids such as rehearsing or elaborating. For instance, in a study where children were asked, "If you wanted to phone your friend and someone told you the phone number, would it make any difference if you called right after you heard the number, or if you got a drink first?" the children responded that it would not matter (Ellis, 1979). It becomes very clear that young children not only neglect to use memory aid techniques but also fail to recognize the need for them. This understanding of how one's own mind works is called **metacognition,** and it typically does not develop until the age of seven or eight.

Playing memory games requires that the child recall the placement of the object and recognize a matching object.

Recognition.   Memory task in which one has to identify (recognize) previously learned information—the "I'll know it when I see it" phenomenon.

Recall.   Memory task in which one must retrieve previously learned information without any cues, such as when giving directions to someone.

Metacognition.   Knowledge about your own thoughts and the factors that influence your thinking.

The following anecdotal record illustrates the toddler's internalization of symbol representation in the mind.

ANECDOTAL RECORD 8–1

Child's Name: Michael

Date: May 10

Time: 10:08 a.m.

Observer: A. Kovacik

Location: Early Head Start classroom

During play in the Early Head Start classroom, Jessica, 26 months, and 30-month-old Jade were placing large plastic pegs into square foam mats at a low, rectangular table. The teacher had placed a spare bucket on the table, telling the girls, "Now there are two buckets so that you can both have a place for your pegs." Twenty-four-month-old Michael meandered past the table, observing the girls play. He stopped, approached the table, and examined the spare bucket provided for the girls. The bucket had originally been used for storage of small metal cars and was labeled on one end with a color picture of cars. Michael picked up the bucket, pointed to the picture, and repeated, "cars, cars, cars." He moved directly to the toy shelves and looked on each shelf. He got on his hands and knees and looked under furniture. He continued to repeat, "cars, cars." Michael approached the table where Jessica and Jade continued to play. Pointing to the cars, he took the bucket to the teacher. "Have you been looking for the cars? We don't have metal cars." Michael persists. The teacher takes Michael to the preschool classroom, where they seek cars until Michael spots an identical bucket arranged on a low, open shelf. He says, "cars, cars, cars," and takes one car in each hand. "Vroom, vroom." Michael takes the cars back to the toddler classroom. While in the classroom he alternately places the cars in the bucket and takes them out to push across the table and onto the floor.

CULTURAL VARIATION

Remembering our past

How do we remember things that happened to us as children? Some people have very vivid autobiographical memories, while some have limited memories of events such as their second birthdays or an early trip to the zoo. Some theorists say that until a child develops a sense of self she cannot recall the memories. Others say that the way in which the culture or family talks about past events has much more to do with if and how we remember (Sutton, 2002). Social interactionists believe that children cannot remember in solitude and that the way in which the reminiscing takes place alters the form and the content of the memories.

For instance, children of parents who engage in more "elaborative" conversation about the past will themselves produce richer, more detailed narratives. In America, mothers and fathers on average use more details about the past, and include more emotional content, with girls than with boys (Fivush, 1994). This may be a reason why women across cultures report earlier and richer memories from childhood than do men (MacDonald, Uesiliana, & Hayne, 2000). Cultural style affects memory over time as well. Caucasian American mothers and children talk more about the role of the self in past episodes than do Korean mothers and children, and the Americans also include a higher proportion of references to their own and others' emotional states in narrating the past (Mullen & Yi, 1995).

Interrelatedness of Domains   The infant that is allowed and has the ability to move may develop object permanence much more quickly. Kermoian and Campos (1988) found that eight-month-olds who could move independently were much more likely to seek hidden objects than those who could not. Hence, movement affects cognitive development.

Table 8–1 lists memory concepts, indications that the concept has been achieved, and the age at which the concept is typically achieved.

TABLE 8–1 **Memory Development**

Age	Concept	Behavioral Indicators
Infant	Sensorial associations	Responds to mother's face
	Sensorial associations after short delay	Infant looks for objects outside of field of vision.
	Representation associations after longer delay	Infant seeks an object hidden in front of her.
	Representation associations with location	Infant seeks object when it is not in typical location.
Toddler	Representation is permanently encoded	Child seeks object after considerable delay until it is found.
	Memory recalled with cue	Child seeks object from a related sensorial stimulus.
Preschool	Memory recalled without cue	Child remembers object or activity without a cue.
	Retrieved memories applied to new situations	Child uses old memory to expand understanding.
	Memories strengthened by unconscious strategies	Child uses self-talk.
School-age	Memories strengthened by conscious strategies	Child will elaborate and rehearse.

What to look for in memory development

❑ What does the infant/child attend to?

❑ How long does the infant attend to the same stimuli?

❑ What kinds of sensory stimuli change the infant or child's focus of attention?

❑ Is the infant/child making associations to objects or people that are out of sight?

❑ Is the child looking for objects or people in the places it is expected they would be found?

❑ Does the child relate past events with a cue? Without a cue?

❑ Can the child relate events that happened yesterday? Last week? How long ago?

❑ What kinds of events or experiences does the child remember?

❑ Does the child use self-talk?

❑ What kinds of strategies does the child use to remember things?

The next two anecdotal records document memory development.

ANECDOTAL RECORD 8–2

Child's Name: Tasha

Date: July 14

Time: 9:35 a.m.

Observer: A. Kovacik

Location: Parkwood Early Learning Center Infant Classroom

Three-month-old Tasha sits securely in her infant seat, located on the floor of the infant classroom. The caregiver sits on the floor with Tasha and two other babies: James, age 7 months and Alex, age 10 months (who are not in seats but are crawling, creeping, and cruising about the room). The caregiver alternately engages the three children. The caregiver talks with Tasha, gaining her attention. She exaggerates her expression as she says "Hello, my wonderful girl, are you ready to play?" Tasha waves her arms and legs, seemingly in agreement. There is a rattle with a thin yellow handle and round colorful balls at the top located on the floor at the caregiver's knee. The caregiver picks the rattle up by the top leaving the handle exposed. The caregiver's arm is suspended in air close to Tasha's face, when Alex cries out. The caregiver turns her attention from Tasha to attend to Alex leaving her arm in place with rattle in hand. Tasha reaches out, grasps the rattle from the caregiver and begins to shake it, creating a jingling sound. The caregiver quickly looks back at Tasha and says, "You did that yourself! You remembered that the rattle jingles—jingle, jingle." Tasha kicks her legs and continues to shake the rattle with her left hand. Tasha watches the rattle as she shakes it.

ANECDOTAL RECORD 8–3

Child Name: Sean

Date: December 20

Time: 8:50 a.m.

Observer: A. Kovacik

Location: Parkwood Early Learning Center Infant Classroom

Nine-month-old Sean plays on the floor of the infant room. The caregiver is standing at the changing table, changing the diaper of another baby. Sean alternately crawls and sits as he moves around the carpeted area in the center of the room. He sits on his bottom, back straight and legs out in front of him in a V, knees slightly bent. He picks up a toy block and places it in an empty bucket. The telephone located on the wall rings three times. The caregiver looks at Sean and says, "I can't get the phone right now, I'm busy changing Monica's diaper. Ring, ring, who will get the phone?" (Meanwhile, the phone stops ringing, presumably answered by someone else at the center.) Sean utters groups of sounds back to the caregiver. He crawls on hands and knees to a low shelf where a small, red toy telephone is stored. He grasps the telephone and holds the receiver to his ear. He makes babbling sounds. The caregiver says, "'Hello, this is Sean. Hello, hello.' Sean will answer the phone." Sean looks at the caregiver, babbles, and drops the telephone. He crawls on hands and knees back to the bucket.

Imitation supports memory development.

Problem Solving

"Problem solving is an attempt to find an appropriate way of attaining a goal when the goal is not readily available" (Santrock, 2005, p. 356). We all use problem solving every day of our lives, from trying to figure out how to get to a concert when we appear to be lost, to how to make a meal in 30 minutes. The child's ability to solve problems develops from mental maturation and from experiences. As children grow, their brains' capabilities allow them to process and store previously learned information and use it to solve problems in the future.

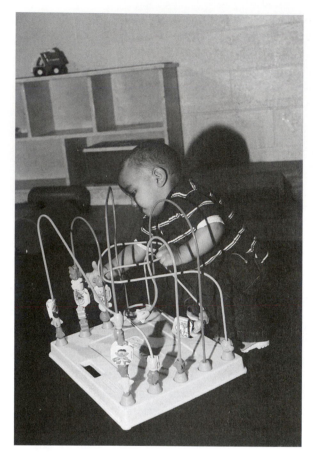

Puzzle-like toys and activities promote problem-solving abilities.

Goal-directed behaviors begin in early infancy.

 In video stream 4 on the accompanying CD-ROM, view children solving problems as they uncover the mystery.

The Developmental Course of Problem Solving

The development of problem solving begins with reflexive connections being made within the brain between stimuli and responses to those stimuli. As this progresses, cause and effect relationships are formed. The infant at first kicks the mobile or puts his foot toward his mouth without having any expectations about what that action will cause or what effect it will have. Infants can learn to associate certain actions with their outcomes as early as two months of age. Thus the beginnings of **goal-directed behaviors** can be seen. In other words, the infant's actions are now intentional.

At approximately eight months of age, the infant begins to develop **means-end behaviors,** problem-solving abilities in which the infant must develop a strategy for reaching his goal. For example, instead of simply moving his arm to make the mobile move, he has to remove or overcome an obstacle in order to make it move. Let's say that the mobile has been moved and now it is out of his reach—how will he get the same

Goal-directed behaviors.   Any behaviors that have intentionality.

Means-end behaviors.   Goal-directed behaviors that require one to overcome obstacles and develop strategies.

results as before? The two-month-old might simply not try, whereas the eight-month-old might use something else in the crib or on the floor to increase his reach, like a stick or pole.

A toddler's problem-solving skills will improve as his experiences and explorations with objects in the environment increase. This is why some people talk about toddlers as being in the "terrible twos." (I would much rather consider it the "terrific twos" because they are experimenting with everything!) They are searching for the rules of cause-and-effect relationships. They are asking the following sorts of questions.

What will happen if . . .

> . . . I put this cheese sandwich into the DVD player?
> . . . I put this block in the toilet then push this button?
> . . . I drop this cup on the floor one more time?

or

How can I . . .

> . . . get those cookies that mom put on the top shelf?
> . . . make the dog smell good?
> . . . get mommy to pay attention to me?

Although it can be frustrating, remember that the child's experiences and explorations are what help them develop more sophisticated problem-solving skills, and through exploration and experimentation the child moves from concrete cause-and-effect relationships to abstraction and application. (See a developmental progression of problem solving in Table 8-2.)

Social Problem Solving

Consider the problem solving that is going on here within the social context.

What to look for in problem solving

❑ Does the infant/child make connections between cause and effect?

❑ Do the cause and effect relationships revolve around their own bodies, other objects, or how objects cause other objects to change?

❑ Does the child exhibit *means-end* behaviors?

❑ What kinds of explorations does the child engage in?

❑ Does the child experiment? With what kinds of materials?

❑ Does the child come up with novel solutions to problems?

❑ Does the child apply previously learned rules to predict outcomes?

Simple materials can support problem solving.

TABLE 8–2 **Developmental Progression of Problem Solving**

Stage	Concept	Indicator	Child's view
Stage 1	Connections form within self from reflexive acts	Child makes raspberries (vibrating sound infants make with their lips).	When I do something I feel something.
Stage 2	Connections form between self and outside of self due to nonpurposeful action	Child kicks mobile and makes it move.	I am surprised.
Stage 3	Purposeful action based on prior reaction	Child recreates the cause-and-effect relationship purposefully.	Hey, I can make this move whenever I do this.
Stage 4	Using a tool for desired response, means-end behaviors	Child uses a tool to cause a reaction.	I want the truck that is out of my reach; what can I use to get it?
Stage 5	Exploration	Child explores cause-and-effect relationships.	How can I make this fit? How can I get to this? How does this taste? How does this work?
Stage 6	Experimentation	Child makes hypothesis.	What will happen if . . . ? If this, then what?
Stage 7	Verification	Child repeats actions and continues to test hypothesis.	This happened before; will it happen again? What if it doesn't happen again?
Stage 8	Application	Child uses past cause-and-effect relationships and then applies them to novel situations.	I want to build something that has a function—how will I do it?

Logical Thinking or Reasoning

Logical thinking is based on the child's ability to carry out mental actions or **operations.** The child will also be able to understand and utilize early forms of **reasoning,** such as: If we do not go to school on Saturdays, and tomorrow is Saturday, what does that mean? As with all cognitive processes, the development of one affects the development of another. The development of logical thinking relies on the development of problem solving, memory, and abstraction.

The Developmental Course of Logical Thinking and Reasoning   The prerequisite to logical thinking is the child's framework of knowledge and the experiences of playing around with information in order to explain the impossible and integrate multiple aspects of knowledge. The onset of logical thinking is marked by the child's ability to stabilize a concept, often represented within a particular schema. The child can hold the representation in order to compare and contrast new objects or ideas, re-classifying and thinking of the concept in new and different ways. Whereas the infant and toddler will rely on concrete objects to carry out actions and experiment with actual objects, the older child will begin to be able to carry these out in his head. He will be able move objects, reverse the order of tasks such as pouring water, and visualize the order of steps for a task not yet presented.

In video stream 4 on the accompanying CD-ROM, view how preschool children deduce who or what has visited their classroom.

The development of logical thinking and reasoning involves attending to stimuli, and includes the concepts of conservation and reversibility.

ATTENDING TO STIMULI   The infant and young child will attend to stimuli that do not seem to make sense to them. Remember that at the beginning of this chapter we discussed how the child is continually trying to make sense of the world. In other words, he is perfecting his logical thinking skills. So, when something appears "nonsensical" he attends to it longer, because he is trying to figure it out. Classic experiments reveal that when an infant or young child is presented with a stimulus that violates what he would expect to see or hear, he will attend to it longer—demonstrating that his preconceived notions about the physical world are being challenged (Kellman and Spelke, 1983; Baillargeon, Spelke, & Wasserman, 1985).

How do we know when an infant is attending to something? Some of the indicators are turning the head, eyes, and body toward the direction of the target, as well as a stilling of body movements, slowing down of the heartbeat, and often changing of the position of the mouth (Reddy, Hay, Murray, & Trevarthen, 1997). The young child tells us he is attending when he concentrates and focuses on the task before him or looks at the source of the information (watching the person talk, watching the animal move) while being relatively still himself. Finally, when a young child is very interested in something he will ask many questions, demonstrating his attempts to make sense of something. A child who can talk has the added ability to ask others and learn in a social

---

Operations.   Mental actions usually involving symbols.

Reasoning.   A particular type of problem solving that involves making inferences in order to draw conclusions.

Children use the power of observation to learn about the world around them.

context, as well. The child in the car continually asking "why" for every answer given is not trying to drive you crazy, he is trying to understand the world around him. The youngest child will ask "what"; the older child begins to ask "why" and "how."

CONSERVATION   When the child can conserve it simply means they can understand that the amount of something stays the same even when the shape of it changes. The child that has developed *conservation* can identify that even though you have poured one glass of water into a taller glass, the amount of water still stays the same. The child who is not yet able to conserve will say, after you have poured the water into a taller glass, that there is now more water. In other words, their judgment is based on appearance rather than on logical thinking.

REVERSIBILITY   **Reversibility** refers to the ability to visualize how an operation or action could be reversed. The following anecdote demonstrates reversibility.

ANECDOTAL RECORD 8–4

Child's Name: Monique

Date: January 15

Time: 10:55 a.m.

Observer: D. Ahola

Location: Happy Times Center, Three-Year-Old Classroom

Children explore concepts of conservation with play dough.

Monique is playing at the play dough table with Tevina, the student teacher. Tevina takes a piece of play dough and rolls it into a ball, then smashes it down to create a pancake or cookie-like object. Monique looks over to see the new object and begins manipulating the play dough, trying to make a similar object. While she is watching, Tevina takes the flat object and rolls it back into a ball. Monique takes her piece of play dough, rolls it into a ball, and smashes it down—finally creating the cookie she wanted to make to give to her teacher. Another child watches as Monique presents the cookie to the teacher and asks Monique, "How did you make that?" Monique answers, "It's easy, make a ball, then make a cookie!"

Table 8–3 shows the stages in the development of logical thinking.

What to look for in logical thinking
Does the child:

❑ classify objects and concepts?

❑ draw conclusions based on logic? (e.g., if it snows then it is cold)

❑ draw conclusions based on egocentric perception? (e.g., it rained because I wore yellow)

❑ question the pluralistic roles of people and objects? (e.g., my teacher is a teacher, so she can't be a mommy)

Reversibility.   The ability to visualize how an action or operation can be reversed.

TABLE 8–3 **The Development of Logical Thinking/Reasoning**

Stage	Developmental Tasks	Behavioral Indicators
Stage 1	Distinguishing same and different	Finds one's belongings among those of others Completes matching tasks
Stage 2	Classifying: placing like items together	Sorts silverware Sorts cars according to color
Stage 3	Classifying objects with several like characteristics	Sorts animals by where they live and by classification (e.g., mammals, reptiles) Sorts cars by color and model
	Distinguishing objects included in a class	Recognizes that the total is a sum of all parts (e.g., in a class of 18 children, 15 of whom are girls, when asked whether there are more girls or more children, child will respond "more children") Classic experiment: Are there more beads or more brown beads?
	Conservation of continuous quantities	Recognizes that quantity remains the same even when shape changes Recognizes that a sandwich cut in four is still equal to one sandwich
	Conservation of numbers	Correctly makes one-to-one correspondence Sets up for snack using one cup with one napkin
	Reversibility	Reverses operations Tells the backward sequence of baking a cookie
Stage 4	Deductive reasoning	Uses multiple criteria in order to predict (e.g., if we don't have school on Saturday, and tomorrow is Saturday, then we don't have school tomorrow)

- ❑ distinguish appearance from reality? (e.g., when I put a mask on, I am still me even though on the surface I look like someone else)
- ❑ demonstrate an ability to conserve?
- ❑ take another person's perspective?
- ❑ explain otherwise magical phenomenon logically? (e.g., when the celery stalk turns orange overnight it is because the dyed water went up through its veins)

A child demonstrates categorizing and placement of numbers.

Theory of Mind

One who can understand and predict another person's mental processes—their thoughts, emotions, motives, beliefs, and intentions—is said to have developed a theory of mind (Berger, 2002). A theory of mind allows the individual to understand why a playmate is crying, know what someone else wants, predict what another will do, and in general be able to know what another person is thinking. The development of a theory of mind is more than likely a critical piece in positive peer relationships and other social interactions. The child who can understand what another person is thinking can navigate through relationships more effectively.

The Developmental Course of Theory of Mind   Although the exact developmental course and onset of a theory of mind is not known, there are some clues as to how this phenomenon unfolds.

PRECURSORS TO THEORY OF MIND   Before 12 months of age, children show a precocious ability to understand intentions and other important aspects of the mind (such as gaze direction, attention, and pretense). At 18 months of age, toddlers demonstrate the ability to understand what others want, not just what they themselves want. In the classic study done by Repacholi and Gopnik (1997), 14-month-olds and 18-month-olds were first tested for their preference for two kinds of foods: raw vegetables and goldfish crackers. They then watched as the experimenter tasted the two foods herself. She showed disgust for one type and delight for another. The experimenter then opened both her hands over each bowl and asked each child, "Can I have some?" The 14-month-olds gave her the food they preferred, while the 18-month-olds gave her the food she actually showed preference for.

At two and a half to three years of age, children make attempts at tricking someone or using strategies to install false belief in others. However, the strategies still rely on the child's own thinking rather than the other person's. Consider Anecdotal Record 8-5 on the following page.

At five years of age most children can pass the **false belief task** which, by many accounts, is the first real evidence of theory of mind. Figure 8–1 gives an explanation of a false belief task. Passing the false belief task means children have reached a stage in

False Belief Task.   A standard experimental instrument for studying children's Theory of Mind abilities. This task tests whether children are able to attribute false belief to someone else. For example a child is presented with a sealed box of crayons. When asked what the box contains the child naturally suggests that the box contains Crayons. The examiner reveals that although the box looks like it might contain crayons it actually contains rubber bands. The rubber bands are sealed back inside of the crayon box and the child is asked to predict what another child will think the box contains. The child without the ability of theory of mind predicts that the other child will think the box contains rubber bands.

FIGURE 8-1 Explanation and an example of a false-belief task.

A **false-belief task** is one in which the child is asked to identify what another person would be thinking given the clues that are present. In order to test this, a child is told a story or given a scene in which they are to learn information about something that someone else may not be privy to. Then they are to predict how the person would react, given that they do not have all the information.

For example, the experimenter reads the following scenario to the child:

Raoul hides a cookie in his kitchen cupboard and then goes outside to play. When he is gone his sister finds the cookie and puts it in the refrigerator. When Raoul comes back inside, where will he look for the cookie?

The child who has not developed theory of mind will say the refrigerator—because she has knowledge that the cookie has been moved and does not realize that Raoul doesn't.

which they can have an "opaque" reading of mind and reality; that is, they can easily distinguish between what *is* the case and what people *believe* is the case. As children enter elementary school they begin to understand the nuances of human thinking. They come to realize that what a person is thinking does not always match what he or she is showing. They can tell, for example, that even a person who is laughing might actually feel sad (Flavell, Miller, and Miller, 1993), and that one person can have different feelings about one situation or topic.

ANECDOTAL RECORD 8–5

Child's Name: Taisha

Date: February 15

Time: 3:15 p.m.

Observer: D. Ahola

Location: Sunshine Center

Twenty-seven-month-old Taisha was the youngest player in the children's hide-and-seek game. As the other three- and four-year-old children ran to hide under exposed tables or behind small chairs, Taisha stood in the middle of the room and placed her hands over her eyes. Giggling the whole time, she said, "You can't find me!!!"

What to look for in the development of theory of mind

❑ Does the child exhibit **joint attention**?

❑ Does the child realize his own preferences over others?

Joint Attention. Paying attention to something that another person is referencing.

❑ Does the child recognize the motives or intentions of others?

❑ Does the child try to trick others?

❑ When the child does attempt a trick, whose beliefs are at the center of it?

❑ Does the child attempt deception or lying?

❑ Does the child identify others' emotions by anything other than appearance?

CULTURAL VARIATION

Theory of mind has been found to emerge in the United States, Australia, and Korea at about four years of age. In Canada and Cameroon it is more like three and one-half years of age. In Japan it appears at age five, and in Quechua, Peru, not until age seven (Wellman, Cross, & Watson, 2001). The difference in onset is probably due in part to a culture's anticipation of the future and its use of deception.

Another factor that affects theory of mind development is family size (Perner, Ruffman & Leekam, 1994). Children from larger families perform false-belief tasks better than do children from smaller families. One possible explanation for this is that the interactions provided by siblings facilitate theory of mind, because siblings are typically in competition for resources, and sometimes this involves trickery. Another explanation is that because of the older siblings' mental advantage, the younger sibling will do well to develop "reverse psychology" types of deception.

Of Special Interest—Symbolic Play in Children with Developmental Delays

In this section we focus on the development of object-based play, from early exploratory manipulations, to planned, symbolic, multischeme sequences—thus zeroing in on cognitive development. The emphasis, then, is on symbolic play rather than social play. Whereas children with developmental delays may show deficits in social play as well, we will concentrate on the cognitive aspect of play and how children with special needs might be affected.

The Development of Symbolic Play

Table 8–4 shows the development of play in typically developing children as delineated by Piaget. As you will note, the ages give the reader some sense of when these play schemas develop; they are to be used as a sort of gage to go by but by no means are they meant to be used to evaluate children. However, the age guidelines can show you how a child should be progressing through symbolic play.

In video stream 2 on the accompanying CD-ROM, identify the symbolic play among toddlers.

TABLE 8-4   **Developmental Taxonomy of Play Based on Piaget (1951)**

2–5 months	Sensorimotor play	Children enjoy causing something to happen with an object: banging blocks together, rolling objects, throwing, dumping, etc.
5–10 months	Coordination of secondary schemes	Children use objects in different ways and begin combining them: stacking cars on a block, dumping blocks from a truck.
10–18 months	Ritualistic action patterns	Children play (pretend) with objects in their conventional way: using a brush to brush their hair, drink from an empty cup, pretend to eat with a fork. The actions are directed toward self.
	Symbolic Play	
18 months	Projection of symbolic schemes onto new objects	Children pretend with objects in a conventional manner, but now they will apply it to another object or something outside of themselves. Children now pretend to feed the baby, comb the baby's hair, pretend the baby is asleep rather than pretending they themselves are asleep.
18 months	Projection of imitative schemes onto new objects	Children now pretend with objects that are not in their typical routines: child pretends to read the paper, answer the telephone, write on envelope.
24 months	Simple identification of one object with another	Children pretend that one object is another: block is telephone, sticks are candles.
24 months	Identification of body with another person or object	Children pretend to be something else: animal, mommy, airline pilot.
3–4 years	Simple combinations	Children put together simple scenes to create one whole task or action. Children pretend to wash baby from beginning to end or pretend to have a birthday party. There is no elaboration; the previously imitated scenes are simply put together.
3–4 years	Compensating	Children attempt to correct reality, rather than reproduce it: child pretends to go mountain climbing and goes all the way to the top, whereas when he actually went they only went up halfway.
3–4 years	Liquidating	Child attempts to undo an unpleasant situation and the negative aspect is undone through the play. For example, child goes over to baby and goes through the whole morning routine reenactment without fighting.
3–4 years	Anticipatory	The actual action of pretend playing—acting out scenes and play themes that have never happened but can be anticipated. Child acts out what will happen when he goes to Disney World next week.

Symbolic Play Deficits in Children with Developmental Delays

How children are developing in terms of symbolic play can have a major impact on their social, language, and motor development. Children with special needs are at times removed from symbolic play either physically or psychologically, meaning that either their physical limitations or mental deficits prevent them from playing.

Playing is central to the development of cognition. When a child has a developmental delay he may not progress through the play stages at a normal rate, and some may not progress at all. When a child does not engage in play or becomes stagnated in a level of play, it is imperative for the teacher or caregiver to intervene. Children with disabling conditions (particularly developmental delays) will show varying signs of play deficits from only being able to use the objects sensorially (banging them, throwing them, etc.), to being "stuck" or using the objects repeatedly in the same way. Consider the following anecdotal record.

Making candles out of golf tees or sticks is symbolic play.

In video stream 3 on the accompanying CD-ROM, note the symbolic play that the toddlers are demonstrating.

ANECDOTAL RECORD 8–6

Child's Name: Adam

Date: March 20

Time: 9:40 a.m.

Observer: D. Ahola

Location: Child's living room

Three-year-old Adam is sitting in his family room playing with the cars and the play garage that his mom just got him. Adam takes the first blue car and carefully places it next to the ramp that extends out from the garage. Next, he carefully picks up the red car and places it side by side to the blue car. Adam continues to place each of the seven cars side by side. After they are all placed he begins to make another line of the cars by starting the whole process over again.

Adam has been diagnosed with autism. If left to himself he will continue to line up the cars time and time again. Determining where the child is can give you a great road map as to where to try to go with the child. By looking at Table 8–4 we can see that Adam is in the "Coordination of secondary schemes" stage. Without some kind of play therapy it will be difficult for him to move out of it. We would need to begin to offer some sort of play therapy that would give Adam cues as to how to play with cars—making the cars roll, making the sounds of the car as it moves, etc.

When you see that a child is not developing in the area of symbolic play it is time to write some goals and objectives that include play development.

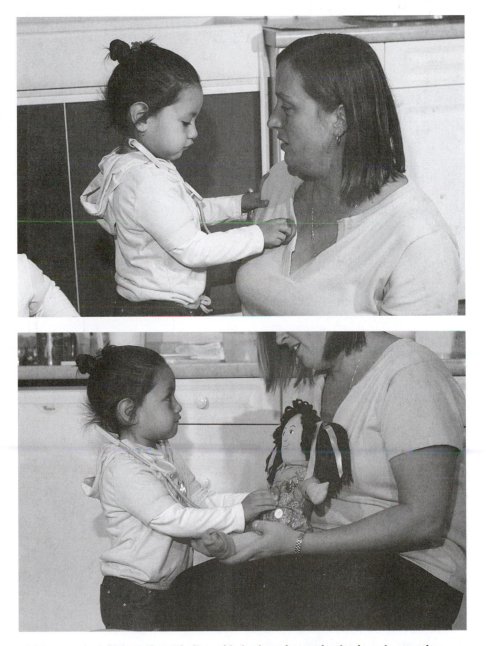

Child's progression through symbolic and imitative schemes begins by using another human and moves to objects.

Until Adam can begin to use the cars in conventional ways he will not move into symbolic play and eventually social play—social play being the ultimate goal.

What to look for in a child's symbolic play

- ❏ How does the child play with objects?
- ❏ Does the child use combinations of play scenes with objects?
- ❏ Are play themes extended to objects outside of the child's self?
- ❏ Does the child pretend?
- ❏ Does the child take on other roles?
- ❏ Does the child put together several imitative actions during pretend play for one complete scene?
- ❏ Does the child alter what really happens (imitate) or does he/she make up other pieces?
- ❏ Does the child make up completely new, unseen **play scripts**?

 Print the Anecdotal Record from the CD-ROM. Highlight (code) the behavioral indicators of cognitive development. Coding can be done best by using highlighters, colored pencils, or thin-tipped markers. Crayons do not work well.

QUESTIONS TO CONSIDER ○ ○ ○

1. Going back to Anecdotal Record 8–1: What was Michael telling us about his memory development?
2. How do brain maturation and life experiences interact to inform cognitive development?
3. How could cognitive development be affected by the development of language? The development of movement?

REFERENCES ○ ○ ○

Baillargeon, R., Spelke, E. S., & Wasserman, S. (1985). Object permanence in five-month-old infants. *Cognition, 20,* 191–208.

Berger, K. S. (2002). *The developing person through childhood* (3rd ed.). New York: Worth.

Ellis, H. C. (1979). *Fundamentals of human learning, memory and cognition* (2nd ed.). Dubuque, IA: W. C. Brown.

Fivush, R. (1994). Constructing narrative, emotion, and self in parent-child conversations about the past. In Neisser, U., & Fivush, R. (Eds.), *The Remembering Self* (pp. 136–157). Cambridge, UK: Cambridge University Press.

Flavell, J. H., Miller, P. H., & Miller, S. A. (1993). *Cognitive development* (3rd ed.). Upper Saddle River, NJ: Prentice Hall.

Play scripts.   Playing out of a familiar scene as if to a script. Examples include birthday party, pet store, ice cream shop, etc.

Kellman, P. J., & Spelke, E. S. (1983). Perception of partly occluded objects in infancy. *Cognitive Psychology, 15,* 483–524.

Kermoian, R., & Campos, J. J. (1988). Locomotor experience: A facilitator of spatial cognitive development. *Child Development, 59,* 908–917.

MacDonald, S., Uesiliana, K., & Hayne, H. (2000). Cross-cultural and gender differences in childhood amnesia. *Memory, 8,* 365–376.

Mullen, M. K., & Yi, S. (1995). The cultural context of talk about the past: Implications for the development of autobiographical memory. *Cognitive Development, 10,* 407–419.

Perner, D. G., Ruffman, T., & Leekam, S. (1994). Theory of mind is contagious: You catch it from your sibs. *Child Development, 67,* 1228–1238.

Piaget, J. (1951). *Play, dreams and imitation in childhood.* London: Heinemann.

Reddy, V., Hay, D., Murray, L., & Trevarthen, C. (1997). Communication in infancy: Mutual regulation of affect and attention. In G. Bremner, A. Slater, & G. Butterworth (Eds.), *Infant development: recent advances* (pp. 247–273). Hove, East Sussex, UK: Psychology Press.

Repacholi, B. M., & Gopnik, A. (1997). Early reasoning about desires: Evidence from 14- and 18-month-olds. *Developmental Psychology, 33,* 12–21.

Santrock, J. W. (2005). *Psychology* (7th ed.). New York: McGraw-Hill.

Sousa, D. A. (1995). *How the Brain Learns.* Reston, VA: National Association of Secondary School Principals.

Sutton, J. (2002). Cognitive conceptions of language and the development of autobiographical memory. [Electronic version]. *Language and Communication., 22,* 375–390.

Wellman, H. M., Cross, D., & Watson, J. (2001). Meta-analysis of theory-of-mind development: The truth about false belief. *Child Development, 72,* 655–684.

9

Social Development

CHAPTER OBJECTIVES

- To understand the sequence of emotional development

- To understand development of emotional regulation

- To define aspects of social competence

- To understand the components of and development of attachment

- To describe the link between early attachment and later cognitive, emotional, physical, and social development

- To define and understand social play

- To understand autistic spectrum disorders

CHILD STUDY OBJECTIVES

Upon conclusion of this chapter the student will:

- code an anecdotal record for social development.

- identify a checklist for social development.

- create a checklist for social development.

- create a structured observation to assess social development.

- gather visual documentation indicating social development.

- create interview questions for the parent regarding social development.

INTRODUCTION TO SOCIAL DEVELOPMENT

Children, like other humans, are social beings. As they grow and develop they form relationships and attachments. Social competence is gained through experience and understanding of a child's social context or culture. The human brain is hardwired to develop within that social context. Human contact is necessary for survival and it helps children thrive. As children grow and develop into social beings they form relationships, learn to regulate their emotions, learn to share, and engage in play. The all-important task of socialization begins during the early years. **Socialization** is the process influenced by parents and others to ensure that children learn the standards of behavior, attitudes, and skills associated with the society or culture in which they develop.

BRAIN CONCEPTS RELEVANT TO SOCIAL DEVELOPMENT

Overview of Neural Transmission

From the moment a child is born, the responses made by others influence the developing brain. The infant's ability to form relationships and attachments and to regulate her own emotions is a function of brain development that is supported by positive nurturing experiences (Gable & Hunting, 2000).

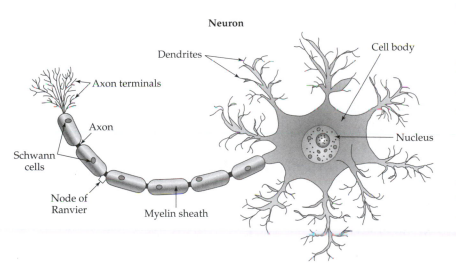

Neuron

In fact, those experiences act as catalysts as the brain establishes and reinforces connections from neuron to neuron. These connections are formed when impulses are sent and received between **neurons.** A part of the neuron called an **axon** sends messages, and spiny neuron structures called **dendrites** receive them. These electrically charged connections are called synapses. As a

....

Socialization.   The process influenced by parents and others to ensure that children learn the standards of behavior, attitudes, and skills associated with the society or culture in which they develop.

Neurons.   Nerve cells that make up the nervous system and allow different parts of the body to communicate with each other.

Axon.   Long fibrous portion of the neuron that conducts nerve impulses.

Dendrites.   Branches out from the neuron, detects electrical signals emitted by other neurons, and transmits them to the cell body.

child experiences rich and varied environmental stimuli, the synapses become more complex, like a tree with expanding branches and limbs.

Pruning

Although the number of neurons remains the same during the first three years of life, there is rapid and prolific synapse development. In fact, the brain develops more synapses than it needs. Synapses or connections that the brain uses frequently become hardwired, or remain, while those that the brain does not use are eliminated.

Experience plays an important role in determining which connections remain and which are eliminated or pruned. **Pruning** is the dying off of some cells and connections due to lack of stimulation. The "use it or lose it" concept of neuron pruning is important to consider when planning activities for young children. By providing positive and nurturing social learning opportunities, we ensure that the synapses associated with these experiences become permanent. For example, a caregiver who responds to an infant's cry in a consistent, warm, and nurturing manner provides the stimulation that sparks the activity between axons and dendrites that creates synapses (Sousa, 2001).

Adult responses during a child's early life are so powerful that they influence what the child learns about herself, others, and the world. Brain connections that lead to healthy social development grow as a result of supportive and predictable nurturance. Conversely, negative or hurtful experiences also become part of permanent brain structure. This is because the brain does not discriminate between positive and negative stimuli when making connections. Those children whose early relationships were neglectful, abusive, and stressful have brain connections that reflect those experiences.

Sensitive Periods

The development of **social competence** begins at birth and continues throughout one's lifetime; however, optimal periods of growth and development occur in this area between the ages of three and six. The preschool years are especially critical in the development of social competence. During these years the child learns how to react and to interact with peers. Research suggests that social adeptness in adolescence and adulthood is highly dependent on social skill development in the early years. In fact, social competence has been linked to the child's early experiences regarding the stability of relationships. Alice Sterling Honig and Kyung Ja Park (1993) of Syracuse University has examined the social competence of children with multiple secure relationships and those with numerous disrupted attachment relationships. It appears that multiple separations, caused by such factors, as high turnover among early childhood teachers, negatively influence the social abilities of the young child. Additionally, caregiver responsiveness is linked to the development of secure relationships (Honig, 2002).

Pruning.   In cognitive science, the natural occurrence of the dying off of some cells and connections due to the lack of stimulation.

Social competence.   A set of skills that include initiating and maintaining satisfying, reciprocal relationships, which are needed to meet the requirements of society.

Interrelatedness of Domains

> #### Relationship of Social Development to Other Domains
>
> Observations in the areas of language, cognitive, motor, and emotional development inform interpretations of a child's social development. As abilities and knowledge grow in each of the domains they affect the child's social functioning. Consider the relationships between social development and language. The child must be able to understand what someone else is saying in order to interact. She must have communicative skills in order to enter into and remain in social situations. How about emotional development and socialization? As we will see, the child must develop **emotional regulation,** or the ability to manage her own emotional responses, in order to negotiate and compromise during play situations. Children's cognitive development, specifically their schema development, contributes to the making of a play theme, such as acting out going to the doctor or to a birthday party. A child's motor development determines whether or not she can stay with the other children in their gross motor play. In conclusion, when interpreting observations in the area of social development, one must consider the other domains and their effects.

CONCEPTS OF SOCIAL DEVELOPMENT

The complexities of social development are evident to anyone who has worked or lived with a growing child. Components of social development include attachment, emotional regulation, and empathy. Gaining social competence, including the understanding of social rules, the formation of friendships, and the ability to sustain play are important developmental tasks. These tasks are critical to the development of all children, including those with developmental concerns.

Attachment

Attachment, as defined by Maccoby (1980) is a "relatively enduring emotional tie to a specific other person" (p. 53). The human tendency toward attachment is linked to the survival instinct. Infants are born helpless, needing to be entirely cared for and protected. Fortunately, they are born with the necessary tools to attain such care. Naturally occurring neural and hormonal interactions assist parents and children with this powerful process. Typically, parents naturally follow their biological instincts, nurturing their babies and maintaining physical closeness.

Emotional regulation.   The ability to alter or control one's emotional response to situations that are overstimulating or provocative.

Attachment.   An emotional connection between people or between a person and an animal or object. Feelings of distress occur during separation.

Oxytocin is a chemical released in the brain in response to social contact, particularly skin-to-skin contact. This hormone promotes bonding and creates desire for further contact between parent and child (Insel, 1992). Increased levels of estrogen during pregnancy influence the multiplication of oxytocin receptors in the expecting mother's brain. This makes the new mother highly responsive to the presence of oxytocin. Hormones continue to increase during labor, delivery, and nursing, helping to create a bond. Breast feeding increases the production of oxytocin in the infant, creating the two-way path for attachment to occur.

The Developmental Course of Attachment

As parent or guardian and child get to know each other, attachment develops. For the first three months of life, infants demonstrate **indiscriminate attachment,** as their behaviors are not directed toward any specific individual. During this time infants display attachment behaviors such as tracking with their eyes, crying, smiling, and cooing. The infant prefers to gaze at a human face as opposed to shapes or colors, but differentiation between individual faces is not yet developed. At three to six months the infant begins to discriminate between familiar and unfamiliar faces and responds differently to each.

In video stream 1 on the accompanying CD-ROM, note the various secure attachment behaviors being demonstrated.

Synchrony refers to the patterns of interaction that develop between the parent or guardian and the infant. Some liken it to a dance between the two, one leading and the other following, but always reading and responding to each other's cues. Synchronization occurs when the adult correctly interprets the infant's cues and then responds appropriately. This is known as **goodness of fit**—in other words, the appropriateness of reciprocal responses. Table 9–1 demonstrates the cues an infant might give and the interpretations the caregiver might make.

At approximately seven months the infant prefers the attachment figure (in many cases this is the mother), and cries or shows distress when she leaves the room. From 7–24 months the infant/toddler shows **separation anxiety** and **stranger fear** and will actively seek out physical contact with the attachment figure. By this time the attachment has clearly formed. Between two and three years of age the child will still seek contact, but now it is not necessarily physical—being able to see the attachment figure and/or hear her is enough. This is a time when we can observe active exploration with the attachment figure as base. Between the ages of three and four years the child

Oxytocin.   A chemical released in the brain in response to social contact, particularly skin-to-skin contact.

Indiscriminate attachment.   Stage of attachment in which babies prefer humans to nonhumans, but do not discriminate among individual people.

Synchrony.   Refers to the harmonious patterns of interaction that develop between the parent or guardian and the infant.

Goodness of fit.   The quality of the match between the child's temperament and the demands of the surrounding environment.

Separation anxiety.   A child's fear of being left by the parent or caregiver. Emerges at approximately eight or nine months of age.

Stranger fear.   Fear of unfamiliar people.

TABLE 9–1 **How Caregivers Interpret the Gaze of an Infant**

Baby's Face	How We See It
Infant gazes with adult face to face	Appears intentional and engaging
Smiling into adult's face	Viewed as the infant being pleased, focused
Infant head and face are turned away from the adult	Viewed as the child taking a break in order to keep the interaction going and maintain interest
Infant looks away completely	Interpreted as the infant needs a break
Infant head is lowered and does not gaze at face of adult	Viewed as an indicator that interaction should stop
Infant rapidly shakes head with no face-to-face gaze	Viewed as the infant not liking the stimulus
The infant glances away and tilts chin up, partially looking away	Interpreted that a different technique to engage the infant should be used
Infant's head is lowered with inactive body	Viewed as the child giving in to unwanted stimulation

From *Guiding Children's Social Development* 5th edition by Kostelnik/Whiren/Soderman/Stein/Gregory © 2006. Reprinted with permission of Thomson Delmar Learning, a division of Thomson Learning.

can stay with a stranger for brief periods of time and by five years of age the child realizes that the attachment figure is permanent and there is no longer a need for constant contact (Bailey & Wolery, 1992). Table 9–2 shows the stages of attachment.

What to Look For in Attachment

- ❑ Does the infant exhibit social smiles?
- ❑ Do the caregiver and infant display synchrony?
- ❑ What kinds of cues does the infant give to signal the mother?
- ❑ What kinds of attachment behaviors does the infant exhibit?
- ❑ Does the infant show any preferences for a particular caregiver?
- ❑ What kind of behaviors does the infant exhibit that suggest preference?
- ❑ Does the infant show distress when the mother (attachment figure) leaves the room?
- ❑ Does the infant/toddler show attachment behaviors to anyone other than the primary caregiver?
- ❑ Does the infant demonstrate anxiety at separation from the primary caregiver?
- ❑ Does the infant demonstrate anxiety in the presence of a stranger?
- ❑ What kind of proximity-seeking behaviors, if any, does the child demonstrate?

TABLE 9–2 **The Development of Attachment**

Stage of Attachment	Concept of Attachment	Indicators/What It Looks Like
Stage 1	Indiscriminate attachment or undiscriminating social responsiveness	Infant engages in attachment-like behaviors, such as crying, cooing, smiling **(social smile),** grasping fingers of caregivers, tracking caregiver movements, and generally testing how others will respond when she displays a specific behavior
Stage 2	Discriminating phase	Infant shows preference for familiar faces by responding differently to those the infant knows—for instance, smiling and cooing now only to the attachment figures. The end of this phase is marked by the infant now showing distress when attachment figure leaves the room.
Stage 3	Proximity-seeking behaviors	Infant/toddler actively seeks out proximity and contact with the attachment figure. She becomes visibly distressed when mother (attachment figure) leaves the room. Will seek proximity by clinging, hiding behind, following, and clutching on to mother. Separation anxiety and stranger fear are evident.
Stage 4	Mother as secure base	The young child looks to attachment figure (mother) as a base to touch back to periodically while actively exploring the environment. Proximity is still desired but not as much physically. As long as child can see or hear mother and touch back to her she is content. Attachments to other caregivers forming.
Stage 5	Initial separation	It is now possible to leave the child alone for brief periods of time with a stranger who is friendly and skilled at separation. A larger circle of caregivers can now give comfort and security.
Stage 6	Abstract attachment	Child now realizes that attachment is formed and there is no longer a need for physical contact or immediate proximity. Attachment to more than one caregiver has developed.

Based on Bailey and Wolery (1992), Ainsworth (1979), Bowlby (1969), and Marvin (1977).

Social smile.   Infant facial expression, characterized by an open mouth and raised cheeks, that indicates interest and pleasure in response to people and stimuli.

❏ Does the child explore and use the primary caregiver as a secure base?

❏ What kinds of behaviors indicate the "Mother as secure base" phase?

Types of Attachment   Observations of attachment have led researchers to conclude that there are several types of attachment patterns that form as a result of *goodness of fit* and the components of the child's culture.

When a young child has formed a **secure attachment,** he can be comforted by a trusted adult and can use that adult as a secure base from which to explore. An **insecure-avoidant attachment** is characterized by the child's relative indifference to the parent or the primary caregiver. An **insecure-resistant attachment** means that the child is overly preoccupied with the primary caregiver or attachment figure but finds little comfort or soothing from the contact. Finally, the child with the **disorganized and disoriented attachment** does not know how to respond to the caregiver and has not formed any patterns of response. This type of attachment is often found in abuse relationships. Table 9–3 gives indicators for each type of attachment.

CULTURAL VARIATION

Cultural Variations in Attachment

The types of relationships that are emphasized and valued between caregiver and child vary among cultures. In some cultures, patterns of interactions considered by American standards as insecure attachments are quite normal. Take, for example, the appearance of insecure-resistant attachments among Japanese children who respond with great protests when their mothers depart. In Japanese culture this response may be due to the fact that historically, Japanese children are rarely left with someone outside the family (Saarni, Mumme, & Campos, 1998). As the culture changes, and as more Japanese children go into child care situations, perhaps a change in attachment patterns will occur. In northern Germany infants display what could be considered insecure-avoidant attachment (Grossman, Grossmann, Huber, & Wartner, 1981) due to the ease at which they separate from the caregiver. Perhaps this is because the German culture emphasizes leaving children alone more frequently than in other cultures. In many European countries parents and caregivers leave children outside while they go into stores briefly. The child views the separation as routine and non-threatening, and the adult views it as healthy.

Secure attachment.   A healthy parent-child connection, signified by the child's being confident when the parent or primary caregiver is present and distressed at the parent's absence.

Insecure-avoidant attachment.   Infant avoids the parent or primary caregiver in the strange situation and fails to greet the parent upon return.

Insecure-resistant attachment.   Infant stays close to the parent or primary caregiver, does not explore, gets very upset when parent leaves, and then RESISTS efforts to comfort.

Disorganized and disoriented attachment.   The child does not know how to respond to the caregiver and has not formed a pattern of responses.

TABLE 9–3 Attachment Classifications and Behavioral Indicators

Attachment Classification	Behavioral Indicators
Secure attachment to caregiver	Child is active and engaged, with purposeful exploration of the environment in the presence of the attachment figure. Child becomes upset when figure leaves and is easily soothed when figure returns. Child may initially demonstrate aversion to stranger but with cues from attachment figure becomes relaxed.
Insecure-avoidant attachment to caregiver	Unsure and tentative play and exploration of the environment. Demonstrates little or no response to attachment figure's absence or return. Child does not seek comfort from attachment figure. The child is uncomfortable with strangers but does not actively resist interactions.
Insecure-resistant attachment to caregiver	Child is agitated, clingy, and anxious without attachment figure. Child is not easily comforted at reunion with attachment figure. Child does not approach strangers and may not separate from attachment figure.
Disorganized and disoriented attachment and other serious attachment problems	Child is unpredictable, with disorganized reaches and responses to attachment figure. Approach/withdrawal interactions with attachment figure. Relationships are disorganized, with no attachment to any significant figure in the child's experience.

Source: McDevitt and Ormrod (2002)

Emotional Regulation

Emotional regulation refers to the control or cognitive monitoring of emotional responses in order to reach a goal, initiate, or extend a social experience. Learning to regulate emotions is an arduous task for most children. The young brain and body is not yet fully capable of controlling emotional reactions in a socially acceptable manner. Individual age and temperament influence the degree of success children experience as they navigate the tides of emotional actions and reactions.

The Developmental Course of Emotional Regulation   Emotional regulation develops from the basic reflexive behaviors such as sucking or gazing seen during infancy to the early attempts at voluntary regulations found in toddlerhood. The older child is much

| TABLE 9–4 | Sequence of Emotional Regulation |

Age	Emotional Regulation Skills
Early weeks	Reflexive sucking, gazing
One month	Deliberate sucking and gazing
Three months	Looks away, turns head, takes a break
Six months	Smiles, grasping, oral exploration, motor control of item
Toddler years	Uses secure base. Laughs. Uses coping skills such as sucking or distracting. Makes efforts to control negative emotions. Use of a secure item such as a blanket.
Preschool years	Emotional response less frequent, less impulsive, greater attention span
School-age years	Understands emotional display rules

more cognitively active in monitoring emotions. He engages in tasks such as remembering the rules or understanding cause and effect. See Table 9–4 for the typical sequence of the development of emotional regulation.

Often the development of soothing mechanisms, such as thumb sucking, is done naturally—in some infants before birth. The young infant finds the sucking behavior soothing and therefore repeats the action. So begins the process of emotional regulation, from accidental to deliberate. Over the first few months of life infants become more adept at regulating emotional responses. The infant regulates crying, attention, and smiles. The acquisition of emotional regulatory skills enables the infant to control the negative or overwhelming aspects of a situation while still engaging with it. Infants may look away, avert their gaze, or turn their head to "take a break" from stimulation that is overwhelming or intrusive. These simple skills help the infant sustain social contact, thus strengthening social development (Stifter, Spinrad, & Braungart-Kieker, 1999).

Smiling is another skill developed early in life that helps the infant relax even when aroused. As the infant develops these regulatory abilities, social interactions increase in complexity with the child reaching out to bring things closer for oral exploration. Increased sensory ability enables the child to grasp, hold, and orally explore items without dropping them. Mouthing and sucking are increasingly more successful as the infant's motor coordination improves and self-soothing by means of sucking is more successful. With this new ability, the infant can attend during play while simultaneously self-regulating through sucking or holding. This whole-body response to emotional stimulation helps the infant control emotional response as well as gain new experiences that will undoubtedly require the use of regulatory skills (Fogel, 2000).

At about six months of age infants use laughter as a response to stimulating situations. Infants may respond in laughter to situations that once made them cry. As children grow, they develop increasingly sophisticated regulation techniques. A toddler, wary of a strange situation, may seek out a trusted adult in order to mitigate his feelings of fear. The security found in the trusted adult allows the child to regulate his fear and explore new experiences.

Greater social pressure for appropriate emotional expression is placed on toddlers and preschool children. Emotional responses become less frequent and more conventional. For example, an infant startled by a loud noise may respond with great distress, whereas a three-year-old child may simply cover his ears. Preschool children engage in temper tantrums less as they gain enough self-control to express their feelings verbally. Impulsivity is reduced, enabling the preschool child to attend for longer periods of time and wait for his turn.

In video stream 1 on the accompanying CD-ROM, note the amount of self-control a toddler must exhibit in order to wait.

Children begin to learn **emotional display rules** that help them know when and how to respond. For example, a four-year-old likely understands that it is not appropriate to laugh when another child is hurt or when something is broken (Saarni, 1989). Children become skilled in separating the visible emotional expression from the person's actual inner response. For example, upon receiving an unsatisfactory birthday gift, the eight-year-old will express appreciation. He also controls his impulse to laugh during science instruction even when the material presented strikes him as amusing.

What to Look For in Emotional Regulation

❑ Does the infant use soothing mechanisms?

❑ Does the toddler rely on a soothing object such as a stuffed animal?

❑ Does the toddler respond to others' moods?

❑ Does the toddler actively show affection?

❑ Does the preschool child verbalize feelings?

❑ Does the preschool child express feelings in symbolic play?

❑ Does the child show empathy toward others?

❑ Does the child understand the socially acceptable expression of emotions?

❑ Does the child show understanding of use of emotional display rules?

❑ Does the child understand that two or more emotions can occur simultaneously?

Empathy

Empathy, quite simply, is the ability to recognize how someone else is feeling and to understand it as if you were feeling it yourself. The old adage directing us to "walk in another man's shoes" requires us to be empathetic. The development of empathy is related to the development of a theory of mind, as described in Chapter 8 on cognitive

---

Emotional display rules.   Culturally specific social rules about how and when one can express certain emotions.

Empathy.   The ability to recognize how someone else is feeling as if experiencing the feeling personally.

development. Empathy, however, unlike theory of mind, develops naturally in the first years of life. For instance, a nine-month-old baby can see another baby fall and have tears well up in his own eyes and crawl off to be comforted by his mother as though he were the one who had been hurt. A 15-month-old child might go get his teddy bear for a crying friend; if the child continues to cry, the security blanket may be retrieved to help stop the crying behavior. Interestingly, infants only a few days old may become upset if they hear another infant crying. Researchers have seen this response as the earliest precursor of empathy (Granacher, 1998).

Another feature of empathy in infants is **motor mimicry.** Motor mimicry is the act of mirroring the emotional expressions of another as a way of expressing support. The crying behaviors of one child can illicit crying behavior from others. Children who witness others bump or fall may act as if the pain or sadness were their own. Even children as young as a year old mirror the emotional responses of others. They may cry and rub their heads after seeing another child bump his head and cry. At about age two and one-half, motor mimicry fades from a toddler's emotional repertoire, as he begins to realize that someone else's pain is different from his own (Granacher, 1998).

Toddlers continue to display distress as another child, or even adult, is crying or in pain and will attempt comforting. For instance, the toddler or young preschooler who is observed patting another's back, saying, "It's OK" is now not only recognizing another's emotions but acting on them as well. Young children also make faces that reflect the emotions others may be feeling. This indicates the beginning of true empathy or feeling

Motor mimicry.   The act of mirroring the emotional expressions of another as a way of expressing support.

what someone else might feel. Often the preschool child is placed in situations that require sophisticated understanding of another's feelings. Consider the following anecdotal record.

ANECDOTAL RECORD 9–1

Child's Name: Joseph, Maggie, and Annie

Date: October 1

Time: 10:15 a.m.

Observer: D. Ahola

Location: Gateway Montessori Classroom

Joseph and Maggie are playing in the dramatic play center. They are pretending to be a pet store owner/clerk and a customer who wants to get some fish food. As they are playing, they laugh and converse. While watching the fish they imagine that they are by the ocean. Annie, who loves the ocean, comes over and asks if she can play (we all know that asking to be in the play will not get you in it). Joseph and Maggie in concert say, "NO, this is only for two people and you don't have any fish!!" Seeing the hurt look on Annie's face and wanting to avoid a social conflict, Mrs. T. enters the play to make repairs. She goes to Joseph and Maggie and asks, "If you were Annie how would you feel?" Joseph gives his usual response, "I'd feel sad?" Maggie says, "I wouldn't care." Mrs. T. realizes that neither of the two children is ready yet to put themselves in her place so she switches gears. "Well, look at Annie's face, what does it look like she's feeling?" Maggie says, "She looks really sad, like she is going to cry." Joseph nods his head in agreement.

The three- and four-year-old child begins to show signs of understanding the feelings of others as they accurately identify overt expressions of those feelings. By age five or six the children begin to notice that other people may not express emotions in a typical manner, yet they can still link behaviors to emotions that may not be as overt.

What to Look For in Empathy

- ❑ How does the infant/toddler react when he hears or sees someone crying?
- ❑ Does the infant/toddler show any motor mimicry when seeing another person's emotions?
- ❑ What emotions given from another person cause a reaction in the infant/toddler?
- ❑ Can the preschool child identify what another person might be feeling?
- ❑ How does the preschool child identify another person's feelings?
- ❑ Does the preschool/school-age child show any behaviors that might indicate he is feeling what someone else is feeling?

❑ Does the preschool/school-age child demonstrate behaviors that might indicate he is trying to comfort or join in another person's feelings?

❑ Does the young child react more to children his own age or adults?

Components of Social Competence

ANECDOTAL RECORD 9–2

Child's Name: Ben, Ezra, Millie, Diana, & Jade

Date: October 11

Time: 10:00 a.m.

Observer: Miss Diane

Location: Stepping Stone Child Center

Ben, Ezra, and Millie play inside a tent erected in the middle of the preschool classroom. They have recreated a camping scene based on a recent vacation experience shared by the boys. Millie has collected a picnic basket, sleeping bags, canteens, and fishing poles to set the stage for the camping play script. Diana and Jade enter the tent and step on the "picnic" set up in the center of the area. Millie stands up and pushes Diana out of the way roughly, saying, "You can't be in here. There isn't enough room for you. This is our picnic." Diana catches her balance and replies, "I know. That's why we are going fishing. You'll need more food. You are hungry campers." She quickly picks up the fishing poles and hands one to Jade. "Let's go." Diana and Jade step out of the tent and Jade turns back, "Anyone want to go fishing with us?" Ezra decides to fish. Millie calls after them, "Hurry back. I'll cook the fish for dinner." When the children return from "fishing" all five children pile into the tent. It is crowded and Ben's fingers get stepped on. Jade suggests that they build another tent and be "neighbors." The children agree and set to finding a blanket to use as another tent.

Social competence refers to the interpersonal skills needed to meet the standards of society. Components of social competence include social knowledge and understanding, social skills, and social depositions or attributes.

Note that in Anecdotal Record 9–2 each child demonstrates different skills in *social competence*. Ben, Ezra, and Millie share the social knowledge of camping. Diana resists Millie's negative behavior by regulating her own response. Jade demonstrated social understanding as she invited others to join the fishing activity. Diana's flexibility created a positive play experience and may have influenced Ezra's own flexibility in switching his play script. Agreeable children are likely to be included in play experiences, which in turn contributes to increased social strengths (Katz & McClellan, 1997). Social competence requires more than flexibility. Diana attended to important social features of the camping play script. She suggested that the hungry campers would want fish. Attention to detail extended the play rather than derailing it. Understanding of the social context helps children navigate the complexities of early social interactions. Although Millie initially rejected the play initiation of Diana and Jade, she ultimately acknowledged and responded to the changed play script. Responsiveness and sensitivity to others is an important component of social competence.

Social knowledge involves understanding the social customs, rules, and habits of a group. For young children this is typically the play group, early childhood setting, or elementary classroom. Knowledge of the language and popular play scripts is helpful. Children who have shared experiences as a group or who bring a common experience to the social setting benefit from that knowledge. For example, boys in a kindergarten extended day program often engaged in active superhero play. Knowledge of superhero powers, characteristics, and behaviors aided children in role negotiation, reversals, and problem solving.

Children who are able to decipher peer interactions through accurate predictions of another's feelings demonstrate social understanding. The understanding of others' feelings, motives, and preferences helps the child negotiate, communicate, and compromise. The simple task of turn taking requires social understanding. One child needs to anticipate the other child's desires in order to establish an agreeable schedule. A socially competent child may create an alternative task for his playmate while waiting. For instance, one child may pretend to be the police officer issuing citations, while the other drives the car. They can switch roles as they take turns driving. The child's social understanding aids in resolving this typical play conflict.

Many of the social experiences of the three- and four-year-old focus on initiating or entering play groups. Children engage in and switch play scripts regularly. Negotiating entry into play requires that the child use skills such as showing interest in another child's work or play, making comments on another child's play activity, or adding to play discussion (Katz & McClellan, 1997). A child may offer a compliment such as "Nice tower" or "Good job building that car" as a means of engaging another child. A child who would like to take a turn at playing checkers may comment, "I have checkers at home" or "I'll play the winner."

Social dispositions are behaviors that children engage in often. These behaviors are intentional and goal-oriented. Some children have dispositions toward creativity, curiosity, or humorousness. Others may be impulsive, assertive, and argumentative. Many dispositions are thought to be inborn. Related to temperament, dispositions to learn, to form attachments, and to explore are likely present at birth. However other social dispositions such as generosity, empathy, and friendliness are learned. Instruction for these social skills does not necessarily occur in a formal manner but through models. Not every disposition learned by a child is positive. Children also learn to be antagonistic, bossy, and self-absorbed. These negative dispositions can lead to serious social difficulties (Katz & McClellan, 1997). Take, for instance, Anecdotal Record 9-3 on the following page.

 In video stream 7 on the accompanying CD-ROM, note the social competence—specifically, compromise and perspective-taking—necessary to complete the task.

....

Social dispositions. Social cognitive behaviors that children engage in often. They include, but are not limited to, creativity, curiosity, and impulsivity.

ANECDOTAL RECORD 9–3

Child's Name: Libby

Date: November 16

Time: 10:00 a.m.

Observer: Miss Maria

Location: Lally Center

Four-year-old Libby sat at the table with other children waiting for snack. Five-year-old John was passing out cups. Libby watched him intently and when he approached her chair she reached out and placed her hands on the stack of cups. Pulling on the stack of cups she insisted, "I want my cup. I want it now. Give me the cups." John held tight to the other end of the stack of paper cups. The cups began to collapse and John let go. Libby threw the crumpled cups one after another on the floor. "John squished the cups," she yelled to the teacher.

After snack, several children stacked cardboard "brick" blocks into a tower. Two groups of children raced to build the highest tower. Libby approached the play and began to shout, "I want those blocks. Don't build them into a tower. I want to make a road." Libby took off her right shoe and threw it at the block structure, knocking it over. On her hands and knees she quickly retrieved as many blocks as she could hold. The other children left the block area.

What to Look For in Social Competence

- ❑ Does the child generally demonstrate a positive mood?
- ❑ Does the child come to the program or setting willingly?
- ❑ Does the child usually cope with rebuffs and reverses adequately?
- ❑ Does the child have a positive relationship with other children?
- ❑ Does the child display the capacity for humor?
- ❑ Does the child approach others in a positive manner?
- ❑ Does the child express his wishes clearly?
- ❑ Does the child assert himself appropriately?
- ❑ Does the child express frustration and anger without hurting others, self, or property?
- ❑ Does the child successfully gain entrance to play?
- ❑ Does the child take turns fairly easily?
- ❑ Does the child show interest in other children and their play?
- ❑ Does the child use nonverbal skills to engage other children?

Source: Katz and McClellan, 1997.

Social Play

Play has an important role in the development of children's social skills. It provides the arena in which children practice turn taking, explore sharing and cooperation, and ultimately come to understand others' thoughts, perceptions, and emotions (Johnson, Christie, & Yawkey, 1999). The child utilizes multiple developmental skills (cognitive, language, social, emotional, creative, and motor) during play, creating a multidimensional spectrum of behavior. Play development cannot be viewed as a series of sequential steps toward the development of scripts, but as qualitative shifts that reflect changes in social competence.

The Sequence of Social Play   Social features of play during infancy and toddlerhood involve an interaction with an accommodating play partner, such as a parent, older sibling, or caregiver. These supportive early experiences of peekaboo or chase provide the foundations for social development in general, and social play development in particular (Johnson et al., 1999). Play for the infant and toddler usually focuses on an object, some favorite or interesting toy. Toys are a sort of transition object as toddlers go from parallel play to interactive play. The toy actually supports the social interaction, helping the child to engage others. Two-and-one-half-year-old Tanner is given a wrench and invited to repair the sink with two other children. The wrench serves as Tanner's "ticket" to play; he interacts with other children around a "fix-it" script. Toddlers are often assigned "prop" roles by older children. The toddler may serve as the sick baby, or the dog in a veterinary script. During the play the younger child is directed, sometimes physically placed in a location, to extend the drama. These early experiences provide toddlers with a framework for play. During the preschool years, children continue to increase their interactive play skills through a wide range of play experiences and social situations.

The Levels of Social Play   Through extensive observation, Carollee Howes and Catherine Matheson (1992) defined six levels of social play. The first level, **parallel play,** is demonstrated when children play in close proximity, engaging with similar toys or activities, but without establishing eye contact or conversing. For example, in a group of toddlers who sit near each other on the floor engaged with trucks, each toddler is focused on his own truck play and is seemingly uninvolved in the play of others. Children may talk during parallel play, but not to each other. Parallel play is different from **parallel aware play,** where children establish eye contact and imitate each other's play. Although children who engage in this level of play acknowledge each other, they are not actually socially engaged with each other.

In the third level, **simple social play,** children engage and interact socially. They talk, exchange objects, smile, or hold hands. Children at this level engage each other in play through discussion of their own play activities, such as reporting how they are

---

Parallel play.   Play in which children are in close physical proximity but do not engage one another.

Parallel aware play.   Play in which children are in close physical proximity, make eye contact, and imitate one another.

Simple social play.   Play in which children engage and interact socially with one another.

building a block tower. In the fourth level, **complementary and reciprocal social play,** one child's behavior echoes the other's as they engage in a responsive pattern. For example, children may "trade" props in doll play as a means of continuing the play as a social activity. Games such as hide-and-seek and run-and-chase fall into this category (Johnson et al., 1999). The development of play scripts is evident at this stage. A *script* is a play theme based on the child's real or fantasy experiences. It is the dramatic portrayal of a sequence of events, with predictable variations. **Cooperative social pretend play,** level five, consists of socio-dramatic role playing. Roles in early dramatizations are not always explicitly labeled, such as when a child says, "I'm the mommy," but rather they are often identifiable by the child's actions. For example, children who play the role of waiter and customer may serve and eat, respectively, giving clues to their play identities. In the sixth level, **complex social pretend play,** children demonstrate both social and pretend structures. During this level of play, children temporarily leave their pretend

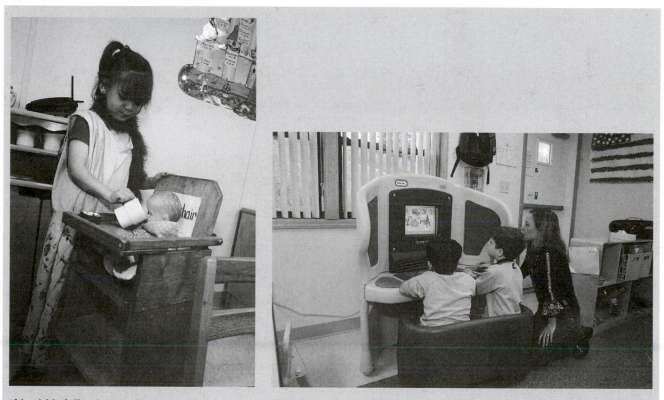

This girl is following a script.   These boys are engaging in complementary and reciprocal social play.

Complementary and reciprocal social play.   Play in which children echo the behavior of others in a reciprocal and responsive manner.

Cooperative social pretend play.   Socio-dramatic role playing among and between children.

Complex social pretend play.   Play in which children demonstrate both social and pretend structures or scripts.

The girls are demonstrating parallel aware play.

roles to talk about the play for the purpose of extending or negotiating. Examples include naming and assigning roles such as "I'm the doctor and you are the sick patient," proposing a new play script such as "Let's pretend that we are cats and the boys are dogs," or modifying play scripts such as "OK, now you are all better and we need to go to the store—let's shop." Prompting other children with "You can't be the mommy, you're a boy" is another example (Johnson et al., 1999). Children playing together make the drama somewhat unpredictable by adding new ideas and dialogue as they negotiate the emerging script with each other (Jones & Reynolds, 1992). Several levels of play are represented in Anecdotal Record 9-4 on the following page. Four-year-old Gabby engages in complex social pretend play, Lisa is struggling to gain entry to the play script, and two-year-old Maddie serves as a prop and play catalyst.

   In video stream 5 on the accompanying CD-ROM, note the complex social play that is being demonstrated by the children in the video.

What to Look For in Social Play

- ❑ Does the infant touch her image in the mirror?
- ❑ Does the infant smile at images in the mirror?
- ❑ Does the child laugh during play?
- ❑ Does the child participate in social games like patty-cake?
- ❑ Does the child play independently with toys?

❑ Does the child play with toys that are like those other children are using?

❑ Does the child create play scripts with other children?

❑ Does the child play games that require turn taking?

❑ Does the child make up games with roles and rules?

❑ Does the child share toys, space, or ideas during play?

❑ Does the child perform for others?

❑ Does the child assume a leadership role when playing?

ANECDOTAL RECORD 9–4

Child's Name: Gabby

Date: October 25

Time: 9:15 a.m.

Observer: Miss Erin

Location: B & H Learning Center

Four-year-old Gabby enters the housekeeping area, where she collects a bowl and a cup. She approaches four-year-old Paula, who is sitting in the wooden doll high chair. Paula reports, "I've got to go." Gabby pleads, "No, don't. You need your hair cut." Gabby swiftly moves to the play sink and swaps the bowl and cup for a yellow plastic rolling pin. She stands alongside Paula, who remains in the doll chair. Gabby moves the rolling pin over Paula's head (as if to curl her hair with curling iron).

Four-year-old Lisa approaches the play area and stands next to Paula. Paula resists her, "Go away." Gabby places her hands on Lisa's shoulders, "Get away from her" (with a slight push). Lisa leaves the play area. Gabby moves close to Paula again and tells her, "Don't worry, you're fine. I'm right here, sweetheart."

Two-year-old Mattie enters the housekeeping area and stands on the ledge of the window seat. Gabby pulls Mattie by her legs to a sitting position and tells her, "Get down. That's not safe, sweetheart." Mattie begins to kick her feet, hitting Gabby in the legs. Lisa re-enters the play area. Standing with one hand on her hip and the other pointing at Mattie, she reports, "She's kicking her feet. Make her go to bed if she doesn't stop." Gabby pulls Mattie to a lying position so that she is lying down on the window seat. Gabby covers Mattie with a baby blanket. Lisa (now on the edge of the dramatic play area) visually searches the area and quickly retrieves a play telephone from the floor. She makes a ringing sound, "ring, ring, ring." Immediately, Gabby placing her hand to her own ear and without a prop says, "Hi, hi, hi. I have no idea." She tilts her head as if to hold the (imaginary) telephone secure on her shoulder as she uses her hands to adjust Maddie's blanket. Lisa speaks into the plastic play telephone receiver, "I'll be home in five minutes so that you can take the baby to the doctor, OK? Bye." Lisa hangs up the play telephone and instantly enters the housekeeping area with a briefcase in her left hand and proclaims, "I'm home."

Of Special Interest–Attachment Disorders

Reactive attachment disorder (RAD) is a complex psychiatric illness that can affect young children. It is characterized by serious problems in emotional attachments to others and usually presents by age five. Often this disorder is diagnosed incorrectly as ADHD or conduct disorder. RAD can develop in a child who is living in a chaotic, unresponsive environment, one that the child learns does not meet his physical, emotional, or psychological needs. Children moving from foster home to foster home, or who live in abusive or neglectful homes, are particularly vulnerable to developing a reactive attachment disorder.

Possible signs of attachment disorders are:

- Indiscriminate affection, often to strangers, but not affectionate on parent's terms
- Problems making eye contact, except when angry or lying
- A severe need to control everything and everyone, which worsens as the child gets older
- Hypervigilant (always on guard against danger)
- Hyperactive (impulsive, exaggerated behaviors)
- Argumentative, often over silly or insignificant things
- Frequent tantrums
- Demanding or clingy, often at inappropriate times
- Trouble understanding cause and effect
- Poor impulse control
- Little or no empathy; often has not developed a conscience
- Cruelty to animals
- Destructive to property or self
- Problems with food, either hoarding it or refusing to eat
- Difficulty making friends
- Sneaks things without permission even if he could have had them by asking

Adapted from Anderson and Anderson, 2005.

Social Competency Deficits

The child with social competency deficits is at great risk for future difficulties and even disorders. Failure to be accepted by peers and others in the environment has an impact on emotional, cognitive, physical, and language development. Does "physical" really belong in that list? Yes! In recent years we have come to understand just how much the social domain affects the physical domain, such aspects as heart and lung function and blood pressure. Therefore, it is very important to observe children in play situations and, in particular, monitor how their behavior affects their socialization.

Reactive attachment disorder (RAD).   A clinically recognized form of severe insecure attachment. Children with RAD are so neurologically disrupted that they cannot attach to a primary caregiver or go through the normal developmental processes.

A video series titled *Hand in Hand: Strategies to Support Play-Based Learning* (Educational Productions, Inc., 1991) identifies specific play problems that children might have, which can be observed by the teachers in the classroom. The following categories of play problems are included in this video series:

- The child who wanders
- The child who dabbles
- The child who is aloof
- The child who is rejected

This is a good tool for teachers of young children, especially those working in inclusive environments. Video scenes show children who are easily overlooked and children who quickly get labeled as problems. Intervention tips are provided to increase the child's social play skill level. The following checklist can be used as a guide for those occasions when further investigation or referral are required to better understand a child's development.

When to Seek Outside Help in Addressing Children's Social Competence

- ❑ Does the child exhibit problems in a number of items listed in "What to Look For in Social Competence"?
- ❑ Is there a long-standing pattern of difficulties, particularly aggressive behavior?
- ❑ Do the incidents of aggression seem to be increasing?
- ❑ Are the social and behavioral problems of concern occurring in more than one of the child's social contexts? At home? At church? In the neighborhood?
- ❑ Do the behavior patterns of concern persist despite the assistance of the parents and teachers?
- ❑ Is the behavior in question having a serious impact on other children? On the teacher? On the classroom?
- ❑ Does the child's behavior jeopardize the safety or rights of other children in the class?

If the answer to one or more of these indicators is *yes*, it may be time to seek outside assistance (Katz & McClellan, 1997).

Autism

Autism refers to a wide range of symptoms with varying degrees and differing ranges of symptoms. The term is used to describe those mildly affected to those profoundly affected. This disorder generally manifests itself prior to the age of three and is observable in a variety of ways, depending on the age and development of the child. Autistic spectrum disorders or pervasive developmental disorders (PDD) include:

- ➤ **Autistic disorder.** The developmental disorder characterized by severe deficits in communication, social interaction, and repetitive/stereotypical behaviors.
- ➤ **Asperger's syndrome.** A disorder in which normal intelligence and language is present, but autistic-like behaviors are exhibited.
- ➤ **Childhood disintegrative disorder.** Rare disorder in which a child is developing typically until approximately 18 months, at which time a regression in

communication and social interaction occurs. This disorder differs from autism in the pattern of onset, course, and outcome.

> ➤ **Rett syndrome.** A progressive brain disorder occurring in girls, characterized by autism, purposeless hand movements, and mental retardation. Manifests between 6 and 18 months.

> ➤ **Pervasive Developmental Disorder-Not Otherwise Specified (PDD-NOS).** A condition in which some, but not all, features of autism or other pervasive developmental disorders are identified.

Autistic spectrum disorders have a range of three central symptoms used for diagnosis. The three symptoms include impairments in *imagination, social communication,* and *social interaction.* There is also a strong tendency toward repetitive behavior, such as word repeating or hand flapping.

Little is known for certain about the exact causes of autistic spectrum disorders and much research is needed. However, in some cases there may a genetic link. There is also unsubstantiated speculation that some cases are caused by certain vaccinations or, more specifically, the substances used as a coagulant in some vaccines. Others hypothesize that environmental toxins or pollution may cause the disorder. It is clear, however, that autistic spectrum disorders are not the result of emotional deprivation or faulty parenting. Although there is the temptation to view the disorder as psychological, its symptoms are related to the child's perception of the environment. Figure 9–1 lists some signs and symptoms that may indicate autistic spectrum disorders.

FIGURE 9–1 **Signs of possible autism.**

Clinical Clues for Possible Autism

- ❏ Delay or absence of spoken language
- ❏ Unresponsive to others
- ❏ Fails to read facial expressions of others
- ❏ Does not engage in pretend play
- ❏ Little or no imagination
- ❏ Does not show typical interest in or play near other children
- ❏ Does not take turns
- ❏ Does not use nonverbal pointing or gesturing
- ❏ Lack of gaze monitoring
- ❏ Unusual or repetitive hand and finger mannerisms (flapping)
- ❏ Intense response or no response to sensory stimuli

Social/Communication Red Flags

- ❏ Absence of smile or expression of joy by approximately six to eight months
- ❏ Babbling and cooing with adults in a conversational (back and forth) manner is absent.
- ❏ Babbling absent at 12–14 months
- ❏ Lack of nonverbal reaching, pointing, or gesturing
- ❏ Absence of words or vocabulary at 16–17 months

Compiled from the following sources: Greenspan and Wieder (1998); Filipek, et al. (2000).

Print the Anecdotal Record from the CD-ROM. Highlight (code) the behavioral indicators of social development. Coding can be done best by using highlighters, colored pencils, or thin-tipped markers. Crayons do not work well.

QUESTIONS TO CONSIDER ○ ○ ○

1. What are some of the reasons a child may or may not form secure attachments with the parent or caregiver?
2. How might you describe the play of a two-year-old and how does it differ from that of a six-year-old?
3. Think about how your own social development was influenced by the play activities and environment that you experienced as a child. List three ways that your play influenced your social development.

REFERENCES ○ ○ ○

Ainsworth, M. (1979). Attachment as related to mother-infant interaction. *Advances in the Study of Behavior, 9,* 2–52.

Anderson, K., & Anderson, M. (2005). *Radkid.org: Reactive attachment disorder and detachment issues.* Retrieved January 5, 2006 from http://www.radkid.org.

Bailey, D. B., & Wolery, M. (1992). *Teaching infants and preschoolers with disabilities* (2nd ed.). Columbus, OH: Prentice Hall.

Bowlby, J. (1969). *Attachment and loss: Vol. 1. Attachment.* London: Hogarth.

Educational Productions, Inc. (Producer). (1991). *Hand in hand: Strategies to support play-based learning* [Videotape series]. (Available from Educational Productions, Inc., 9000 SW Gemini Drive, Beaverton, OR 97008-7151.)

Filipek, P. A., Accardo, P. J., Ashwal, S., Baranek, G. T., Cook, E. H., Jr., Dawson, G., et al. (2000). Practice parameter: Screening and diagnosis of autism. Report of the Quality Standards Subcommittee of the American Academy of Neurology and the Child Neurology Society. *Neurology, 55*(4), 468–479.

Fogel, A. (2000). *Infancy: Infant, family, and society* (4th ed.). New York: Wadsworth Publishing.

Gable, S., & Hunting, M. (2000). Nature, nurture and early brain development. *Human Environment Sciences Extension.* Columbia, MS: Missouri University Extension, University of Missouri–Columbia.

Granacher, R. P. (1998, January). *How to raise a moral child.* Retrieved April 17, 2005, from http://www.2preslex.org/GRANACH1.HTM

Greenspan, S. I., & Wieder, S. (1998). *The child with special needs. Encouraging intellectual and emotional growth.* Reading, MA: Perseus Books.

Grossmann, K. E., Grossmann, K., Huber, F., & Wartner, U. (1981). German children's behavior towards their mothers at 12 months and their fathers at 18 months in Ainsworth's Strange Situation. *International Journal of Behavioral Development, 4,* 157–181.

Honig, A. S. (2002). *Secure relationships: Nurturing infant/toddler attachment in the early care setting*. Washington, DC: National Association for the Education of Young Children.

Honig, A. S., & Park, K. (1993, March). *Preschool aggression and cognition: Effects of infant care*. Paper presented at the biennial meeting of the Society for Research in Child Development, New Orleans, LA.

Howes, C., & Matheson, C. (1992, September). Sequences in the development of competent play with peers: Social and social pretend play. *Developmental Psychology, 28*(5), 961–974.

Insel, T. R. (1992). Oxytocin: A neuropeptide for affiliation. Evidence from behavioral, receptor, autoradiographic, and comparative studies. *Psychoneuroendocrinology 17*(1), 3–35.

Johnson, J. E., Christie, J. F., & Yawkey, T. D. (1999). *Play and early childhood development* (2nd ed.). New York: Longman.

Jones, E., & Reynolds, G. (1992). *The play's the thing: Teachers' roles in children's play*. New York: Teachers College Press.

Katz, L. G., & McClellan, D. E. (1997). *Fostering children's social competence: The teacher's role*. Washington, DC: National Association for the Education of Young Children.

Kostelnik, M., Whiren, A., Soderman, A., Stein, L., & Gregory, K. (2006). *Guiding children's social development* (5th ed.). Clifton Park, NY: Thomson Delmar Learning.

Maccoby, E. E. (1980). *Social development: Psychological growth and the parent-child relationship*. New York: Harcourt Brace Jovanovich.

McDevitt, T. M., & Ormrod, J. E. (2002). *Child development and education*. Upper Saddle River, NJ: Pearson Education.

Marvin, R. S. (1977). An ethological-cognitive model for the attenuation of mother-child attachment behavior. In T. Alloway, P. Pliner, & L. Kramer (Eds.), *Attachment behavior* (pp. 25–60). New York: Plenum.

Saarni, C. (1989). Children's understanding of strategic control of emotional expression in social transactions. In C. Saarni, & P. Harris (Eds.), *Children's understanding of emotions*. New York: Cambridge University Press.

Saarni, C., Mumme, D. L., & Campos, J. J. (1998). Emotional development: Action, communication, and understanding. In W. Damon (Editor-in-chief), & N. Eisenberg (Vol. Ed.), *Handbook of child psychology: Vol. 3. Social, emotional and personality development* (5th ed., pp. 237–309). New York: Wiley.

Sousa, D. (2001). *How the brain learns* (2nd ed.). Thousand Oaks, CA: Corwin.

Stifter, C. A., Spinrad, T. L., & Braungart-Kieker, J. M. (1999). Toward a developmental model of child compliance: The role of emotion regulation in infancy. *Child Development, 70* (1), 21–32.

Emotional Development

CHAPTER OBJECTIVES

- To define emotion
- To understand the influences of emotion on brain development
- To describe components of emotions
- To define and describe dimensions of temperament
- To understand the development of emotional competence
- To describe the link between emotional development and the developing sense of self

CHILD STUDY OBJECTIVES

Upon conclusion of this chapter the student will:

- code anecdotal records for emotional development
- identify a checklist for emotional development.
- create a checklist for emotional development.
- create a structured observation to assess emotional development.
- gather visual documentation indicating emotional development.
- create interview questions for the parent/family regarding emotional development.

INTRODUCTION TO EMOTIONAL DEVELOPMENT

An **emotion** is a feeling that involves physiological reactions such as elevated blood pressure, cognitive structures such as thinking about falling in love, and overt behavior such as smiling. Thinking about emotion usually elicits ideas of joy, anger, or boredom, to name a few. There are 200 words for emotions in the English language, words young children are only just beginning to understand. Emotions greatly influence development, influencing all aspects of a child's growth and well-being.

BRAIN DEVELOPMENT CONCEPTS: THE RELATIONSHIP BETWEEN TRAUMA AND USE-DEPENDENT DEVELOPMENT

The brain develops from low to high; that is, the lower portions of the brain are most developed at birth and the higher parts are less developed. When we talk about the lower parts of the brain we are typically referring to the **brainstem.** The brainstem consists of structures primarily involved in reflexes and autonomic functions, such as breathing, heart rate, glandular secretions, and drives such as hunger and sleep. The higher portion of the brain is referred to as the **cortical regions** of the brain. The cortical regions of the brain are involved in thoughtful, organized thinking. The development of the cortical regions of the brain makes way for moderating the reactions of the brainstem. In other words, the infant reacts immediately to stimuli in the environment in a primitive or instinctual manner. In contrast, the older child has the ability to react after thinking about the situation—with less impulsivity, aggression, or hyperactivity. The capacity to moderate frustration, impulsivity, aggression, and violent behavior is age-related and, as a function of brain maturation and growth, continually develops.

Perry (1998) writes: "A frustrated three-year-old (with a relatively unorganized cortex-cortical region) will have a difficult time modulating the reactive, brainstem-mediated state of arousal and will scream, kick, bite, throw and hit. However, the older child when frustrated may feel like kicking, biting and spitting, but has built in the capacity to modulate and inhibit those urges" (p. 5).

In a nurturing, predictive environment the child develops the circuits in the brain to effectively modulate outside stimuli that cause emotional reactions, and thus the child learns to react appropriately. Likewise, the child in a responsive, nonviolent environment develops the circuitry to allow her to focus, manage impulses, and attend to what is important. This occurs because the brain develops according to usage, and if the child is continually activating the higher regions of the brain while reacting to outside stimuli, those cortical regions of the brain eventually take over and the child/adolescent will be governed by thoughtful emotional responses (Perry, 1998).

....

Emotion.   A feeling that involves physiological reactions, thinking, and overt behavior.

Brainstem.   The lower part of the brain, which receives sensory input and monitors vital functions such as heartbeat, body temperature, and digestion.

Cortical regions.   Area of the brain's cerebral cortex involving thought and organized thinking.

However, if the child is developing in a chaotic, unpredictable, and violent environment the brain circuitry will develop much differently. The concept of **use-dependent development** is a key concept in this case, because the more exposure the child has to the chaotic and violent environment the more permanently the brain is affected.

The neurophysiological changes that take place when a child is exposed to stressful situations are very complicated and involve chemical as well as electrical changes in the brain. However, the result of those changes has become very clear. When the child is in a stressful situation she will respond to it as a fearful event. The fear sets off a chain re-action in the brain that basically ends with the brainstem being activated and the corti-cal regions of the brain being deactivated or not used. After continued exposure to the fear—whether it be from being a subject of violence or witnessing violence—the brain's use-dependent process kicks in. The circuitry promoting aggressive, impulsive, and otherwise primitive survival acts is strengthened and the circuitry promoting the more thoughtful, focused acts is weakened. The result then is a child or adolescent who learns to react immediately in a violent, impulsive manner to many kinds of stimuli. Because many actions are perceived as threats, the child/adolescent develops **hyperarousal** and **hypervigilance** (Perry, 1998). It has been shown that children who have developed in a violent, unresponsive environment interpret many cues to be threats—the way some-one looks at them, the tone of voice someone uses, the gestures one makes—because they are always ready for fight or flight, the typical reaction to stress. The child who is hyperaroused will not be able to focus on or attend to the learning environment, be-cause the cortical regions of the brain concerned with memory, emotional regulation, and attention have been turned off and the brainstem, which is responsible for arousal, adrenaline rushes, and anxiety, has been turned on.

Unfortunately, when a child is continually exposed to a violent, unresponsive envi-ronment, the brain changes that take place can be enduring. Although we know that there is much plasticity in the brain, once the circuitry is laid down it is hard to change. Of course, the earlier the child can be taken out of the violent environment and placed in a nurturing one, the more hope there is that the child will develop the brain connec-tions that foster appropriate, effective emotional responses.

THE COMPONENTS OF EMOTIONAL DEVELOPMENT

Emotional development involves aspects of the child's temperament or inborn traits, the emergent expression of feelings, emotional understanding, and emotional competence.

Temperament

While observing infants and toddlers, it becomes apparent that they have unique per-sonality traits right at birth. Some infants seem to always be happy and responsive. You can set your watch by their eating and sleeping habits, and they play with a single toy

---

Use-dependent development.   The concept that the development of the brain is dependent on stimulation.

Hyperarousal.   The brain's heightened response to continuous stimulation.

Hypervigilance.   The brain's continual fight-or-flight response to stimulation.

for extended periods of time. Other infants cannot seem to get into a routine or follow a schedule, they cry a great deal, and they do not seem to get interested in anything for more than seconds at a time. These traits that make babies and toddlers so different are referred to as the child's **temperament.** Temperament is defined as "constitutionally based individual differences in emotional, motor, and attentional reactivity and self-regulation" (Rothbart & Bates, 1998). Each of us is born with a temperament, and while as we mature we may learn how to cope with our less than optimal temperamental traits, they will remain fairly stable. Most of us at one time or another have heard our parents say of our behavior, "Oh, she's always been moody like that," or "Well, he's been constantly moving around since he was a baby," or "She's always been happy—even when she was a baby." Of course, these little quips usually come out at embarrassing moments, but nonetheless they give us insight into how our temperament has remained stable throughout the developmental period. Table 10–1 describes the dimensions of temperament.

What to Look For in Temperament

- ❑ How does the infant respond to changes in the environment?
- ❑ How does the infant respond to stimuli such as sights or sounds? Does the infant seem to withdraw? Show distress when there are sudden noises or flashes of light?
- ❑ How much does the infant/young child move? Is the movement constant? Are there periods of intermittent quiet?
- ❑ Is the infant/young child on a schedule? Is this schedule predictable?
- ❑ Does the infant/young child like to try new things, such as foods, activities, experiences?
- ❑ How does the infant/young child react to new activities or seeing new people?
- ❑ How long can the infant/young child stay with one activity? What kinds of stimuli distract the child?
- ❑ What is the typical mood of the young child?
- ❑ If the child were observed for an entire day, what percentage of the time would the child be smiling and alert? How much time would the child be frowning and disengaged?
- ❑ How much emotional intensity does the child demonstrate?
- ❑ What kinds of behaviors are observed when the child is having a disagreement with family or peers? What kinds of behaviors are observed when the child is excited about something?

Emotions

Emotions are physiological and psychological responses (feelings) that individuals have in reaction to experiences and events that have particular relevance to them. The manifestation, or what we see, from that response or feeling is called **affect.** You may hear

....

Temperament.   Individual traits or styles of reaction.

Affect.   Physical manifestation of an emotional response.

TABLE 10–1   **Dimensions of Temperament**

Dimension of Temperament	Extremes on Both Ends
Activity level: Amount of movement and bodily activity	High activity: This child prefers games and play with a lot of movement, splashes around in the bath, and gets restless and distressed if made to sit quietly in one spot for long periods of time.
	Low activity: This child moves slowly, can sit for long periods of time looking at a book or coloring.
Biological rhythms: Regularity or irregularity of such functions as sleep-wake cycle, hunger, and bowel movement	Regularity: Child sleeps through the night, takes a regular nap, eats about the same amount and time each day.
	Irregularity: Unpredictable sleep and wake patterns, eating patterns, and bowel movements.
Approach/Withdrawal: How the child responds to new situations or other stimuli	Approach: This child responds positively to a new food by swallowing it, reaches for a new toy, smiles at strangers, and when first joining a play group, plunges right in.
	Withdrawal: This child is typically cautious about exploring new objects, is likely to push away a new toy or spit out new food for the first time. Around strangers or in a new situation the child might cry, fuss, and strain to get away.
Adaptability: How quickly or slowly the child adapts to a change in routine or overcomes an initial negative response	High adaptability: Child adjusts easily to family moves or visits to strange places and is agreeable to changes in schedules such as feeding and sleeping.
	Low adaptability: Child takes longer to adjust to changes or to accept something new. This child is sometimes misjudged as willful or stubborn, when in fact she is more cautious.
Quality of mood: The amount of pleasant, cheerful, and openly friendly behavior (positive mood) as contrasted with fussing, crying, and openly showing unfriendliness (negative mood)	Positive mood: This is the easy to care for child. She smiles, laughs, and shows pleasure in interactions and activities. Negative mood: This is the child who tends to fuss and complain a lot and may show little to no pleasure. He may exhibit a deadpan expression (this can be deceiving, however, because even though the child does not express pleasure during an activity or exchange he may report it later to parents or friends as an exciting or happy event).
Intensity of reactions: The energy level of mood expression, whether it is positive or negative	Low intensity: This child expresses both pleasure and discomfort in a low-key way. Again, this can be misjudged, in that mild expressions can mask strong emotions.
	High intensity: This child expresses her feelings with great intensity—laughing loudly, even bubbling. When upset, she cries loudly or throws a tantrum.

(Continued on next page)

TABLE 10–1   Dimensions of Temperament (*Continued*)

Dimension of Temperament	Extremes on Both Ends
Sensitivity threshold: How sensitive the child is to outside and internal stimuli	Low threshold: Child may be easily upset by loud noises, bright lights, a wet or soiled diaper, or sudden changes in temperature.
	High threshold: Child has apparently little or no reaction to loud, bright, moving stimuli. This child may not give signals that something is painful or irritating. This is the child who may have an ear infection, and will not show distress or cry, but may only tug on his ear.
Distractibility: How easily the child can be distracted from an activity like feeding or playing by some unexpected stimulus	High distractibility: Child looks away from eating at the slightest sound or sight. She doesn't attend to a toy for any period of time because something always takes her attention away from it.
	Low distractibility: Child stays with something and does not let anything distract her from it—other noises, people around her, or conversations do not sway this child from continuing to engage in her activity.
Persistence: How long a child will stay with a difficult activity without giving up, and Attention span: How long the child will concentrate before his interest shifts	High persistence: Child with a long attention span will continue to be absorbed in what he is doing for long periods of time. This child does not require much adult attention once he gets involved in an activity. He may become upset if asked to quit an activity while in the middle of it.
	Low persistence: Child has what appears to be a short attention span. He will not stick with an activity and will give up easily when he cannot reach the goal of the activity.

Adapted from WestEd California Department of Education (2002); Thomas and Chess (1998).

someone say about a child, "She has a flat affect," meaning that the child does not express much feeling outwardly on her face. Remember the discussion in chapter 2 concerning taking anecdotal notes, and how important it was to record exactly what you see rather than what you think you see? Because a child's actual emotion may not always fit in with what we see, it is imperative to understand the patterns of children's emotional responses in order to really understand their emotional development. However, we know that facial expressions depicting the basic emotions of happiness, anger, sadness, and fear are universal to all cultures. The motivation to show these emotions later in early childhood and beyond, however, depends on the child's individual temperament and the culture in which she is developing.

The Development of Emotions   An infant is not born with all the emotions she will ever have. Initially, the infant will have two global arousal states: one is attraction to pleasant stimulation and the other is withdrawal from unpleasant stimulation (Berk, 2005). At about six weeks the infant will begin showing joy or happiness, at four months she will

| TABLE 10-2 | Core Emotions and Related Emotions | | |

Joy	Anger	Sadness	Fear
happiness	frustration	dejection	wariness
delight	jealousy	unhappiness	anxiety
contentment	disgust	distress	suspicion
satisfaction	annoyance	grief	dread
pleasure	fury	discouragement	dismay
elation	boredom	shame	anguish
pride	defiance	guilt	panic

Source: From *Guiding Children's Social Development* 5th edition by Kostelnik/Whiren/Soderman/Stein/Gregory © 2006. Reprinted with permission of Thomson Delmar Learning, a division of Thomson Learning.

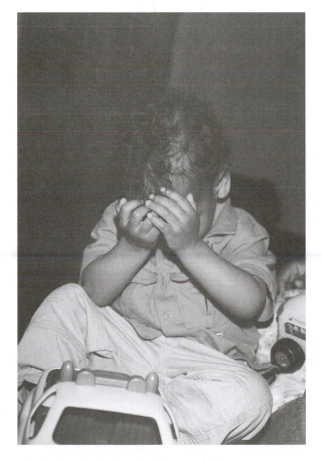

Toddlers' emotional expressions are intense.

demonstrate anger, sadness will show itself around five to seven months, and fear at approximately six to nine months (Kostelnik, Whiren, Soderman, Stein, & Gregory 2006). From these four core emotions, joy, anger, sadness, and fear, all other emotions will develop (Izard, 1991). Table 10–2 identifies the core emotions and the corresponding emotional clusters.

Evidenced by smiles, happiness is the first emotion demonstrated in the infant. The infant smiles when content and close to the caregiver. At approximately two to three months of age the infant engages in *social smiling,* which occurs when interacting with people. Laughter begins around three to four months of age and initially in response to very active stimuli such as a tickling game or a cause-and-effect toy. Later, the young child begins to laugh at surprise events and when people in the environment act silly or playful. Around one year of age, the child demonstrates several different smiles, depending on the context. For instance, she may show a broad, "cheek-raised" smile to a parent's greeting, a reserved, muted smile in response to a friendly stranger, and a "mouth-open smile" during stimulating play (Dickson, Fogel, & Messinger, 1998).

Anger is first demonstrated by intense reactions to situations in which the infant is distressed, such as being hungry, feeling pain (those first shots at the doctor's office), being too cold or hot, or being over- or understimulated. As the infant develops, the signs of anger become more pronounced and more intense. Situations that bring about these feelings and reactions are more about the toddler's drive to become independent. Situations in which we see a toddler becoming angry include blocking her goal, taking away something that she wants, or restraining her movement (Berk, 2005). Around three years of age, young children's emotions are very intense because they hold one emotion at a time. So the preschooler who is angry is very angry—there is nothing else—but she quickly moves to another emotion. The quick changes children make from one emotional state to another are universally recognized as typical for children this age (Gonzalez-Mena & Eyer, 2003).

ANECDOTAL RECORD 10–1

Child's Name: Joey

Date: December 1

Time: 10:15 a.m.

Observer: Mrs. T.

Location: Gateway Montessori Classroom

It was a tough morning for Joey. We have been working on giving Joey language strategies for dealing with his frustration when he can't play with something he wants. He has been doing well with it—however, this morning he came in and he was yawning and very tired. (I think it affected his coping skills.) At one point I asked him to begin cleaning up. He screamed in a very loud voice and with his face getting red, "NO, NO, NO, I don't want to!" I said, "Joey, we need to clean up so we can go outside." Joey, again screaming and with a hint of crying as well replied, "I hate you and I hate this school!" He kicked his leg out toward me. I said, "I cannot let you hurt me or anyone else in this room, Joey. You need to go to the quiet corner and calm down." Joey stomped over to the book area and threw two books while looking at me the whole time. He then sat down, crossed his arms, and maintained an angry (fixed eyes, tight jaw, flushed skin, pursed lips) look on his face. After the children cleaned up, the student teacher began to read a story and I sat on the floor with the other children. After about one minute Joey walked over to where I was sitting and slowly curled up in my lap and I think without even knowing it, he began to stroke my hair.

Sadness is mainly seen in the infant and toddler when the caregiver is not present or does not engage in communication; this is typically seen around three to four months of age. Although sadness can be a response to the same situations which evoke anger, more often it is a response to the removal of the caregiver's attention.

Finally, the affect related to fear emerges around the sixth month and is usually in response to strangers in the environment. The manifestation of *stranger anxiety* depends a great deal on the child's temperament, the culture, and the child's past experiences with strangers. Like anger, fear increases throughout the first year of life.

Emotional Understanding

As the infant is developing her own emotional manifestations, she is also beginning to recognize and understand the emotions of others. **Emotion knowledge/emotional understanding** includes such skills as accurately perceiving and understanding emotion signals in oneself, others, and various contexts. Initially, in face to face interactions, the infant shows she understands emotions by matching the emotional signals given off by the caregiver with her own, similar signals. Similarly, the infant matches the emotions of others with whom she is not necessarily interacting through the process of **emotional contagion** (Berk, 2005). Although in an infant these responses are considered more reflexive and automatic in nature, they do signal the infant's tuning in to others' emotions and the emergence of responding to the emotions of others. At approximately eight months of age, when the infant has developed the ability to perceive facial expressions and can also match the voice with an emotion, she will begin to engage in **social referencing.** The infant/toddler will now look to a trusted caregiver to determine how she should feel about an experience or situation. When the child falls she will look at the parent/guardian or caregiver (if it was not a serious fall) before exhibiting a reaction. If the adult reacts with intense fear or concern, the child will follow with crying or anxiety herself. If, however, the caregiver simply reacts with mild concern—"Oh, you fell. Are you OK?"—the child will respond with less anxiety.

The toddler will also refer to the caregiver when introduced to a stranger. Oftentimes the way the caregiver interacts with the stranger will direct the toddler's reaction. By about 18 months the toddler will begin to indicate that she realizes others' feelings may be different from her own. For example, the toddler, seeing the face someone makes when eating a particular food, will determine what food she will offer that person, even if it is not what she prefers herself.

The young child at first will identify a person's emotion by the outward signals, such as facial expressions or other behaviors. By about four years of age the child can start to identify how a person might feel given the context or the situation. For example, the three-year-old might know that a person is happy or sad by his or her expression but she may not understand why she feels that way. The four-year-old, on the other hand, can now identify how a person might feel in a particular situation. As the child develops she becomes more attuned to the way a person feels and begins to understand the complexity of human emotions. Specifically, understanding how a person could have conflicting emotions about a particular situation will not emerge until middle childhood.

The Significance of Emotional Understanding   The result of emotional understanding is the development of sympathy, empathy, and morality as well. Recent research has shown that the development of emotional understanding is critical to positive social relationships and to peer acceptance in early childhood and the early school years (Eisenberg et al., 1997; Hubbard & Coie, 1994). Empirical evidence also supports the

Emotion knowledge/emotional understanding.   Includes such skills as accurately perceiving and understanding emotion signals in oneself, others, and various contexts.

Emotional contagion.   Modeling or reflecting emotions observed in others.

Social referencing.   The child's use of the caregiver's response to regulate her own.

connection between emotion knowledge and verbal ability, an important component of cognitive ability (Izard, Fine, Schultz, Mostow, Acerman, & Younstrom, 2001; Schultz, Izard, & Ackerman, 2000). A study by Mostow, Izard, Fine, and Trentacosta (2002) demonstrated that the path to social acceptance is reliant on the development of emotional knowledge as defined by the ability to understand, predict, and interpret the emotions of others. The authors of the study rated children's level of emotional understanding in three ways. First a child would identify an emotion based on facial cues—so pictures of people making various faces were shown to the children and they were to respond as to how the person was feeling. Second, the child was to identify how the person was feeling by watching his or her behaviors. For example, if she were to see another child skipping and singing down a hallway, how would that child be feeling? And thirdly, the child would identify how someone would feel if put in a particular situation. For instance, the child would be told that a boy has just gotten an ice cream cone and he takes one lick and then the ice cream falls out—now how would the boy feel? In determining the level of emotional understanding that your particular child is at you could try these tests as well.

What to Look For in the Development of Emotion and Emotional Understanding

❑ What kinds of emotions do the facial expressions and behavioral gestures that the child exhibits express?

❑ At what intensity are emotions expressed?

❑ In what kinds of situations does the infant/toddler/young child express happiness, anger, sadness, or fear?

❑ Does the infant demonstrate emotional contagion?

❑ Does the young child demonstrate swift changes in intense emotions?

❑ How does the infant match others' emotions?

❑ How does the infant/toddler react to strangers?

❑ Does the child react to stimuli, experiences, or situations immediately or does he look to others for cues on how to respond?

❑ Is the young child able to identify her own emotions?

❑ Can the young child identify how another person might be feeling given his or her facial cues? The situation that person might be in? Other behavioral signs?

Emotional Competence

Children demonstrate emotional competence as they become aware of their own emotions. Being able to identify feelings of sadness, happiness, frustration, glee, boredom, excitement, etc. supports the child's emotional understanding. This cognitive task requires that the child make associations between internal emotional responses and external social manifestations. Children grow increasingly aware that they may experience multiple emotions at once or that emotional expressions don't always match what one is actually feeling. These children have an extensive emotional vocabulary and implement the use of emotional labels accurately.

Emotionally competent children accurately read social and cultural cues regarding what people are feeling or how to respond to such feelings. These children understand the cultural meaning of emotional behaviors. For example, emotionally competent children may stop to help pick up papers or books dropped by another. In this way the emotionally competent child deciphers the social code for kindness and responds. The child's expression of kindness is evidence of the child's capacity for empathetic involvement.

ANECDOTAL RECORD 10–2

Child's Name: Joseph & Alex

Date: October 21

Time: 11:15 a.m.

Observer: Mrs. J.

Location: Park School Playground

While playing tag on the school playground at recess, seven-year-old Joseph was suddenly excluded from the game. The other boys decided that Joseph could no longer play because his fast running made it difficult for them to escape. Joseph became upset and angry. Close to tears, he stomped over to the bench and sat with his arms folded across his chest. Several classmates approached him asking, "What's wrong?" Joseph did not reply but simply turned away from them. Joseph's friend Alex, who had also been playing tag, approached the bench and silently sat next to him. The boys sat in silence, side by side, for the duration of recess. When asked about why he thought Alex sat on the bench with him, Joseph responded, "He understands how I feel and doesn't bother me by talking about it."

Alex demonstrated social competence as he tailored his empathic response to Joseph's needs. Alex may have also been aware of the socially acceptable options for the male expression of sadness as he avoided talking about the feelings with his friend.

Emotionally competent children adapt and regulate their emotional expression to match social expectations. They employ self-regulatory strategies to reduce stress and increase coping behaviors. A child who is feeling angry with a friend for breaking her toy uses coping mechanisms such as, "It was only an accident," "The toy wasn't very good," or "I wonder if it can be fixed" to regulate her response to the angry feeling.

What to Look For in the Development of Emotional Competence
- ❑ Does the child demonstrate awareness of her own emotions?
- ❑ Does the child talk about her own abilities?
- ❑ Is the child beginning to manage her own emotional responses?
- ❑ Does the child understand global ideas of "right" and "wrong"?
- ❑ Does the child engage in new ideas or activities?
- ❑ Does the child strive to achieve new goals?
- ❑ Does the child persist even when experiencing setbacks?

INTRODUCTION TO SENSE OF SELF

The concept of self-esteem is complex. Expressed as an individual's personal feelings, perceptions, and evaluations of worth, this concept takes on many dimensions. Each aspect of a person's self is evaluated separately. The physical self may be highly valued by an individual, yet the working self may not receive the same celebration. Self-evaluations determine personal impressions of competency (Branden, 1994). Self-evaluations usually come in the form of questions such as:

- Am I a good friend?
- Do I have the skills to win the swim competition?
- Can I contribute to my community in a meaningful way?
- Do I have the basic skills to be successful on life's journey?

Self-esteem is not stable. Success or failure can change how a person views himself. Those who continually challenge their current capacities or seek new experiences create opportunities to demonstrate competence in ways that they may never have imagined. Of course, there are those who hold a high opinion of their ability when it is undeserved. Conversely, there are those who demonstrate a high level of competence and assign little value to it. How people think and feel about themselves is important. Feelings of confidence, mastery, and worthiness are critical to healthy emotional development. Those who feel competent in their abilities are better able to face life's challenges (Curry & Johnson, 1990).

Developing self-esteem is a lifelong process. Our self-concepts change as new challenges and experiences shape our growth and development. All humans, from the infant to the elderly, are actively engaged in developing a sense of self and are influencing the development of others. Although these are lifelong issues their roots are in the early years. Infants and toddlers are developing and growing to understand an initial sense of self. Preschool children are negotiating their understanding of how that self coexists with others, what dimensions it takes, and what perimeters define it. School-age children are assessing their abilities, talents, and interactions with new standards and possibilities.

The Development of Sense of Self

Infant's and Toddler's Sense of Self
The infant's earliest sense of self grows out of her first experiences with others. Responsive, nurturing caregiving reinforces that the infant has worth and value. As the infant grows and develops, the cognitive task of object permanence makes way for **self-differentiation,** or the infant's discovery that she is separate and independent of others.

The toddler's developing sense of self includes the **categorical self,** which comprises gender, age, physical features, and competences. It is not uncommon at all to

....

Self-differentiation. The infant's discovery that he or she is separate and independent of others.

Categorical self. Includes the child's identification of his or her own gender, age, physical features, and competences.

hear toddlers identifying their body parts, such as nose, ears, and mouth, or proclaiming, "I do it." By age two toddlers know if they are boys or girls and will identify others by gender. Appearances may still be confusing, however, and toddlers may think that a boy dressed in girl's clothing is actually a girl. Toddler girls can be heard to say, "When I grow up I will be a daddy." This is primarily due to the fact that among toddlers **gender constancy** has not yet formed.

Preschool Children's Sense of Self   Three-year-olds have a much more stable understanding of gender than toddlers do. In fact, preschoolers are quite rigid in their portrayal of **gender stereotypes.** In a 1989 Australian study of gender, Bronwyn Davies found that preschoolers may form stereotypic notions of gender to better internalize concepts of gender constancy. Davies read a collection of storybooks depicting characters in nontraditional gender roles to children aged three, four, and five. On several occasions children listened to the reading of *The Paper Bag Princess* by Robert Munch. When asked to relate how they felt about the main characters, Princess Elizabeth and Prince Donald, the children overwhelmingly stated that Donald was the hero, although he was clearly the victim and that Elizabeth, the real hero, ought to have known better than to visit the prince without cleaning herself up after battle with the fierce dragon! Even children who displayed nontraditional gender behaviors in their own play and interests strongly identified with stereotypic storybook characters as models of the correct gender. See Table 10–3 for the development of gender awareness.

Three- and four-year-old children are becoming more adept at understanding information about themselves or forming a self-concept. The preschool child may say "When I get angry I feel like hitting someone" or "When I am happy I sing and sing and sing." The child's perception is limited, however, because at this age behavior is viewed as "good" or "bad" by the child. Much of the preschooler's focus on self-worth centers on friendships. A child's ability to make friends may reflect her self-esteem, but friendship experiences may contribute to the child's ability to define how she feels about herself (Curry & Johnson, 1990).

Kindergarten and Primary Grade Children's Sense of Self   Early school-age children are optimistic regarding their abilities and expectations for academic success. They have little ability to accurately judge their own strengths and weaknesses and are often

Gender constancy.   The concept that one's gender is a permanent feature and does not change as a result of outward appearances such as clothing or action.

Gender stereotypes.   Fixed, conventional notion of gender.

TABLE 10–3	Development of Gender Awareness
5–6 months	Differentiates between a male and a female face of adult and of another baby
9 months	Associates female face with female voice
10 months	Associates male face with male voice
12 months	Indicates understanding of own gender by gazing longer at other babies of their own gender, i.e., girls gaze longer at girls and boys gaze longer at boys
18 months	Notices differences in sexual organs
22–24 months	Identifies own gender but does not yet understand that gender is constant
24 months	Prefers to play with other children of the same gender
2–3 years	Identifies with adults of the same gender. Takes on gender-related clothing and play preferences. Does not understand gender constancy
4 years	Aware of gender differences with a tendency toward rigid gender roles
5 years	Understands that gender is constant
6–7 years	The start of gender identity. Begins to take on characteristics associated with the child's particular gender, including aspects of social, psychological, biological, cultural, and cognitive factors that make up what is considered male or female

overly optimistic. A five-year-old may report that she can drive a race car, when in fact she has never actually even been in a race car. The older child might query, "How do you know that you can drive a race car?" knowing that such statements need to be supported with evidence to gain acceptance.

School-age children are increasingly concerned with status as a means of gaining power. Social status is one means by which children gain power, but they also gain a sense of power as a result of their personal accomplishments and expanding skills. Peer acceptance is important to the school-age child. Play among school-age children involves more sharing, less conflict, and fewer physical aggressions than the play of the preschool child. School-age play, however, involves threats to the self-esteem of the players. Children may be friendly one minute and mean or hurtful the next. Children seem to tolerate the ups and downs of such social interactions (Curry & Johnson, 1990).

What to Look For in the Development of Sense of Self

❑ Does the child identify herself in a mirror?
❑ Does the child point to body parts when named?
❑ Does the child seek out other toddlers to look at or play with?

- ❑ Does the child identify herself by gender, age, or ability?
- ❑ Does the child label aspects of ability?
- ❑ Does the child seek to extend positive play relationships?
- ❑ Does the child evaluate her own behavior?
- ❑ Does the child derive power from her own accomplishments?
- ❑ Does the child accurately access her own performance?

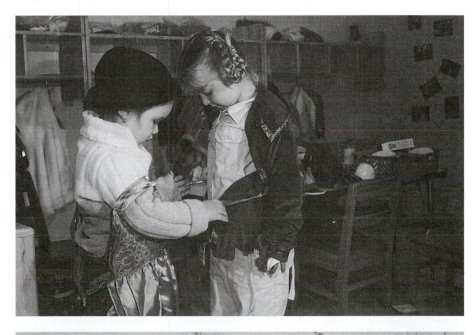

As children approach three years of age, gender roles become more significant.

Of Special Interest–Anxiety Disorders

Anxiety is a subjective sense of worry, apprehension, fear, and distress. It is normal to have these sensations on occasion, and so it is important to distinguish between normal levels of anxiety and unhealthy or pathologic levels of anxiety. For instance, it is perfectly normal and developmentally appropriate for a child between the ages of 18 months and 4 years of age to have separation anxiety. However, the six-year-old child who does not want to leave his mother to go to a friend's birthday party may be experiencing a separation or social phobia disorder.

TABLE 10–4   **Anxiety Disorders Seen in Childhood and Prevalent Signs**

Anxiety Disorder	Description	Prevalent Signs
Generalized anxiety disorder	A child or adolescent with this disorder experiences extreme, unrealistic worry that does not seem to be related to any recent event.	Feels self-conscious, feels tense, has a strong need for reassurance, and complains about stomachaches or other discomforts that don't appear to have any physical basis.
Specific phobias Social phobias	A phobia is an unrealistic and excessive fear of some situation or object. Phobias can center on animals, storms, water, heights, or situations, such as being in an enclosed space. A child with social phobia is terrified of being criticized or judged harshly by others and avoids social situations.	Intense avoidance of object of fear—or any representation of fearful object (e.g., pictures of animals), such that daily living is severely affected. Obvious agitation.
Panic disorder	Panic disorder is marked by repeated panic attacks without apparent cause.	Panic attacks are periods of intense fear accompanied by pounding heartbeat, sweating, dizziness, nausea, or a feeling of imminent death.
Obsessive-compulsive disorder	A child with obsessive-compulsive disorder becomes trapped in a pattern of repetitive thoughts and behaviors.	The compulsive behaviors may include repeated hand washing, counting, or arranging and rearranging objects.
Post-traumatic stress disorder (PTSD)	Post-traumatic stress disorder can develop in a child or adolescent after she experiences a very stressful event. Such events may include physical or sexual abuse, being a victim of or witnessing violence, or being caught in a disaster, such as a bombing or hurricane.	A child suffering from PTSD may experience the event again and again in strong memories, flashbacks, or troublesome thoughts. She may also overreact when startled (*hypervigilance*) or have difficulty sleeping.

The signs of an anxiety disorder take on two forms. Physical sensations and signs include headaches, nausea/vomiting, sweating, accelerated heart rate, diarrhea, weakness, stomach pain, difficulty breathing, and other assorted aches and pains. Emotional sensations and signs include nervousness and fear. Behavioral manifestations include intense withdrawal, school refusal, and refusal to leave the house or caregiver's side.

Anxiety disorders, when severe, can affect a child's thinking, decision-making ability, perceptions of the environment, learning, and concentration. They raise blood pressure and heart rate, and can cause a multitude of health-related illnesses.

Table 10–4 identifies the most common types of childhood anxiety disorders and the signs of each. When a child manifests signs over a prolonged period of time (6 weeks or more), and when the behaviors or physical symptoms increase to a level that affects normal functioning, a parent should consult a pediatrician or child psychologist.

 Print the Anecdotal Record from the CD-ROM. Highlight (code) the behavioral indicators of emotional development. Coding can be done best by using highlighters, colored pencils, or thin-tipped markers.

QUESTIONS TO CONSIDER ○ ○ ○

1. Discuss the ways nature and nurture interact in the development of gender identity.

2. Discuss the relationship between temperament and emotional regulation.

3. Discuss the circumstances under which a child's temperament may contribute to maladaptive or phobia-like behaviors.

REFERENCES ○ ○ ○

Berk, L. E. (2005). *Infants and children* (5th ed.). Boston: Pearson Allyn & Bacon.

Branden, N. (1994). *Six pillars of self-esteem*. New York: Bantam Books.

Curry, N. E., & Johnson, C. N. (1990). *Beyond self-esteem: Developing a genuine sense of human value*. Washington, DC: National Association for the Education of Young Children.

Davies, B. (1989). *Frogs and snails and feminist tales: Preschool children and gender.* Sydney: Allen & Unwin.

Dickson, K. L., Fogel, A., & Messinger, D. (1998). The development of emotions from a social process view. In M. F. Mascolo (Ed.), *What develops in emotional development?* (pp. 253–271). New York: Plenum.

Eisenberg, N., Fabes, R. A., Shepard, S. A., Murphy, B. C., Guthrie, I. K., Jones, S., et al. (1997). Contemporaneous and longitudinal predictors of child's social function from regulation and emotionality. *Child Development, 68,* 642–664.

Gonzalez-Mena, J., & Eyer, D. W. (2003). *Infants, toddlers and caregivers: A curriculum of respectful, responsive care and education* (6th ed.). Columbus, OH: McGraw-Hill.

Hubbard, J. A., & Coie, J. D. (1994). Emotional correlates of social competence in children's peer relationships. *Merrill-Palmer Quarterly, 20,* 1–20.

Izard, C. E. (1991). *The psychology of emotions*. New York: Plenum.

Izard, C. E., Fine, S. E., Schultz, D., Mostow, A. J., Acerman, B. P., & Younstrom, E. (2001). Emotion knowledge as a predictor of social behavior and academic competence in children at risk. *Psychological Science, 12*, 18–23.

Kostelnik, M., Whiren, A., Soderman, A., Stein, L., & Gregory, K. (2006). *Guiding children's social development* (5th ed.). Clifton Park, NY: Thomson Delmar Learning.

Mostow, A. J., Izard, C. E., Fine, S., & Trentacosta, C. J. (2002). Modeling emotional, cognitive, and behavioral predictors of peer acceptance. *Child Development, 73*(6), 1775–1788.

Munch, R. (1980). *The paper bag princess.* Toronto: Annick Press.

Perry, B. D. (1998). *Violence and childhood: How persisting fear can alter the developing child's brain.* Retrieved March 22, 2005, from http://www.terrylarimore.com/PainAndViolence.html

Rothbart, M. K., & Bates, J. E. (1998). Temperament. In W. Damon (Series Ed.), & N. Eisenberg (Vol. Ed.), *Handbook of child psychology: Vol. 3. Social, Emotional, and Personality Development* (5th ed.) 105–176. New York: Wiley.

Schultz, D., Izard, C. E., & Ackerman, B. P. (2000). Children's anger attribution bias: Relations to family adjustment and social adjustment. *Social Development, 9*, 284–301.

Thomas, A., & Chess, S. (1998). Temperament and personality. In G. A. Kohnstamm, J. E. Bates, & M. K. Rothbart (Eds.), *Temperament in childhood.* Chichester, UK: Wiley.

WestEd, & The California Department of Education (2002). *The program for infant and toddler caregivers.* Sausalito, CA: WestEd.

Language and Literacy Development

CHAPTER OBJECTIVES

- To understand the development of language
- To identify components of language
- To reflect on cultural variations of language
- To understand brain functions related to language

CHILD STUDY OBJECTIVES

Upon conclusion of this chapter the student will:

- code the language and literacy development for each of the existing anecdotal records.
- develop a checklist or rating scale for language or literacy development.
- gather and label visual documentation relating to language and literacy development.
- prepare a plan for (identify goal and objective) and conduct a structured observation for language or literacy development, interpreting the results (by completing an assessment form and writing a brief summary).
- prepare 5–7 questions for families regarding their child's language and/or literacy development.

INTRODUCTION TO THE LANGUAGE DOMAIN

"Language refers to a form of communication in which we learn to use complex rules to form and manipulate symbols (words and gestures) that are to generate an endless number of meaningful sentences" (Plotnik, 1999). Basically, language is a vehicle for communication. Language allows us to convey our thoughts, emotions, and needs to others. It is how we share information and how we transmit the culture from one generation to the next.

Language serves a wide variety of purposes for the developing child. It helps the child express desires, feelings, and needs; it helps to transmit meaning; it is a framework for social interactions and connectedness; and it helps children explore their environment. Language helps children sharpen their memory, control their behavior, and direct and organize thoughts. Language is critical in helping children to learn.

Language development moves from simple to complex and from external utterances to internal thought. For example, a toddler may repeat the word *truck* as he pushes his plastic toy across the floor in an attempt to understand the concept of large moving vehicles with multiple wheels, trailers, and loud horns. Ultimately this language cue will be internalized and spoken language will not be needed when thinking about an object's "truck-ness." The development of language is interconnected with development in other domains. A young child with the motor ability to climb to the top of the climber may use more complex language to communicate with other, likely older children, who play at the top of the climbing structure. A child who has many words to express her feelings may better regulate her emotions during complex peer interaction, such as during unstructured play or recess, than those children who struggle to find words to describe their anger or frustration.

Social Construction of Language

Although language comes in many forms (written, oral, sign, pictures, etc.), all forms are made up of symbols. The symbols are arrived upon by a particular culture and the rules that govern the use of symbols are also constructed by that culture. In other words, the symbols are particular to a culture and the way those symbols are put together to form meaning are specific to the culture as well.

Language and Cognition

Language and cognition are inextricably linked—in fact, in many texts of child development you will find language listed in the cognitive domain. Some believe that language drives cognition and others believe the opposite, that cognition drives language. Either way, the development of one is directly linked to the development of another.

Language and Culture

As a culture becomes more complex and diversified, language becomes more specific and complex itself. It is also clear that the terminology used by a culture reflects that culture's interests and concerns. For example, Native Americans in Canada's Northwest

Territories typically have at least 13 terms for different types and conditions of snow, while most Southern Californians use only two terms: *ice* and *snow*. Although the English language has many different words that refer to different states of frozen water, all these words are rarely used in a place or culture where the only time people ever experience any type of frozen water is in their glasses in the form of ice cubes (O'Neil, 2005). Therefore, children growing up in a particular culture learn vocabulary that is significant and useful to them.

The Ability to Learn Any Language

Language acquisition is an amazing process. The infant comes equipped to learn the language to which he is exposed and in the absence of sensory impairments, such as in hearing, develops spoken language. However, even if the child cannot hear the sounds of language he can learn to communicate via another sense. The child who is exposed to the components of a language will learn it naturally, without any formalized teaching. Because the drive to learn language is so strong, infants and children can overcome many obstacles and still acquire language.

BRAIN DEVELOPMENT AND LANGUAGE

Language takes place throughout the entire brain. There are those who say that the primary processing centers for language reside in the left hemisphere. However, we know that processing language is a team effort, with both the left and right hemispheres being utilized. Both hemispheres are needed to perform the tasks necessary to master language comprehension and expression. One area of the brain interprets the sounds of the language, another interprets the visual piece of language such as gestures and facial expressions. There are centers that search for word meanings and areas that produce the sounds of the language. Although researchers are still trying to uncover the mysteries of language and language acquisition, two brain development concepts related to language development are fairly well established. First are the concepts of a **critical period** and a **sensitive period** and second, the notion of **plasticity.**

Critical Periods for Language Acquisition

The "critical period of language acquisition" hypothesis asserts that the crucial period of language acquisition ends around the age of 12 years. According to this hypothesis,

Language acquisition.   The manner in which a person obtains language.

Critical period.   Fixed period of time in development when certain experiences need to occur in order for development to proceed normally.

Sensitive period.   Any time when a child is particularly receptive to certain kinds of environmental experiences.

Plasticity.   The ability of the brain and nervous system to change with experience and to adapt to deficits and injury.

if no language is learned before then, it can never be learned in a normal and fully functional sense. That is, if a child is not exposed to the components of language by 12 years of age, he will have lost the ability to ever use language. The critical periods can be viewed as windows of opportunity during which regions of the brain are flexible and specific connections are made easily. Once a region matures, it is difficult, if not impossible, for new connections to be made. For example, we know that there is a critical period for the development of visual perception. If the child does not receive visual stimulation during the first seven months of life, some aspects of visual perception may never develop—hence the importance of surgically removing cataracts from an infant's eye.

In other words, when it comes to language development the optimal time for learning a language is between the ages of birth to 12. It is important to note that although children who have not been exposed to language during the critical period may develop some means of communication such as signing or naming objects, they will not experience optimal language development.

Critical Periods for Sound Discrimination

An infant comes equipped to learn any language to which she is exposed. We know that there are critical periods for learning to discriminate sounds of the language. The newborn's brain begins making dedicated connections in the auditory cortex when the baby hears a phoneme (the smallest units of sound, such as [p] or [s]) over and over. By six months, a Swedish baby will have different connections than a Japanese baby. By 12 months, infant babbling has acquired the sound of the infant's own language and he is unable to discriminate sounds not heard in his language—this is likened to the "use it or lose it" concept presented in Chapter 7. Numerous studies have demonstrated that by 12 months of age if a child hasn't heard a specific sound in a given language he will lose the ability to hear it. Many of us have had the experience of trying to learn a new language but not being able to make some of the sounds of the language because we cannot discriminate that sound.

The ability to discriminate sounds has lasting effects on language and literacy development. A child who has been prevented from hearing language for the first two years is more susceptible to language delays and future reading difficulties. This is why it is so important to have a child's hearing checked regularly and to prevent ear infections as much as possible.

Plasticity

Now here's the interesting piece—even though there are critical periods for language development, the brain possesses a tremendous ability to change and learn, and this is called *plasticity*. Basically, "plasticity refers to the brain's capacity to change" (Restak, 2003, p. 7). Remember the old saying, "You can't teach an old dog new tricks?" Well, apparently you can't apply that saying to all animals because when it comes to people, you can! The brain will literally change its structure and function when necessary to compensate for brain malfunction or loss of brain tissue. In some cases, the brain will automatically begin to change, but sometimes intensive intervention is needed to help the brain relearn. For instance, in the case of *dyslexic* individuals researchers have found that the neurological deficits underlying the disorder can be reversed after intense intervention lasting as little as two months (Restak, 2003). Reversing the deficit is accomplished by intensive phonetic instruction in which the left hemisphere of the brain is activated. By doing this over and over the left side of the brain learns to activate itself during the reading process. In other words, due to the brain's incredible ability to change, it can learn how to respond more efficiently given the appropriate cues. More on the signs of dyslexia can be found at the end of this chapter in the "Of Special Interest" section.

MODES OF LANGUAGE

Language can be divided into two general categories: *receptive* and *expressive*. **Receptive language** refers to listening and comprehending language. Receptive language includes the baby's awareness of sounds, turning toward her caregiver when she speaks, responding to one word like "no," recognizing the names of familiar objects, and listening to stories and music. Expressive language is the ability to communicate emotions and messages. Expressive language includes the baby's crying and making certain sounds to indicate specific needs, babbling in a turn-taking fashion with a caregiver, saying first words like "mama," asking questions, and finally creating complex sentences. It is amazing, but the child displays both receptive and expressive language abilities at birth and basically masters both by five years of age.

Receptive Language Development

Infants are born predisposed to understand language. Newborn infants respond to sounds in their environment. Environmental sounds such as speech or a loud noise elicits a response from the infant. Infants remain still while listening to a familiar sound or cry when startled.

Early in infancy babies learn to turn toward a voice and gaze or smile. In fact, young infants can recognize familiar voices and are soothed by their predictability. Additionally, infants as young as three months of age attend to unfamiliar voices as they discriminate tones. Four- to six-month-old infants respond to the word *no*. They are responsive to changes in voice tone and carefully attend to environmental sounds.

The exciting and fun receptive language development of the 7- to 12-month-old infant is marked by obvious listening behavior. The infant turns and looks at faces when called by name and enjoys games such as patty-cake and this-little-piggy. It is during this period that the infant recognizes the names of familiar objects such as car, keys, or daddy and begins to respond to simple requests such as "Get the ball."

At age one the child points to named pictures in books or displayed in the environment and responds to instructions to identify body parts such as "Where are your eyes?" or "Get your nose!" He can follow simple commands such as "Get your hat" and

---

Receptive language.   Includes learning to listen to, recognize, and understand the communication of others.

TABLE 11–1 **Receptive Language Development**

Stage of Development	Adult/Peer Stimulus	Child's Reactions to Adult/Peer Stimulus
Stage 1	Make sounds	Infant will turn head toward sound
	While facing the infant, react to some sound the infant has made	Infant will react with same sound to continue the play
Stage 2	Play music	Infant will show signs of excitement, such as moving hands, smiling, or making sounds
	Reference the name of an object that is in sight	Infant will look at or attend to the object
Stage 3	Environmental sounds	Toddler will associate with person or activity
	Present a known object and say its name	Child will nod as if to agree with the name of the object
	Say name of object that is not in sight	Child will associate by showing she knows what is being talked about—getting the object or showing excitement that someone is coming
Stage 4	Tell the child to get an object that is out of sight	Child retrieves object
	Give a two-step direction	Child carries out the direction
	Ask questions with who or what	Child shows answer by pointing or retrieving

understands simple questions like "Where is the ball?" At approximately 16 months the child will understand 100–200 words but will only say (*express*) less than 50.

The toddler understands two-part commands such as "Pick up the blocks and put them in the basket" and understands contrasting meaning such as *stop/go, in/on,* or *hot/cold.* The toddler notices and responds to environmental sounds such as the telephone or trash truck and will indicate understanding by attempting to answer the phone or engage in trash collecting. Receptive language continues to develop as children continue to process sounds and assign meaning to those sounds. Table 11–1 shows the stages in the development of receptive language.

What to Look For in Receptive Language

- ❑ Does the infant turn toward familiar voices?
- ❑ Does the infant seek novel sounds?
- ❑ Does the toddler identify named objects?
- ❑ Does the child identify action-related words?
- ❑ Does the child follow simple directions?
- ❑ Does the child react to music?
- ❑ Does the child follow simple two-step directions?

Baby Talk

One familiar question is the role of baby talk, also known as *motherese*. Baby talk is a variety of English spoken by adults (not by babies), primarily to infants and occasionally to pets. Some of the linguistic characteristics of baby talk are listed below. The use of motherese has been shown to advance the development of language in children.

Characteristics of Motherese

- High-pitched voice
- Exaggerated pitch patterns, often ending on raised pitch
- Slow tempo
- Whispering
- Nicknames and endearments directed to the child
- Reduplications (e.g., *night-night*, *choo-choo*)
- Word repetition rather than use of pronouns
- Short, simple sentences
- Frequent repetition
- Expansions of children's utterances (expatiation)

Expressive Language Development

Expressive language is communicating by voice, gestures, facial expressions, or other signs. Receptive language develops prior to spoken language but, like everything else in human development, the two are inextricably linked.

The first stage of expressive language development can be termed **early vocalizations.** The newborn begins self-expression through reflexive communication modes such as crying and making body movements and facial expressions. The two-month-old makes meaningful sounds such as cooing during a pleasant exchange, crying when something is not pleasurable, and laughing to pull the caregiver into more interactions. Between three and six months new sounds begin, such as squeals, growls, croons, and the vowel sounds "ooo" and "eeee." This is the time of experimentation. The infant explores a variety of sounds and matched responses.

At around six to ten months of age the child begins babbling. Babbling consists of consonant sounds, particularly the sounds we consider the "hard sounds" like [b], [d], and [g], followed by a vowel, producing the sounds "bababa," "dadada," and of course, "mamamama." At one year of age the infant produces his first words that are recognizably part of the native language and that are paired with an object. First words and **protowords** are not always recognized by the families or caregivers. For instance, 13-month-old Catherine hears from her mom that her aunt Marilyn is coming over to visit. Catherine quickly runs to the window and begins saying, "Nananana? Nananana?" Mom explains that "Nananana" is her word for her aunt Marilyn.

Expressive language.   Communication by voice, gestures, facial expressions, or other signs.

Early vocalizations.   The first stage of expressive language development.

Protowords.   Repeatedly occurring words bound to specific contexts, with fixed meaning for individuals familiar with the context in which they are spoken.

FIGURE 11–1   **An example of underextension.**

Twenty-two-month-old Rebecca came into school with her pajama bottoms on. There were dogs and puppies printed on the fabric of the pajama pants. I said, "I see you have puppies on your pajamas." Rebecca said "Fala." Because Rebecca has a language delay I looked to mom wondering what she had said. Mom said, "That is what she calls all dogs, because we have a picture of FDR's (Franklin Delano Roosevelt's) dog Fala at home. She calls all dogs 'Fala.'"

First words appear between 10 and 16 months of age. These are words that are used consistently and are intelligible to parents and sometimes to other listeners. First words are restrictive in use and very context-specific. The addition of more words is a slow process up until around 18 months, or the point when the child has about 50 words.

Around thirteen to eighteen months, or at the 50-word mark, the young child's vocabulary grows tremendously and reflects the particular culture in which the child is developing. (see the "Cultural Variation" box later in this chapter). This phase is sometimes called the **naming explosion** or **vocabulary spurt.**

Between twelve and eighteen months the child begins to use **holophrases**—one-word utterances that express a complete meaningful thought. The child that whispers "(s)leep" could mean, I want to sleep, I don't want to sleep, I will put the baby doll to sleep, or mommy is sleeping. During this period the child will also exhibit **overextension,** using one word to label a wider collection of similar objects, such as calling anything that flies "birdie," and **underextension,** using a word too narrowly, such as only using the word *truck* to refer to the orange Ford pickup that dad owns. Figure 11–1 gives a humorous example of this concept.

During the vocabulary spurt (18–24 months), the child begins using **telegraphic speech** in which two words convey meaning, such as "baby sick," "daddy home," or "mommy go." The two words are typically high content words and the pattern leaves out words that are not important to actual meaning, such as *the, is,* and *can.* It is also at this time when the child will employ the technique of **fast mapping,** which allows the child to add a word to his lexicon after only one exposure.

By 24 months the toddler begins putting together three-, four-, and five-word utterances that may contain nouns and verbs. Although subject/verb agreement between the components is not yet perfected, the child is now able to get messages across to anyone. Table 11–2 shows the stage in expressive language development during the period of birth to 24 months.

....

First words.   Words used consistently that are understood by parents and others.

Naming explosion or **vocabulary spurt.**   Tendency for rapid vocabulary growth reflective of the child's experiences and culture.

Holophrases.   One word utterances that express a complete meaningful thought.

Overextension.   The use of one word to label a wider collection of similar objects.

Underextension.   The use of a word too narrowly.

Telegraphic speech.   Combinations of two words that convey meaning.

Fast mapping.   The addition of a word to the child's lexicon after one exposure.

TABLE 11–2   **Expressive Language Development, Birth to 24 months**

	Early Vocalizations	
1	Crying sounds	Related to physiological state
2	Cooing Laughing Crying	Internal state response
3	Patterned vocalizations	[ah], [ee]
4	Babbling Turn taking	Internal state response Infant can understand intonation
5	Yell Squeal	Intonation pattern of native language
6	Canonical babbling	"Ba," "dah," and "ma ma ma" Consonant sounds used are [m], [d], [b], [g] Back to front shift in sound production Canonical babbling has true syllable structure
7	Sound blend	[ma], [na], [ga], [da] Period of verbal play
8	Variegated babbling	Variation of consonant/vowel pattern Dah-de-ba-be
	First Words	
1	Comprehension of speech-sound sequence	Responds predictably to some words, such as own name and "No"
2	Double syllables	Easily made words consisting of a consonant and vowel *Mama, dada, bye-bye* Word association
3	Jargon	Mix of real words and vocal activity that is not real words Largely a connection of vocal sounds with meaning only to the child
4	Holophrases	Single words that are used to express complex thoughts
5	Telegraphic speech	Utterances that leave out many words: "Mommy come?" "Daddy ball." "Want juice."
6	Simple sentences	Two-, three-, and four-word utterances that contain nouns and verbs.

(Continued on next page)

TABLE 11–2   **Expressive Language Development, Birth to 24 months (*Continued*)**

Linguistic Speech		
Term	**Characteristics**	**Examples**
Naming explosion	Increase in an infant's vocabulary, especially in the number of nouns, that begins at about 18 months of age	dad, mama, nana, cup, bottle, dog, kitty
Holophrases	Single words that are used to express complex thoughts.	"Down" is used to mean "Get me down from here."
Overextensions	The application of a word beyond its true meaning.	Child calls multiple people "mama."
Underextensions	The too-narrow application of a word	Toddler uses *cat* to refer to the family cat and no other feline.
Fast mapping	Cursory meaning of a word after just one exposure	Child uses *speckled* to describe a turtle after only a single hearing of the word.
Telegraphic speech	Utterances that leave out many words	"Mommy come?" "Daddy ball." "Want juice."

Source: Deiner (1997)

What to Look For in Expressive Language from Birth to 24 months

- ❑ Does the infant cry when in need of something?
- ❑ Does the infant express utterances that sound like vowels?
- ❑ Does the infant babble consonant-vowel patterns, such as "ma-ma" and "ba-ba"?
- ❑ Does the infant make new and unusual sounds—squeals, squawks, and croons?
- ❑ Does the infant string sounds together?
- ❑ Does the infant use short utterances to express a word that maybe only parents understand?
- ❑ Does the toddler repeat new vocabulary words?
- ❑ Does the toddler use new words in other contexts?
- ❑ Does the toddler use one word to express an entire thought?
- ❑ Does the toddler put together two to three words to convey meaning?

CULTURAL VARIATION

Children developing language experience a period of time when their vocabularies "explode" or increase at a very high rate. Children going through this period usually exhibit either a referential style of vocabulary development or more of an expressive style. A *referential* style reflects a child's preoccupation with naming objects, whereas an *expressive* style (note that this is a style rather than a judgment on how effectively meaning or feeling is conveyed) reflects the child's concern more with social norms. For example, a child with a referential style may point at a toy car and say, "car, car," meaning he wants the car, and a child with an expressive style may point at the car saying "I wannit," meaning he wants the car. Both convey the same message but in a different style. English-speaking children typically demonstrate a referential style, while Japanese, Korean, and Chinese toddlers typically exhibit an expressive style. Both styles are reflected in adult language, as well (Berk, 2005).

DEVELOPMENT OF GRAMMAR

During the preschool years children continue to increase their vocabulary, comprehend more of what is being talked about, and expand their use of expressive language outside of original contexts. At the same time they begin to play around with the rules of the language. This can be considered **grammatical development.**

Every language has rules for how words are put together to form sentences, how individual sounds completely change word meaning, how to change tenses, and so forth. While these rules are typically complex and exceptions are numerous, children learn these rules naturally through exposure and usage. During the preschool years the child learns how to ask questions, change tenses, use negatives, increase the number of words in a sentence, use tags on sentences, use pronouns and prepositions, and refer to indirect objects. The scope of understanding is incredible when you consider that the child is learning to master an entire language in a very short time.

Most people would agree that we learn through our mistakes. The preschool child will make many mistakes while learning to apply and use the rules of the language. **Overregulation** occurs when the child uses the rules of the language in the wrong way while he is learning. When a child overregulates, the typical response from the adult is, "Isn't that cute?" For example, the child might say things like, "I runned more faster that time," "My friend is very cryey today," or "This dress is very beautifulist." As time passes and without any formal instruction the child will repair the grammar. Some will ask, "Should I correct the child?" In some cases you might want to restate what the child said in a correct format. For instance, if Juan said, "Yesterday I goed to the fair," I might

....

Grammatical development.   Developing an understanding of the rules of language.

Overregulation.   Applying a language rule to a word or phrase that does not follow the rule.

TABLE 11-3   Examples of Overregulation

Grammar challenge	Correct example	What you might hear from the child	Why this is a challenge
Changing tenses	Yesterday I went to the store	I goed to the store	To make most verbs into past tense you usually add -ed, but not with the verb go
Creating plural	Two men came into our room	Two mans came into our room	Usually to make a plural you add an -s, but not with irregular nouns
Asking questions	Where is daddy going?	Where daddy is going?	Statements are subject-verb-object, questions change the word order
Negating a sentence	I don't want to go to bed	I no want to go bed	Putting no in front usually negates

come back with, "You went to the fair yesterday? I went last week!" The child will naturally pick up the difference and after several exposures will adjust. By the time the child reaches age six, most of the rules have been learned and are reflected in his language.

Table 11–3 gives some of the rules that are learned during this time and the overregulation that can occur.

What to Look For in Grammatical Development

- ❑ Does the child use pronouns? (e.g., *him, her, she, his*)
- ❑ Does the child refer to indirect objects (e.g., "I got him a present")
- ❑ Does the child ask *wh* questions?
- ❑ How does the child negate a sentence?
- ❑ How does the child ask *wh* questions?
- ❑ Does the child use tenses?
- ❑ How does the child change tenses of verbs?
- ❑ How does the child make plurals?

COMPONENTS OF LANGUAGE

The modes of language are further broken down into the components of language. Figure 11–2 gives an overview of the four components. After examining the box, try to apply these components to sign language. What would phonology look like? What would pragmatics look like?

Phonology

The smallest unit of sound that can be altered to change the meaning of a word is called a *phoneme*. In English, for example, the words *gin, kin, pin, sin, tin,* and *win* all have

FIGURE 11–2 **The components of language.**

> **Phonology.** The smallest unit of sound that can be altered to change the meaning of a word.
> **Semantics.** The meaning of words and word combinations.
> **Syntax.** Syntax refers to the standardized set of rules that determine how words should be combined to make sense to speakers of a language.
> **Pragmatics.** Strategies and rules for effective and socially acceptable interaction.

different meanings due to the fact that the initial sound, or phoneme, is different. Phonemes do not have meaning by themselves. The sounds represented by the *g, k, p, s, t,* and *w* in the words are meaningless alone but they can change the meaning of words.

The actual phonemes, the number of phonemes, and the clusters of phonemes used in a particular language can vary slightly or considerably. For instance, Polynesian languages use about 15 phonemes and favor vowel clusters rather than consonant clusters in words. This pattern can be observed in the Polynesian place names *Kauai, Maui,* and *Samoa.* In contrast, English speakers use 40–46 phonemes and combine consonants into clusters. This can be heard in the English words *schedule, months,* and *shrill.* The San languages of southwest Africa (spoken by the Ju/'hoansi) use some sounds that are not found in English or most other languages. These are click sounds that serve as consonants (O'Neil, 2005). As discussed earlier, if one's native language does not contain certain phonemes it becomes difficult, if not impossible, to distinguish those sounds after 12 months of age.

Semantics

Semantics refers to the meaning of words and word combinations. Some would also call it vocabulary and still others refer to the child's lexicon or "semantic dictionary" as the words they know and understand. Although many words enter a child's vocabulary, they are not considered part of the child's semantic dictionary until he knows how to use the word in various contexts. The child has close to 50 words or more in his expressive vocabulary by 18 months of age and during the second year of life may add up to 20 new words a day to his semantic dictionary (McDevitt & Ormond, 2004).

Syntax

Syntax refers to the standardized set of rules that determine how words should be combined to make sense to speakers of a language. All native speakers of a language learn the basic rules of syntax as they grow up. It is difficult to understand unfamiliar languages not only because the vocabulary is different but also because each language is governed by different rules. Word order is critical to convey meaning. For example, the words *you, are,* and *there* can be combined in three different ways to alter meaning:

There you are.   You are there.   Are you there?

Pragmatics

Pragmatics is the component of language that includes the functional use of language in the social context. Let's face it, what is said with words only covers part of what one is trying to communicate. Have you ever heard someone say, "It wasn't *what* she said, it was *how* she said it that made me mad!" The "how" of what we say is considered pragmatics.

Research suggests that pragmatic development is closely linked to play skill development in children. The child who can communicate a message that can be understood by many people has more opportunities for positive social interactions. Think of people you love to talk to. Why do love to talk to them? Chances are because they know when to talk and when to listen, they know to change topics when the current one has become boring, and they know how to engage you in the conversation—these are pragmatic skills. For the sake of simplicity, pragmatic development is broken down into *speech acts, conversational acts,* and *social sensitivity.*

Speech Acts   **Speech acts** are the behaviors that enable us to use various means to make ourselves understood or to get the point across. These include the intonation of the voice, the volume, and nonverbal cues such as body language. Body language is the language of gestures, expressions, and postures. In North America, we commonly use our arms and hands to say goodbye, express size or proportion, express excitement, give commands, call attention to something, warn, threaten, etc. We use our head to say yes or no, to smile, frown, bow, and flirt. Our head and shoulders in combination may shrug to indicate that we do not know something, we don't care, or we are bored.

Another example of a speech act is tone of voice. Tone of voice can significantly change the meaning of speech. We can say to someone, "Take that" and it can mean many different things simply by how it is spoken. Think of it this way, let's say you're at your parents' house and as you're leaving your mother holds out $20 to you and says, "Take that." If she said it with a quiet, kind voice you might think she feels a bit sorry for you. If she says it quick and loud it might mean that she is mad at you for still needing her money. And if she says it very quietly and hunches her shoulders, she might not want your father to hear her. All these different meanings from these two little words.

A baby less than one year of age has developed three different intonation styles, that of making a statement, making a command, or making a request. Finally, a child develops the ability to change his style of interacting depending on the audience. This is called **code switching.** Typically, this will develop around age five, but hints of this can be seen earlier. For instance, the four-year-old who will talk to the baby using a high-pitched motherese voice and then return to her peers and begin using a normal tone of voice again is demonstrating code switching.

....

Speech acts.   The behaviors that enable us to use various means to make ourselves understood.

Code switching.   Changing the tone or style of one's speech from one form to another when the audience changes.

Conversation   Conversational acts include turn-taking behaviors and the ability to stay on topic. Turn-taking behaviors, such as making vocalizations when an adult pauses or focusing on the face of a speaker, can be observed in infants as young as three months. As the child develops he becomes more proficient at adding pauses and information to a conversation at appropriate times. The ability to stay on topic and offer relevant remarks to a particular topic relies heavily on a child's cognitive development as well as his experiences with a topic, yet should be emerging by three to four years of age.

Social Sensitivity   **Social sensitivity** includes the social conventions that govern appropriate verbal interactions such as talkativeness, style of interacting with adults, eye contact, and personal space. Because these conventions are determined primarily by the culture, there are great variations in development. In some cultures, for instance, children are not included in adult conversations at all and children do not focus on the adult-adult conversation. In some cultures making eye contact is a sign of respect, in others a sign of disrespect. In order to assess pragmatic development, especially in the area of social sensitivity, it becomes imperative to learn the ways of the culture. See the box below for a discussion of several cultural variations in pragmatic development. Table 11–4 then gives the progression of pragmatic development.

Cultural Variations in Pragmatics

➤ The distance tolerated when engaged in personal conversations is closer in Latin America than it is in other cultures or among non-Latin populations in the United States.

➤ Gestures may be differently interpreted from culture to culture. For example, spitting on another person or even at all in public is a sign of disrespect in North America but can be an affectionate blessing if done in a certain way among the Masai of Kenya.

➤ Personal contact such as touching and hugging are also dictated by culture. North American adults generally avoid touching each other except in intimate relationships or when greeting each other with a handshake or hug. Asian and Northern European adults avoid physical contact more than Southern European or Latin Americans, among whom physical contact is expected.

➤ Eye contact is, in many cultures, a way to let others know that you are attending or interested in communicating. However, some Mexican American, Puerto Rican, and Native American cultures discourage children from looking in the face of an adult and consider such behavior disrespectful.

➤ In some cultures, particularly in Native American cultures, answering a question immediately is rude, indicating that the question was not worth thinking about.

➤ *Generally, a smile communicates the same message worldwide.*

Sources: O'Neil (2005); McDevitt and Ormond (2004)

Social sensitivity.   The ability to adapt to cultural expectations or standards.

TABLE 11–4   **Pragmatic Development**

Approximate Age	Concepts and Indicators		
	Speech Acts	**Conversation**	**Social Sensitivity**
0–18 months	Quiets when spoken to Shakes head no Shows toys to adult Extends arms to be picked up Cries differently when in different states	Focuses on face Coos and babbles in response to a voice Responds to own name	Varies response to someone else's voice Gives eye contact Waves bye-bye Smiles to engage another person
18–36 months	Displays emotion Points to objects Uses a word to command: "Go," "Mine" Uses a gesture to convey a message: stomping feet, hands on hips	Says, "What's that?" Uses attention-getting words like "Hey" Uses two-word phrases to convey a message	Uses language in imitative ways, like imitating the speech pattern of an adult Moves another person's face to secure attention Uses eye contact to engage or avoid interactions
3–4 years	Uses gestures such as pointing to provide emphasis Uses volume of voice to convey a message Understands the message behind voice tone	Attends to topic of conversation Corrects peer's language or conversations Asks questions to sustain conversation	Uses body to communicate or gain admittance to play Understands other people's nonverbal communication
5–6 years	Uses complex gestures to communicate Whispers	Describes objects and their functions in detail Takes up to four turns in a conversation Engages the listener with references to objects and people	Begins using the conventions of courtesy: indirectly requests something rather than asking for something Asks to use another's belongings Recognizes when people need help

Source: Marasco, O'Rourke, Riddle, Sepka, and Weaver (2004)

What to Look For in Pragmatic Development

❑ Does the infant follow a person with her eyes?

❑ Does the infant have different cries for different needs?

❑ Does the infant localize the sound's source, such as the speaker?

❑ Does the infant make a vocalization in response to speech?

❑ Does the infant use different vocalizations for different states?

❑ Does the infant shout or cough to gain attention?

❑ Does the infant reach to request an object?

❑ Does the child apparently take turns with communication?

❑ Does the child use volume and intonation to signify the meaning of utterances?

❑ Does the child give eye contact?

❑ How much space does the child prefer to have during conversations?

❑ Can the child stay on topic by adding relevant remarks?

❑ Does the child answer questions? If so, how long does he wait before answering?

❑ Does the child use humor or jokes or sarcasm?

❑ Can the child repair a conversation when she has been interrupted?

❑ Does the child code-switch?

INTRODUCTION TO LITERACY

Literacy encompasses the skills of reading and writing. These skills grow from meaningful cultural experiences and contexts. Children who pass the golden arches on a family trip to the store understand that the towering *M* stands for McDonald's, a place most children enjoy visiting. Long before the child conventionally spells the word *restaurant* he understands the cultural code for such places. The corporate symbol is one way that American children begin to understand written language.

Literacy concepts are developing simultaneously with many skills, forming in an overlapping manner rather than one at a time. In other words, children are speaking, listening, and reading at the same time that they are writing. As children grow they gain an understanding of how written language is used. Children begin to understand that written language helps us share information, remember, and make connections, such as writing out party invitations or thank-you notes (Schickedanz, 1994). Typically children engage in functional writing approximations as they imitate adult behavior. They may "write" a bank check, make a grocery list, or issue traffic citations as part of their exploration of the written language. For example, four-year-old Hannah used a small spiral notepad to record all of her two-year-old sister's traffic violations as she peddled a pink car around the circumference of the kitchen table. On each pass Hannah put up her hand to stop the car's movement and handed her sister the "ticket" as she reported "This is for going fast" or "No parking." The small scraps of paper had horizontal scribbles across the page representing the writing. In this manner, children work to coordinate physical and cognitive skills as they focus on letter formation. Given many opportunities to write, children concentrate on the "hard work" of letter formation in their daily play schemes. The following anecdotal record demonstrates how children use functional written language.

ANECDOTAL RECORD 11–1

Child's Name: Donald

Date: March 3

Time: 9:00 a.m.

Observer: Mrs. Rivers

Location: Head Start Program

During play Donald entered the dramatic play kitchen area. He slipped a white butcher's apron over his head and asked a friend to tie it in the back. Donald picked up a small broom and began sweeping the floor. Other children smiled and picked up their feet so that he could sweep under them. Donald stood a moment surveying the area. He went to the writing area and on a large white paper he wrote "CLZD." Donald returned to the kitchen and taped the sign to the back of the play refrigerator. Pointing to the sign he informed the others: "The store is closed for inventory, time to leave." Children filed out of the dramatic play area, wishing Donald a good day. Donald took all of the food items, dishes, and empty food containers out of the refrigerator and cabinets. He arranged them on the small table. Donald took a small spiral notebook and pencil out of his apron pocket. He carefully counted the items on the table and made horizontal scribbles on the paper. Each scribble was followed by a number. Donald engaged in this task for several minutes. He took the "CLZD" sign down and on the back side wrote, "OPNCMN." He announced to the group, "The store is open, you can come in now."

INTRODUCTION TO WRITING

Writing, like reading, develops over time and not in a magical, enlightened moment. From the very beginning of life children begin to experience and experiment with language. Games of peekaboo, board books, and songs are all met with delight. Children gain understanding of a variety of symbols from these very simple beginnings. Ultimately, children come to know that the symbols, i.e., letters, have meaning. *Emergent* or *early literacy* is the term given to circumstances in which children begin constructing knowledge about the uses of written language long before they begin decoding familiar words and writing in a conventional manner (Gleason, 2004).

In video stream 6 on the accompanying CD-ROM, note the early literacy activities that are taking place in this preschool classroom.

The Components of Writing

Writing extends children's spoken language and is a conscious, purposeful activity. From the time that children begin to show interest in writing, their scribbles represent efforts to write as well as draw. Children write in order to communicate. For example, during block building four-year-old Jessica yelled at Mark and David when they took wooden blocks from her play space. She loudly objected, reporting that she intended to use the blocks. The boys quickly returned the blocks. Jessica retrieved a piece of paper and crayon from the art shelf to create a notice for all to read. Simple lines of squiggles covered the paper. Jessica taped the notice to the block shelf and announced for all to hear as she pointed to the paper and "read": "Don't take the blocks." She turned to the teacher and said: "Now, nobody will do that bad thing again."Jessica made her message quite clear and helped others to understand what her "writing" meant. Eventually Jessica's writing will take on a more conventional form and others will be able to read her warning as well.

 In video stream 6 on the accompanying CD-ROM, take note of how the children are writing for meaning.

The Development of Writing

Children progress through the stages of writing at individual rates. First children draw and name pictures. Eventually children make drawings for the purpose of communicating ideas to others. A child who sets up a pretend post office or library may draw a picture to label the play so that others can join the fun. Children may ask adults to write labels on their drawing as a way of letting others know what the picture depicts. Children progress to labeling parts of a drawing, perhaps naming a fire truck and a dog as a means of recording the events of a recent trip to the fire station. Unconventional spelling is common among children who label their drawings. Children use one alphabet letter to "stand for" a syllable in a word or use one letter to represent a group of sounds. For example, a child might represent the word *car* as "cr" or *truck* as "trk."

As children begin to understand that symbols carry meaning, they demonstrate knowledge that there is a difference between drawing and writing. Additionally, they notice that print proceeds in a linear fashion, and they begin to use this principle in their writing. Young children may use shapes, lines, and squiggles to represent writing. As children examine environmental print they notice that letters vary and occur in strings. These small observations influence children's own writing. Children begin to experiment with how print looks, as well as what it means. They may think that words in large print represent a big object and that small print represents a small object (Schickedanz, 1999). This is visual and not sound-based knowledge.

The Stages of Writing

Scribbling behavior demonstrates children's understanding of literacy forms. Scribbling looks much more like writing than it does drawing. Often children begin scribbles on the left side of the page and move horizontally across the page. Both Hannah's traffic tickets and Donald's inventory, examples shared earlier, demonstrate characteristics of "writing."Children may engage in card making or letter writing, where drawings and alphabet letters are both used but look very different from one another. Children may indicate differences by saying: "This is my picture and it says . . ."as they point to the "words." Often letters and scribbles are represented in the same work. Writing long strings of letters is another way that children approach literacy skills. However, letters are not always formed in a conventional manner; some are backward or upside down. These letters are random in nature and don't conventionally spell words, yet they do represent a message

Scribble of a 28-month-old girl

meant for others to read and are an important precursor to invented spelling. *Invented spelling* characteristic of young writers uses one letter or syllable of a word to represent meaning (Salinger, 1996). For example, the word *car* is written "CR," the word *people* may be represented as "pepL" and the word picture may be "p HR."

Children often rely on creative or invented spelling (Richgels, 2004) in early writing. Invented spelling is a system of representations that follow rules created by the child. Initially spelling includes mostly beginning consonants to relay messages; for example, "I will go to the store" may be written as "I g t s." Early attempts at encoding language reveal that children are active learners who seek methods for representing the sounds that they hear in oral language (Gleason, 2004).

SHEWAZ PAIEN
WE V ϤR TOG
AND I WAZ
PA I N WIV
HR AND DA
STEEFOFASIP

"She was playing we to and I was playing with her and she fell fast asleep."

Today's snack is:

Bagels
Cream Cheese
Crackers

You may have:

IBBY

1 Bagel

Beginnings of invented spelling.

At the same time that children are exploring the function of writing they are seeking to understand written form. They examine relationships between letters and sounds, and practice forming letter characters. Often children include letters in their drawings as they examine the picture-like qualities of written language. To the young child, letters are pictures, much like a drawing of a tree or boat. Because children understand that pictures and drawings are named, they simply refer to alphabet drawings as letters. Ultimately children begin to understand that print has meaning. Two-year-old Kara may believe that all words with the letter *K* are her word or name. Clearly this is an incorrect assumption but an important first step in learning to write. Children younger than two understand that symbols carry meaning. Eventually they come to understand that pictures differ from drawings and that they are arranged in space in different ways. Gradually children write or scribble in a linear fashion and, like the example on the previous page, they begin to use this principle in their writing. Children grow increasingly focused on the form of their writing and ultimately discover that words written in a string are difficult to read. They may use punctuation or dashes between words to help create meaning in their writing. For example rather than writing "weshodshrblocksandtos," a child who understands the importance of spacing might write, "we.shod.shr.blocks.and.tos" to communicate that "we should share blocks and toys." Ultimately, with practice and support, children unlock the mysteries of conventional written language used in their culture, and they use it in every form and for every function imaginable (Salinger, 1996). Table 11–5 shows the stages in the development of writing.

TABLE 11–5 **The Development of Writing**

Stage	Components
Random drawing	Children draw pictures and label them with no specific intended meaning.
Purposeful drawing	Children use drawing to stand for writing. Drawings communicate messages to others. Children may "read" their drawing as if it is writing.
Drawings with labels	Children create drawings and either ask an adult to label parts of the drawing or use unconventional spelling to label pictures themselves.
Scribbling	Children scribble in a manner that differs from drawing.
Letter-like forms	Children write actual letters within their scribbles.
Random letters or letter strings	Random letters take on a story or letter form. Only actual letters are used, although with some errors.
Invented spelling	Children create their own spelling when they don't know the conventional spelling. One letter may represent an entire syllable.
Conventional spelling	Writing is much like that of an adult.

Source: Salinger (1996)

Child's progression of writing over two years

What to Look For in Writing Development

☐ Does the child name drawings?

☐ Does the child label drawings?

☐ Does the child use letters and pictures differently?

☐ Does the child identify letters?

❑ Does the child use a letter to represent a word or object?

❑ Does the child use "writing" to communicate?

❑ Does the child scribble in a linear fashion?

❑ Does the child imitate written form?

❑ Does the child write strings of letters?

❑ Does the child make uniform letters?

❑ Does the child use punctuation between words?

❑ Does the child leave space between words?

❑ Does the child use inventive spelling?

❑ Does the child ask an adult to spell words?

INTRODUCTION TO READING

Learning to read is a complex and multifaceted process that begins with listening and speaking and evolves into being able to ascertain meaning from the printed word. As the child becomes more proficient at mastering her own language, she is also laying the foundation for reading. Burns, Griffin, and Snow (1999) identify three main accomplishments that characterize good readers. First, they understand the alphabetic system of their language to identify printed words; second, they have and use background knowledge and strategies to obtain meaning from print; finally, they read fluently. Now we will discuss the components of each of these accomplishments.

Enjoyment of Reading Activities

The enjoyment of reading activities may not appear to be a component of reading but it is perhaps the most important one. When children are held close and read to from birth,

Shared reading experiences heighten reading enjoyment.

they develop an affinity for reading. Babies will listen to stories, especially if the reader can alter his voice to fit the baby's preferences. As children develop they will begin to ask to be read to, pretend to read themselves, seek out quiet places to look at books, and use books as a resource to get more information. Children anticipate with great excitement when someone is going to tell a story with props, but will listen attentively to someone such as a Native American storyteller who uses only her voice to create the visual experience. Children "read" familiar stories to each other, to adults, and even to pets. Although the stories are not verbatim recitations, they contain the main ideas of the story and are an indicator of **emergent reading.**

ANECDOTAL RECORD 11–2

Child's Name: Suncana

Date: May 6

Time: 10:00 a.m.

Observer: D. Ahola

Location: Gateway Montessori

Four-and-one-half-year-old Suncana called out to me, "Deb, can I read you a story?" "Sure," I said, never willing to pass up a good story. She went over to a basket of books and pulled out an early reader entitled, "The Butter Battle Book," by Dr. Seuss. We sat on the floor together and she began the story. Moving her finger across the title on the cover she read slowly and deliberately, "Theeee BBBButter BBBBBBattle Book." She turned to the first page and again used her finger to move across the words on the page. "Once upon a time there were some little creatures." As she moved her finger across and told the story she was actually looking at the picture and every so often would look back to me for verification—"They liked to live in trees." She continued on in the book, never really reading the words but using the cues from the pictures and her memory of how the story was read to her the day before.

Phonological Awareness

Phonological awareness means that the child is able to think about the sounds of the words apart from their actual meaning (Burns, Griffin, & Snow, 1999). Children begin to pick out sounds and recognize that words contain different sounds. They are delighted when they discover the "hidden" sounds in everyday words. They rhyme sounds

....

Emergent reading.   Reading-related activities demonstrated by children prior to the achievement of conventional reading.

Phonological awareness.   The ability to think about the sounds of words apart from their actual meaning.

to make new and funny words, and they make up words that start with a certain sound or end with a particular sound. Children make connections between sounds that are alike in different words. This is evident when for the first time the child becomes aware of the first sound in her name and how it is the same as someone else's.

ANECDOTAL RECORD 11–3

Child's Name: Anthony

Date: May 10

Time: 9:00 a.m.

Observer: D. Ahola

Location: Gateway Montessori

While working with Anthony on sandpaper letters and finishing the sound of "m" we began to brainstorm together all the things that start with the sound [m]. I said "mom," Anthony said "mmmmmmote!" I said "monkey," he said "mmmmmmoney!" I said "Muhammad," he looked around the room and said "mmmmmmmMolly!!" Then, all full of excitement, he ran over to Muhammad and said, "You and Molly have the same sound!"

Identifying sounds using sandpaper letters

Print Awareness

As the child becomes more and more exposed to written materials, she begins to understand that print carries meaning. This may begin with the child matching labels to objects in the classroom, identifying how many crackers she may take for snack by counting how many crackers are on the sign above the snack table, or by seeing the sign for three people at the water table and then realizing that she will have to wait until someone leaves. Print awareness can be ever present in the dramatic play area, where children pretend to read menus, letters, and sale item flyers. Finally, the child develops the ability to identify specific words in very specific contexts, such as being able to recognize the other children's names in the class by seeing the name on the printed name card. The child may not recognize the name in another context, yet she has learned to match the name with the child purely by the shape of the word. This is called **logographic reading.**

Labeling objects in the environment

Alphabetic Awareness By three years of age many children can identify letters of the alphabet by name, particularly the letters in their own names. They sing the alphabet song and recite the letters in rhythmic patterns. By the age of three or four children begin to distinguish the letters from one another and link the letter to its shape. Again, children delight in matching the letters, such as finding all the *T*s in the house. Often children recognize uppercase letters before lowercase just as they will begin writing uppercase before lowercase.

Sound-Letter Correspondence Around the age of three years, the child begins linking the sounds of the letter to the actual letter shape. Past experiences and the type of learning environment the child is in greatly influence the age at which this begins. A child with a great deal of experience with the written language naturally begins to link the sound [s] with its slithery, snakelike letter *S*.

Book Knowledge The toddler demonstrates knowledge of books by asking adults to read a favorite story. He points out pictures and identifies the objects in the book, shows delight when he knows what is on the next page, and, even though he is not reading yet, he knows when a section of the book has been skipped. Understanding the parts of the book and their functions is also book knowledge. The preschooler begins to identify the author, the illustrator, and the title of the book. The five-year-old begins to distinguish different types of books by function. For instance, books with many words and few colorful real-life pictures provide information on such topics as volcanoes, whereas books with drawn pictures and fewer words are probably more story-like.

....

Logographic reading. Reading that relies on context and visual cues.

ANECDOTAL RECORD 11–4

Child's Name: Breanna

Date: April 2

Time: 9:00 a.m.

Observer: D. Ahola

Location: Gateway Montessori

Today was a day when Breanna wanted to work with sandpaper letters at the sound table. We started with the s letter. We made the sound, thought of things that started with the [s] sound, and traced it in glitter. Next, Bre wanted to make the s in her sound book. I wrote the s and she drew a picture of something that started with the [s] sound. I watched as she drew a curved line with a brown marker, then I asked, "What did you draw?"—thinking that it was a snake. Bre said, "It's a briny branch." I said, "Can you say it again?" Again she said, "It's a briny branch, I saw one on my tree before I came to school today." Then it hit me, she was saying it was a spiny branch! I made a note of this because it is unusual for a three-year-old to think of an adjective for something that starts with a sound.

Story Knowledge   Children better comprehend stories as they develop skills for selecting parts of a story that are most relevant and meaningful. Evidence of the development of story knowledge includes answering questions such as *who, what, where,* and *how,* being able to predict what might happen next, demonstrating comprehension of what happened previously, and defining new words based on the context of the story.

Decoding and Sight Word Recognition

Decoding can be likened to the standard response given to a child who comes across a word they do not know by sight: "Sound it out." Decoding requires the skill of connecting the sound and letter, then blending all the sounds of a given word into a meaningful whole. Once a child begins matching simple words with a consonant-vowel-consonant pattern, such as *CAT,* to a picture or replica, she is then ready to read from a page. Children will first begin to identify simple words, where the spelling closely matches the sounds of the words. Again, when this happens depends a great deal on experience, but by age five the child should have some decoding and sight word knowledge. Next they will begin reading words with long vowels, blends, and dipthongs. At the same time their sight-word vocabulary will grow. The first sight words typically recognized are words that can be difficult to sound out yet are very common, such as *the, a, as,* and *once.*

....

Decoding.   The ability to figure out how to decipher unknown words through the understanding of letters and sounds.

"The monster came and ate all the food and then the monster came and ate other things and then the monster came and told one story. The story was all told and the dog came chasing the ladies."

A dictated story

Orthographic Reading   The final stage of reading development occurs when the child can read on an automatic level. This occurs when the child develops an internal sense of letter patterns and the words they produce—this is termed **orthographic reading.** When the child has internalized the patterns, then reading becomes fluent and comprehension is acquired.

What to Look For in Reading Development

- ❑ Does the infant/toddler/preschooler/school-age child enjoy being read to?
- ❑ Does the child listen to stories?

Orthographic reading.   An internal sense of letter patterns and the words they produce.

Building word patterns

- ❑ Does the child pick up books independently?
- ❑ Does the child point to objects in the book?
- ❑ Does the child pretend to read a book?
- ❑ Does the child pick out characters from a story?
- ❑ Can the child answer comprehension questions about the story?
- ❑ Does the child recognize printed material as carrying a message?
- ❑ Does the child recognize words by the shape of the word?
- ❑ Can the child recognize words in a specific context?
- ❑ Does the child show enjoyment when being read to or when reading?
- ❑ Does the child predict what will happen next in the story?
- ❑ Does the child have any sound-letter discrimination?
- ❑ Can the child identify initial sounds in words?
- ❑ Does the child read short, consonant-vowel-consonant words?
- ❑ Does the child recognize any sight words (*said, the, where, one*)?
- ❑ Does the child read easy reader books?
- ❑ Does the child decode irregularly spelled words?
- ❑ Does the child read for information?
- ❑ Can the child, after reading a sentence, comprehend the meaning?

Table 11–6 identifies the stage of reading development in terms of enjoyment or participation in reading, alphabetic, or phonetic knowledge and finally, writing development.

TABLE 11-6   The Development of Reading

	Stage 1	Stage 2	Stage 3	Stage 4
Book/Reading behaviors	Recognizes books by covers and labels objects in books; talks about characters in the books; asks to be read to	Listens to stories in a group or with one other adult; might read storybooks on own; identifies characters in the stories and the story line; may dictate own stories	*Emergent reading;* recalls a story and may act it out; predicts text; may read early reader books; connects what happens in a story to things in own life; may have some sight words	Reads texts, uses nonfiction informational texts; reads for own purposes; comprehends meaning from implied text
Print/ Alphabetic/ Phonetic awareness	May distinguish between writing and drawing; may pick out specific letters in puzzles or signs	May recognize own name; *logographic reading;* understands that print carries meaning; may have some sound-letter correspondences; identifies letter names; has sensitivity to specific sounds within words	Labels all letters and sequence of alphabet; has sound-letter correspondence with most letters; can blend several letters together to read words	*Orthographic reading;* decodes new words; reads words that are spelled irregularly (dipthongs, vowels, etc.)
Writing/ Spelling	Engages in purposeful scribbling; scribbling may take on form of conventional writing (left to right)	Scribbles/writes as part of an activity; may make picture to go with story; may attempt writing letters; copies letters or name	Writes names independently; uses *invented spelling;* writes lists when dictated by another; writes most upper- and lowercase letters	Now spells from an orthographic perspective; moves from transitional spelling to correct spelling
Language development	Asks and answers *who, what, where* questions; engages in conversation with several interchanges; communicates personal experiences when given a cue	Talks about things that happened yesterday; engages in complex conversations; asks questions relevant to a conversation; uses new vocabulary; may rhyme words	Can say word families (*cat, bat, hat,* etc.); makes up nonsensical words and rhymes	Clarifies own points; creatively uses language to get points across; uses humor, idioms; understands and uses the difference between written and spoken language

Source: Burns, Griffin, and Snow (1999)

Language development is included in the table because the development of reading is known to be contingent on language development. The development of writing is included because it is understood that early on the use of writing or spelling drives the reading process and later reading drives the development of correct spelling. This integrative theory will be discussed more in chapter 13, "Cognitive and Language Theory."

Of Special Interest—Dyslexia

Restak (2003) defines *dyslexia* as, "a persistent difficulty in acquiring word-reading skills" (p. 184). It is characterized by difficulties primarily in reading and writing due to a language–phonological processing deficit. Well, what does that mean? Essentially, it means that the child with dyslexia will have difficulty processing the sounds of the language and therefore when it comes time to read the words by decoding, the child is at a disadvantage. The result is poor reading comprehension, less fluency in reading and speaking, and difficulty holding a word in memory well enough to link the beginning and ending of the sentence.

It is very important to identify what could be dyslexia in a young child, because early intervention is the key to him becoming a proficient reader and, ultimately, a successful student. The young child with a language delay is particularly at risk for having dyslexia. Research has shown that a child with a processing disorder such as dyslexia can overcome the barriers to learning to read if given proper phonetic instruction. Reading programs that stress phonetic instruction can be very effective, but the earlier the child receives intervention, the better. Below are some signs to look for in children. Remember, if a child is exhibiting many of these signs, it could be time to talk to the family and arrange for further evaluation.

Common Signs of Dyslexia: Preschool Children

The preschool child with dyslexia may:

- talk later than most children.
- have difficulty pronouncing words.
- omit, substitute, or add sounds to a word.
- have difficulty with new vocabulary words.
- have oral word-finding problems.
- not be able to rhyme words.
- have difficulty learning sequences such as days of the week or the alphabet.
- have difficulty identifying colors or shapes.
- have trouble following multi-step directions or routines.
- have fine motor skills delay.
- not be able to sequence a story.
- have difficulty identifying specific sounds from words (sound-letter discrimination).

Common Signs of Dyslexia: Kindergarten to Fourth Grade Students

The school-age child with dyslexia may:
- have difficulty pulling out sounds of words.
- have difficulty matching sounds with the corresponding letter.
- not be able to decode words.
- have difficulty with invented spelling.
- reverse letters, e.g., *b* for *d.*
- reverse words, e.g., *tac* for *cat.*
- invert letters, e.g., *m* for *w, u* for *n.*
- read using substitutions, e.g., *back* for *behind.*
- guess words given the context.
- exhibit difficulty in learning new vocabulary.
- transpose number sequences and confuse arithmetic signs ($+ - \times / =$).
- forget necessary tools, equipment, materials.
- rely on memorizing without real comprehension.
- show difficulty in planning, organizing, and managing time.
- have significant fine motor delays and/or disabilities.

 Print the Anecdotal Record from the CD-ROM. Highlight (code) the behavioral indicators of language and literacy development. Coding can be done best by using highlighters, colored pencils, or thin-tipped markers.

QUESTIONS TO CONSIDER ○ ○ ○

1. Describe how aspects of language development might differ from culture to culture.

2. List and describe four ways that pragmatics are used to aid in communication.

3. Identify the ways in which a child's culture can affect literacy acquisition.

REFERENCES ○ ○ ○

Berk, L. E. (2005). *Infants and children* (5th ed.). Boston: Allyn & Bacon.

Burns, M. S., Griffin, P., & Snow, C. E. (Eds.) (1999). *Starting out right: A guide to promoting children's reading success.* Washington, DC: Committee on the Prevention of Reading Difficulties in Young Children, National Research Council.

Deiner, P. L. (1997). *Infants and toddlers: Development and program planning.* New York: Harcourt Brace College Publishers.

Gleason, J. B. (2004). *The development of language* (6th ed.). Boston: Allyn & Bacon.

Hall, E. (1959). *The silent language.* New York: Doubleday.

Marasco, K., O'Rourke, C., Riddle, L., Sepka, L., & Weaver, V. (2004, March). *Pragmatic language assessment guidelines: A best practice document.* Early Intervention Council of Monroe County. Retrieved August 26, 2005, from http://www.advocacycenter.com

McDevitt, T. M., & Ormond, J. E. (2004). *Child development: Educating and working with children and adolescents* (2nd ed.). Upper Saddle River, NJ: Prentice Hall.

O'Neil, D. (2005, July). *Language and culture: An introduction to human communication.* Retrieved July 24, 2005, from http://anthro.palomar.edu/language/default.htm

Plotnik, R. (1999). Thought and Language. In *Introduction to Psychology* (5th ed., chap. 14). Belmont, CA: Wadsworth. Quote retrieved January 25, 2006, from http://www.psy.pdx.edu/PsiCafe/Areas/Developmental/LanguageDev

Restak, R. M. (2003). *The new brain: How the modern age is rewiring your brain.* New York: Rodale.

Richgels, D. J. (2004). *Meaningful writing: Invented spelling and its antecedents.* Paper presented at National Reading Conference, San Antonio, TX.

Salinger, T. S. (1996). *Literacy for young children* (2nd ed.). Upper Saddle River, NJ: Prentice Hall.

Schickedanz, J. A. (1994). *More than the ABCs: The early stages of reading and writing.* Washington, DC: National Association for the Education of Young Children.

12

The Creative Arts

Mark Ahola

CHAPTER OBJECTIVES

- To define creativity and how children create
- To understand art, music, and movement development
- To identify the developmental stages of art, music, and movement skills
- To relate stages and creativity to child observations

CHILD STUDY OBJECTIVES

Upon conclusion of this chapter the student will:

- code anecdotal records for creative arts development.
- identify a checklist for creative arts development.
- create a checklist for creative arts development.
- create a structured observation to assess creative arts development.
- gather visual documentation indicating creative arts development.
- create interview questions for the family regarding creative arts development.
- identify the child's current developmental level related to creative expression.
- conduct developmentally appropriate creative arts activities.

BRAIN DEVELOPMENT: THE MOZART EFFECT

The aspect of brain development to be discussed in this section is the "Mozart effect." This term has been widely used in books and on the Internet, and even resulted in CD-ROMs for babies, all claiming music's positive effect on brain development. Media and public interest was primarily due to a study by Rauscher, Shaw, and Ky (1993). In it, a small sample of college students listened either to a W. A. Mozart sonata, a tape of relaxation instructions, or silence. It was shown that students who listened to Mozart scored higher on a **spatial-temporal reasoning** test (the paper-folding task of the Stanford-Binet Scale of Intelligence) than the other groups. Results from listening to music were immediate and brief, and nonspatial tasks were not affected. Subsequent studies to replicate the effect have had mixed success, depending on the testing and method used; some have begun to question and doubt the study's validity. Other studies of children who learn to play piano, percussion, and other instruments have been more fruitful (Schellenberg, 2004). Harvard Project Zero's extensive review of music research determined that learning to play music shows a "large causal relationship" with spatial-temporal reasoning (Hetland & Winner, 2001). How could it be that music has this direct effect?

The neural impulses of music travel from the ear through the auditory nerve to the **auditory cortex** of the brain, where it is initially processed and interpreted. The cortex is located in the temporal lobe, an area also responsible for memory, language comprehension, and emotion. While some fibers from each ear cross to both sides, the left ear primarily follows a pathway to the auditory cortex in the right hemisphere and the right ear links to the left hemisphere's auditory cortex.

There does not seem to be a "music processing" center of the brain. PET (positron emission tomography) scans have been used to track blood flow, oxygen use, and glucose consumption in the brain as persons respond to music. It appears that the right hemisphere primarily interprets melody, pitch (sound frequency or the highness or lowness of a note), **timbre** (tonal quality of a note), and pulse (the primary beat of music). Rhythmic and harmonic (chordal) processing may be more associated with the left brain. That being said, the location of music processing seems to differ depending on familiarity with the music, one's musical training, and other variables. Research and PET scans agree that music is a "whole brain activity."

If considered valid, possible reasons for the Mozart effect could be either that music helps by exercising areas of the brain responsible for spatial reasoning, or that it instills a relaxation or arousal response that allows information to be more easily accessed. Researchers such as Rauscher believe that when children listen to music, they organize notes into melody as in a puzzle. Music's "mathematical" characteristics are thought to make the same neurological connections or synapses as those used in spatial reasoning.

....

Spatial-temporal reasoning.   The ability to fit items into space and time.

Auditory cortex.   The part of the brain that interprets nerve impulses from the auditory nerve as sound; there is one for each temporal lobe.

Timbre.   Tonal quality of a music note that gives it distinction.

The **limbic system,** the emotional center of the brain, is also stimulated by music. This system contains the amygdala and the hippocampus, found in the lower temporal region. Besides being associated with learning, memory, and emotion, the hippocampus seems to be involved with spatial reasoning. This could be affected by an increase in neurological connections caused by music. On the other hand, music is known to affect emotions and the limbic system. When in a relaxed state, memory is more easily accessed. More research is being done to determine just how and where music affects brain development. It seems that much of this interest began with the Mozart effect.

INTRODUCTION TO CREATIVITY

According to Webster (1990), "Some regard creativity as a term best reserved for geniuses, while others look to the spontaneous songs of the three year old." Can three-year-olds really be creative? Is creativity synonymous with intelligence? Many feel that intelligence is a necessary ingredient for creativity because creative products are high in quality (Sternberg, 2001). However, a painting created by someone may be very high in quality yet not "novel." Also, children who are considered intelligent do not all become successful, creative adults. The environment seems to be a stronger influence on the child's creativity.

Creativity can be viewed in terms of the person who creates, the process that it involves, and the product that is created. There is also a systems element to creativity, because someone, a field of experts, must judge the product as truly novel. In this chapter, we will look at creativity from psychometric, personality traits, cognitive, and systems perspectives. Creativity can be thought of as a way of thinking, a way of being, a way of doing, and a way of interacting.

A Way of Thinking—Psychometric Approach

One way to measure creativity is to quantify it using a psychometric approach. Typically, intelligence or achievement tests are best able to assess **convergent thinking,** in which there is one best solution. In **divergent thinking,** a child brainstorms many possible solutions to an open-ended problem. We can perhaps count the solutions in order to measure creativity. For example, a child can think of many possible ways to mix colors or to play a piano, which can be tallied. Divergent thinking can be viewed as elaborative or creative thinking and easily relates to the arts and creativity.

 A list of commercially available tests of creativity can be found on the accompanying CD-ROM.

In video stream 5 on the accompanying CD-ROM, note how children are using divergent thinking to make structure.

....

Limbic system.   Structures in the brain responsible for emotion and memory.

Convergent thinking.   Deriving one solution from a given problem.

Divergent thinking.   Generating several possible ideas or solutions from a given problem.

A Way of Being—Personality Traits Approach

There are also many characteristic traits of creative persons, as noted by theorists such as Guilford, Torrance, Gardner, and Csikszentmihalyi. These include:

- Fluency in thinking (can produce many ideas)
- Flexibility (can shift from one type of thinking to another)
- Originality (can find unusual and novel ideas)
- Independence (can find ideas without help from others)

What other traits could also be present? The example below demonstrates some characteristics observed by a teacher.

In a group dance circle, flexibility *occurs when a child imitates a three-step movement pattern with the group, and then* independently *improvises her own movements during the song's refrain. Perhaps she comes up with a sequence of four new movements, showing* fluency. *The teacher views her moves as very* original *for her age.*

It certainly seems that this child demonstrates creative traits. Yet, Csikszentmihalyi (1997) notes that children are not truly capable of creativity. It takes many years for the performer or artist to learn his craft and the aesthetics of expression. Certainly, W. A. Mozart was a gifted prodigy at age five. Yet, he did not compose music that would be considered creative in the sense of originality until he first mastered his art form.

A child needn't be contrasted with Mozart. He can discover innovative ways to improvise or create music without first becoming a virtuoso. Thus, we can also view creativity from the child's perspective. He can innovate given his current experience and abilities. The child can change the rules only as he knows them (Beattie, 2000).

In addition to these elements, the child also has the following personality traits, which are noted by Csikszentmihalyi and others:

- Has lots of energy yet can rest and focus diligently on a task
- Is intelligent and playful
- Has a keen imagination and enjoys dramatic fantasy play

A Way of Doing—Cognitive Approach

In order to create or to solve a problem, a person's thinking process must go through the four necessary steps of *preparation, incubation, illumination,* and *verification* (Wallas, 1926; Webster, 1990). These chronological events came from Wallas's theory on discovery.

> ➤ Preparation: Collect ideas and think of a problem.
> ➤ Incubation: "Mill over" ideas at an unconscious and conscious level. Perhaps time away from the task at hand even occurs.
> ➤ Illumination: Discover the solution through insight (the "aha" moment).
> ➤ Verification: Try out the new idea.

In addition, some view evaluation and elaboration of the solution as part of this last stage.

In video stream 7 on the accompanying CD-ROM, note the creative process taking place during this lesson.

The following scenario illustrates the steps involved in creative thinking when working in a group music setting.

During an after school program for primary children, Kelly led her students in singing and performing movements to the song "Down at the Beach." Most students had never seen the ocean or the beach, so afterwards, she asked students to name activities that they enjoy at the local city park. In the preparation *step, Kelly listed each activity on the chalkboard. When one student repeated, "I like to play soccer," after the idea was already given, she validated him and asked what he liked most about soccer. "Scoring a goal" was then written on the board. Through* divergent thinking, *the students listed eight activities that occur in the park. During the* incubation *phase, the group reflected on the activities. Kelly suggested, "If we made our own song, what ones would we put in it?" As the children developed and performed actions for each activity, one child spontaneously replaced the lyric of "Down at the Beach" with "Down at the Park." This was a moment of* illumination. *The children welcomed the idea and, when facilitated by Kelly, created their own* **piggyback** *version. To* verify *the creation, students performed the new song with accompanying movements.*

Perhaps student creativity or contribution to this task could be measured using a chart similar to Table 12–1.

| TABLE 12–1 | Contribution to a Creative Task |

Step in Creative Process	Observed Behavior
Preparation	Gathering materials, brainstorming
Incubation	Problem solving, extending ideas, manipulating materials, experimenting with spatial awareness, developing ideas
Illumination	"The aha experience," making choices, completing tasks
Verification	Performing, presenting, preserving (keeping works), soliciting feedback, recording, videotaping

Piggyback.   A set of new lyrics created to go with a preexisting song melody.

A Way of Interacting—Systems Approach

According to Mihaly Csikszentmihalyi (pronounced "Me-high CHICK-sent-me-high-ee"), three elements (culture, individual, experts) are necessary for creativity to occur:

> ➤ The culture contains aesthetic and symbolic rules such as within an art or music genre.
> ➤ The individual brings novelty to the genre by creating something outside of the norm.
> ➤ The group of experts recognizes it as a valid innovation.

So, creativity does not reside within an individual. It is actually systemic and involves society and culture (Csikszentmihalyi, 1997). It should be pointed out that the teacher is an excellent creativity model for children. The expert can help the individual learn the rules.

What to Look For in Creativity

FLUENCY

- ❑ How many different ways does an infant use to sound a tambourine?
- ❑ A toddler plays how many different rhythms on the drum?
- ❑ How does the child complete a picture theme on different days?

INDEPENDENCE

- ❑ How long does an infant scribble on paper without leaving the work area?
- ❑ What songs does the toddler create during solitary play?
- ❑ Given a piece of construction paper with a shape on it, how does the child complete a picture without assistance?

ORIGINALITY

- ❑ What vocalizations does the infant demonstrate that were not imitative?
- ❑ How does the toddler's dance differ from others of her age group?
- ❑ How does a child's Sculpey figure differ from those made by peers?

DIVERGENT THINKING

- ❑ How many different melodic patterns can a toddler play on the xylophone during a "hello" song?
- ❑ Count the child's number of ideas for ways to use a small kettledrum other than tapping it.
- ❑ How many different drawings can a child demonstrate while incorporating circles on a page?

FOUR-STEP PROBLEM SOLVING

- ❑ How does the child find his theme and elaborate his ideas for a clay sculpture?

❑ What steps does the child show in order to compose a poem or song about a preferred activity?

❑ List what you observe when a group of children create a dance accompaniment for a song.

INTRODUCTION TO ART AND MUSIC DEVELOPMENT

In this chapter we will also look at how art, music, and movement develop in children. It's true that each child is unique and develops at her own pace and according to her own interests. When observing the child, we should be aware of the manner in which she creates.

In the early childhood setting, simply provide the child with a creative environment, lots of materials (i.e., big paper, paints, xylophones, drums), and lots of interest and support without limiting with rules (Gardner, 1982; Lowenfeld & Brittain, 1987). And, while learning art for art's sake, the child also grows cognitively, physically, and socio-emotionally. Researchers are now studying how the creative arts affect cognitive development and perceptual awareness, and how the brain functions when responding to or when making music or art.

DRAWING DEVELOPMENT

You may have noticed that a three-year-old can draw a straight line and may even copy a circle if requested. He may create a more intricate pattern of loops and circles. If you watch carefully, you will see that he is holding his crayon in a more adult-like grasp (pincer grip). He will spend more time on his drawings. The child is developing his motor and cognitive skills as he reaches general benchmarks of drawing development. Although art and all development is continuous, stage theories help define the child's abilities (Kellogg, 1970; Lowenfeld & Brittain, 1987; Malchiodi, 1998).

Before he learns that sounds and sights can be organized as art forms, the child initially has only sensorimotor experience with it. He draws for **kinesthetic** pleasure only at around 18 months of age, pushing a crayon or marker on a large piece of paper repetitively. He pushes a musical toy to

Kinesthetic.   Feeling sensation of gross motor movements, such as in the arms.

get the effect of lights and sounds it emits. Also, he is vocally imitating sounds that he hears. He will learn to express himself and hear and see the immediate feedback from his creations. He will also learn to interpret and influence his world as he moves from kinesthetic to imaginative thinking. We typically view children's two-dimensional and, to a lesser-reviewed extent, three-dimensional artwork in developmental stages. In looking at these, be aware that art development is continuous and, as with all development, context will affect how a child draws (e.g., investment in subject matter). Table 12–2 identifies the stages of drawing development.

TABLE 12–2   Stages of Drawing Development

Stage	Characteristics of Two-Dimensional Art	Pertinent Concepts	Approximate Age
Disorganized or random scribbling	Random marks, large arcs across the paper; horizontal or vertical lines	Kinesthetic pleasure; gross motor movements	1 1/2 years old
Controlled scribbling	Longitudinal or circular patterns; dots on paper; visual awareness of drawing; drawing with intent	Imaginative thinking; increased fine motor control; emotional attachment	6 months after initial scribbling
Named scribbling	Naming scribbles though title/subject matter changes; still appears as scribbling to adult; can copy a circle	Symbolic, abstract thought	3 years old
Early representational (pre-schematic)	Graphic symbols are easier to discern; symbols are constantly changing; "tadpole" human figures are drawn; child exaggerates size or omits according to significance to him; objects seem to revolve around child; color is used subjectively; objects consist of geometric shapes; can copy a square and later a triangle and diagonal	Pincer grip is used; child is egocentric; art is subjective	4 years old
Representational form (schematic)	Symbols are usually drawn in the same manner; color is used more realistically; baseline depicts ground and skyline depicts sky; x-ray and folding over of images are used to depict awareness of environment	Formal operations begin; adult grip is mastered	6–8 years old

Scribbling Stage

At perhaps around 12 or 18 months old, a child scribbles for kinesthetic pleasure only. He enjoys the gross motor movements involved and becomes aware that his motions cause marks to appear on paper. This is *disorganized scribbling*. He does not use fine motor or wrist/hand movements, so big paper (or a wall if not available) is a good surface. You will see him hold the crayon with his fist. He does not visually control his scribbling. Scribbles are initially horizontal, because he moves his arm from side to side. Later scribbles will show vertical patterns.

After a few months, the child discovers that his motions directly affect the marks on the paper. You see that he makes large circular figures and takes his crayon off of the paper to make dots. He is definitely aware of the cause/effect of his scribbling. This is called *controlled scribbling*. Since the child does not name his scribble (which should be accepted), he is not yet thinking symbolically. He just explores and has fun with materials. He reaches for the biggest crayon or the closest cup of paint. (This may account for his choice of color.) You may also observe him filling the entire page with his marks.

Named scribbling occurs at around age three, when the child draws with intent. You will see him hold his crayon with more of an adult grip. He still seems to enjoy the bodily movement in drawing. However, now he perceives that his scribbles have meaning. Perhaps adults saying, "What is that?" or suggesting, "Look at that sun you drew!" prompt

An example of controlled scribbling

An example of named scribbling

Louis draws a tadpole-like figure and a house—early representational art.

this. Once he begins thinking imaginatively, the product will become as important as the process. However, the title for his drawing is somewhat of an afterthought; he will probably even change the title of what his drawing represents later, depending on his emotional state or his current interaction with others or his environment. Although naming scribbles after the fact has been called **romancing**, Davis and Gardner (1992) feel that the child's creation is still credible, that scribble and symbol are not haphazard. These early scribbles are the foundation of later realistic drawings. Also, early scribbles lead to writing and reading.

Early Representational Stage

At around age four, the child intends to represent when he draws. He is in the *early representational* or preschematic stage. Typically, the child's first symbol is a person who is significant to him. The human figure takes on a "tadpole" shape, wherein a circle and lines represent the head and legs. Hands and feet are omitted and eyes are drawn very large. Perhaps these are from the viewpoint of the child who looks down at his own body or of parts that are most significant to him. By age six, his human form will have more detail.

Given paper and magic markers, the child in the early representational stage draws objects according to his subjective views. When you look at his drawings, it is difficult to recognize his subject matter. Items appear randomly arranged on the paper, though they probably revolve around his space and what is significant to him. He may exaggerate size or omit objects according to significance. Color is still subjective, so he may choose yellow because he likes the color or because it represents happiness. However, to a child at this stage, color is not as important as the forms that he creates. When you ask him to tell you about the colors or what he drew, he will readily explain it.

Perhaps you observe a six year old drawing a baseball scene. The pitcher who is throwing a ball may have an arm larger than the other body parts. Children in this stage overexaggerate what is emotionally significant to them. When drawing his family, you may see the child drawing his mother first

---

Romancing.   Labeling or interpreting a created object independent of its creation, not according to its likeness.

Late pre-schematic art

and largest. He places himself immediately next to her. He may even include his pet hamster and almost forget his sister. Yes, the child's drawing is very subjective and egocentric at this age. Objects in his drawing seem to revolve around him.

When the child draws a picture of himself walking or of his family, he may relate an elaborate story to you about the subject matter. He is a *dramatist* and enjoys the social outcomes of creating. Other children are more visual and concerned with the details of their drawing—how it is put together. These children are known as *patterners*.

CULTURAL VARIATION

 Many times we may question a child's interest or motivation to draw because we see her avoiding the art materials, or because we see her being very rigid in her approach to creating and generally lacking in spontaneity. Although some of that has to do with the child's age and general temperament, many times it is related to the child's culture.

Malchiodi (1998) identifies several of the sociocultural influences on children's motivation to draw and attitudes about making art. First, she notes that when compared to children from the United States, children from China preferred to copy from a picture drawn for them rather than to draw freely. She attributes this to a demonstration of respect given to an adult, which is an important quality within Chinese culture. In addition to this collectivism, Su (1995) notes that the practice of learning to write sophisticated Chinese language through copying also affects this. In fact, Su found that at age four, 40 percent of children from China use erasers to correct "errors" when drawing, while only 15 percent of American children use erasers. In traditional Buddhist preschools of Japan, children neatly color in predrawn figures in crayon and then layer it with watercolor (Golomb, 2002).

Therefore, sociocultural influences include how the child is presented or taught art. In China, the brushstroke and the use of washes are significant aspects of painting, while in the United States children are encouraged to develop realism in their work. What the child is taught about art is what is valued in that particular culture, so the child's art will more than likely reflect those values.

Representational Form (Schematic) Stage

By around age seven, the child begins to repeat the same form concept, a **schema,** when drawing objects such as a person, house, or landscape. He is now using *representational form*. In chapter 8, a schema was defined as an organizational or structural pattern in the mind. In art, it refers to drawing a person or landscape in the same order and with the same form. Persons or houses are formed from many geometric shapes, more elaborate than in the previous stage. You may observe that instead of randomly arranging objects on the page the child organizes them on a straight line across the bottom of the page, called a **baseline.** This represents the ground, floor, or wherever the drawn objects are standing. The baseline also can show time or motion. When drawing a hill, the baseline curves, yet objects remain perpendicular to the baseline. Some children draw two baselines to designate depth or may use a skyline to represent the horizon.

Child's self-portrait—representational stage

Schema.   When creating art representing an object, the child uses the same form every time unless an experience changes it.

Baseline.   A drawn line which represents the ground and on which figures stand.

Objects still relate more to the child, the drawer, than to each other. However, he is becoming more aware of his environment. He is so aware that he draws X-ray pictures to show what is going on inside the house that he draws. In order to show objects across the street or river, the child folds over figures so that they are upside down. He is now creating from his perceptions of occurrences rather than the concepts of objects themselves.

Development of Three-Dimensional Artwork

Golomb (2002) studied three-dimensional artwork of children between the ages of two and seven. According to her studies, a two-year-old would probably hold play dough or polymer clay passively, manipulate it without intent, or perhaps hit a table with it (in addition to mouthing it!). At around three years of age, he actively manipulates the clay by pulling, flattening, squeezing, pounding, etc. He gains kinesthetic pleasure, yet does not yet use the clay symbolically. Excitingly, he discovers that rolling the dough on a table makes a long figure, a snake. As imaginative thinking progresses, his lump of clay may represent a car for him. During his third year, similarly to the *named scribbling* stage, the child begins to mold clay into the human figure. Initially, he lengthens the play dough into a crudely shaped column that can be placed upright on a table.

When using clay, the child who is in the early representational stage begins to take clay apart or put pieces together to form objects. When putting pieces together, he typically can add more detail than in the first method. However, there is no right or wrong way.

When working with clay, a child in the representational form stage models a human figure in the same manner repetitively. As in the previous stage, he may assemble the figure by adding pieces (arms, legs, etc.) to a trunk. This is called the analytic method. Or, he may pull the parts out from one lump of clay. This is called the synthetic method (Lowenfeld & Brittain, 1987).

What to Look For in Art Development

SCRIBBLING STAGE

- ❏ How does the small child hold and use art/drawing materials?
- ❏ Does the toddler make horizontal, vertical, or circular marks or dots?
- ❏ Does the small child name the scribble after she draws it? Does the title change over time?
- ❏ When scribbling, how much of the paper does the child cover?
- ❏ What materials does the small child prefer?

EARLY REPRESENTATIONAL STAGE

- ❏ Do the child's human figures have a tadpole shape?
- ❏ How does she arrange drawn objects on the paper?
- ❏ What shapes are used in the child's drawings?
- ❏ What colors does the child use?
- ❏ What items does the child exaggerate or omit when drawing?

REPRESENTATIONAL FORM STAGE

❑ What forms does the child repeat across drawings?

❑ Does the child draw a baseline to represent the ground?

❑ How does the child use color, realistically or subjectively?

❑ How does the child depict things inside a drawn house?

❑ How do the child's drawings differ when she draws preferred subject matter?

THREE-DIMENSIONAL ART

❑ How does the young child manipulate play dough?

❑ Does the young child imitate others around her when forming shapes with clay?

❑ Does the child mold figures by adding or subtracting pieces of clay?

❑ In what order does the child create clay figures of her family?

❑ Does the child create figures in the same way across activities?

MUSIC DEVELOPMENT

Sound is the first sensorial experience for a fetus. While *in utero*, the unborn is first exposed to the rhythms of mother's heartbeat, the sound of her voice, and even the music that she hears. The fetus responds consistently to auditory stimulation by the 28th week. After birth, the newborn baby can recognize and differentiate his mother's voice from other females. Mother probably interacts using motherese, wherein musical and melodic qualities of speech are exaggerated. She sings simple and repetitive lullabies directly in front of the baby, so he can watch her face and mouth intently. The baby's first babbling has musical qualities (Gordon, 1986). This may be imitated by mother, which the baby further assimilates and imitates, closing circles of communication and connecting the two emotionally. Over time, the child will clap hands rhythmically, sing spontaneously during play, and even play a musical instrument. Developing children respond to and create music through all of these actions. We will look at music as it occurs in three primary ways: listening, singing, and moving.

Listening

Music development first begins with *sound awareness*. Does the infant reflexively react to loud sounds by becoming startled and crying? Does she coo when soft, pleasant sounds are heard? At four months, she probably turns her head and locates the source of sounds. This is called *sound localization*. She will then begin to track as sound sources move through her environment (*auditory tracking*). If you sound a rattle or talk while moving past her, she will visually and auditorally follow your path. Or you may find that the infant identifies your voice and that of others through the tonal quality or timbre of sounds (*sound discrimination*).

When a two-year-old listens to music, especially a single voice or instrument without a complex figure ground or background accompaniment, he can discriminate the gross aspects of music. That is, he recognizes melodies and basic concepts of tempo (fast/slow), dynamics (loud/soft), register (high/low), and contour (up or down direction of pitches). Although these concepts are recognized, the young child cannot verbalize them. What other ways can we know that the child discriminates? When rapid notes or high squeaky pitches are played, the young toddler laughs. The child imitates pitches as they are sung to him. He plays the drum loud or soft when modeled. He sounds a kazoo in a wide **glissando** to imitate a siren or fast car. Thus, he is discriminating.

By kindergarten, the child will begin to show awareness of the scalar and rhythmic organization of music. She learns simple songs on the xylophone or piano. She sings "Do Re Mi." She plays a steady rhythm on the drum to a popular song. And she will soon be able to articulate these music concepts as she reaches the stage of formal operations. Table 12–3 shows the development of listening skills.

TABLE 12–3   **Listening Development**

Age	Skill Level	Action	Sample Materials/Procedure for Tester
Birth to 4 weeks	Startle response	Infant turns head toward drum.	Drum/Stand behind child and strike drum
1–2 months	Sound awareness	Turns head to find tambourine.	Bells/Stand behind child and lightly shake tambourine.
3–4 months	Sound localization	Turns head to left or right side, depending on instrument location.	Resonator bells/Stand to the side of child and play bells
4–5 months horizontally, 7–9 months vertically	Auditory/Visual tracking	Maintains eye contact with and follows instrument as it is sounded and moved through space.	Maracas/While shaking maracas, move them through space horizontally or vertically
5–8 months	Sound discrimination	Reacts to sound source according to timbre/tone qualities	Percussion instruments/Play instrument out of view of child
6 months– 1 year	Pitch discrimination	Recognizes phrases of music, melodic contour, and rhythmic differences	Voice or drum/Sing nursery songs; play rhythmic patterns on drum
1.5–4 years	Gross discrimination	Recognizes songs from melody and rhythm; discriminates between fast/slow, loud/soft, same/different; knows rhythmic structure of music	Voice or instrument/Sing folk melodies to child; play contrasting rhythms and dynamics; reinforce concepts with movement
4–8 years	Melodic and rhythmic discrimination	Becomes aware of pitch sets (scales) rather than melodic contours; perceives rhythm and pulse of live and recorded music	Xylophone/Play ascending and descending scales; clap to the beat of sound recording

Adapted from Coleman and Brunk (1995); Hodges (2002); and Campbell and Scott-Kassner (2005)

....

Glissando.   A slide between two pitches or series of notes.

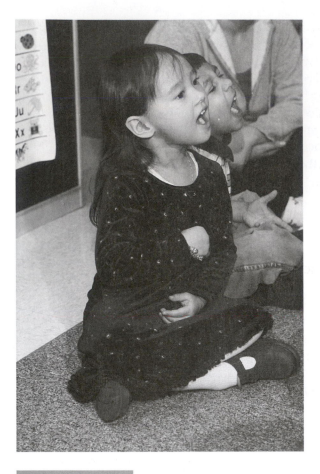

Singing

At three to six months, many infants can successfully match and imitate pitches that are heard. While not yet able to sing melodies, the infant's listening skills are such that he recognizes songs, showing an awareness of the **melodic contour** of music. Through sensorimotor play, the infant or toddler begins to understand music and create it. And even though his motor skills and coordination have not yet developed to make the product "musical," it is the process of making and exploring music that the child enjoys.

A two-year-old sings parts of songs with limited accuracy. He slides in and out of notes. He has difficulty singing large melodic skips and leaps. He may sing along with simple nursery rhymes with few pitches. While he improves at imitating the music of others, he will begin to invent his own songs by age three.

By kindergarten, the child will control his inside/outside voice. He sings loud and soft on cue. His range continues to increase, also. During these primary years, boys typically sing less than girls. It is also difficult to concentrate on singing while performing movements or playing instruments. Refer to Table 12–4 for a hierarchy of vocal development.

TABLE 12–4   **Vocal Development**

Age Range	Observed Behavior
Birth	Produces vocal sounds, babbling
2–3 months	Matches pitch and intensity of music for brief periods
1–2 years	Imitates vocal sounds; does not sing accurately, though imitates melodic contour of songs; when singing, uses glissando between pitches
2 years	Babbles/sings in longer melodies and in small steps; imitates discrete pitches at times
3 years	Invents spontaneous songs; sings entire nursery rhymes and chants; sings accurately at times within four-pitch range (d–g); sings using overall melodic contour consistently
4–5 years	Knows difference between speaking and singing voice; can sing soft and loud; sings in tune within five-pitch range (d–a) and can sing two octaves spontaneously; can sing entire song in the same key
6–7 years	Sings in tune from C to b (almost one octave); has more vocal control of expression

Sources: Adapted from Hodges (2002); Campbell and Scott-Kassner (2005); and Kim (2000)

Melodic contour.   The pattern of higher and lower pitches over time in music.

Moving

A child can both move to music (recorded or performed by others) or can move through music (while creating the sounds herself). Both actions require the child to use her fine or gross motor skills. (Motor development was covered in Chapter 7) Many skills can be applied to music and movement. For example, if the child has stability difficulties, she would be more successful if a conga drum were directly at midline and at a height where she did not have to twist or bend. If a toddler with developmental delays cannot use the pincer grip, she should play a drum with her hands rather than holding a mallet. Understanding motor development can help the child achieve success while being sufficiently challenged.

A baby needs to concentrate intensely when learning new movement tasks. For a toddler, clapping hands requires conscious effort. She does not sustain the claps, clap to the beat, or sing while clapping. Refer to Table 12–5 for stages of movement learning as they relate to music.

Movement has been an important element of learning in music education. For example, music education methods pioneered by Dalcroze, Kodaly, and Orff used movement to help teach children rhythm,

TABLE 12–5   **Movement Learning**

Stage of Movement Learning		Features	Examples
Stage 1	Unknowing inability or ability	Is not aware of the movement; has not attempted the movement.	Child hears guitar but does not realize that it is strummed.
Stage 2	Knowing inability	Is aware of the movement; perceives task as too difficult and has been unsuccessful	Child watches teacher strum; when attempting to strum, fingers become caught between strings
Stage 3	Conscious ability	Thinks about specific aspects of the movement; is moderately successful	Child deliberately draws hand across strings using arm movements; has difficulty controlling dynamics and rhythm
Stage 4	Unconscious ability	Movement is automatic; can attend to or perform other tasks at the same time	Strums for short periods without looking at hand or strings; can sing a simple song while strumming downbeats

Source: Adapted from Landy and Burridge (1999).

melody, and form in an active way. Once rhythm is experienced in the body, it can be generalized to playing instruments, singing, and dancing.

We will classify movement into two main areas: **non-locomotor** and **locomotor.** In non-locomotor movements (axial movements), the child remains in a fixed point on the ground. This typically consists of body percussion activities and instrument play, or dance-in-place (twisting, swaying, etc.). In locomotor movements, the child moves in space along the ground such as walking to the beat and swinging a partner to music.

Non-Locomotor Skills   The toddler probably enjoys banging his fists and hands repetitively on the piano keyboard or hitting pots and pans with a wooden spoon. He is not yet judging or interpreting the sounds; rather, he is exploring through sensorimotor play. At first, rhythm (the beat) of music is not sustained for long periods of time. He may imitate a simple rhythm briefly, but probably prefers to play his own rhythm. In other words, he plays to his own internal beat rather than matching to an external beat (such as a recorded song). Physically he does not yet have the fine motor control to create distinct melodies on a piano or to sustain rhythms on a drum.

When she taps her drum to nursery rhymes or chants, the kindergartner learns about rhythm patterns. In music education, speech is often used to help learn the pulse or beats of music. Perhaps the class chants each student's name, favorite animals, or a classroom theme. A four-step language process to learning movement can be used— *say, say and do, whisper and do, think and do* (Weikart, 2003). The following example illustrates the four steps used in learning rhythm on the drum.

The music teacher needs to assess the children's rhythmic accuracy in his second grade class. He presents a chant, wherein each child takes turns saying breakfast foods rhythmically and repetitively, accenting syllables as needed. One student, Allison, successfully repeats,

SCRAM-bled EGGS and PAN-CAKES

Non-locomotor.   Movement occurs around the body while staying in one place.

Locomotor.   Movement occurs by traveling through space along the ground.

"SCRAM-bled EGGS and PAN-CAKES" (emphasizing downbeats). The teacher then intro-duces a movement to accompany the food chant (tapping knees in a single alternating fashion). Allison says it but does not maintain a beat for each syllable. This is her current ability. After the teacher's modeling and practice, Allison says the chant and taps *the rhythm on her knees. In later sessions, Allison* whispers the chant and taps *it on the drum. She enjoys playing it at dif-ferent tempi and dynamic levels. Lastly, she will* think *of the food and* tap *it on the drum. Per-haps then the skill will generalize to other phrases, rhythmic motives, or instruments.*

In a classroom using the Orff-Schulwerk method, the child learns rhythm and pulse through body percussion. First, hands tap knees or thighs bilaterally on both sides (at the same time) as a **patsch.** It is easier to do this than clap hands at midline for some children. When playing a drum or xylophone, the patsch movement is used to manipu-late or give force to the instrument. For a more complex rhythmic pattern, a clap/patsch or patsch/clap can be used. Later, fingers can snap or feet can stomp to create even more complex patterns. Hands or feet can also tap rhythm unilaterally (one side at a time). Rhythmic competency as it relates to basic non-locomotor movements is out-lined in Table 12–6.

Locomotor Skills   Rhythmic movement combines two elements. One is the element of rhythm, employing time. The other is the element of movement, employing space. For a young child, simple walking in one direction to music is a basic prerequisite skill.

TABLE 12–6   **Non-Locomotor Movements**

Progression of Skills	Non-Locomotor Movement	Without Instrument	With Instrument
Earlier	Single coordinated (parallel bilateral)	Taps hands on legs at the same time	Strikes drum or hand percussion to rhythm of music for brief periods
	Single alternating (alternating bilateral)	Taps one hand on leg, followed by tapping other hand on other leg	Alternates hands and maintains a pulse while drumming; plays piano or xylophone unilaterally (with one hand)
	Double coordinated	Taps hands on legs at the same time, followed by clapping hands or snapping fingers	Strikes two drums in alternating or parallel manner
Later	Combined double coordinated	Taps head, shoulders, knees, and toes	Plays piano bilaterally, with one hand fingering simple melody

Patsch.   Tapping thighs or knees with hands.

The child does not walk to the rhythm or pulse of the music, as he has not reached that stage of listening development. However, he is able to walk as the music is played and stop when the music stops.

As with playing a drum, first a child moves or dances to his own internal beat. His steps will generally be faster than what is comfortable for adults. He can sing or play an instrument while moving, though the rhythm will not be exact. It is difficult for the child to multitask. By early elementary years, the child can perhaps drum while walking to the same pulse. Anyone who has been in a marching band may realize how difficult this can be! Locomotor movements can be found in Table 12–7, arranged from simple to complex.

TABLE 12–7   **Locomotor Movements**

Progression of Skills	Locomotor Movement	Description
Earlier	Simple walking	Locomotion without changing direction, level, or intensity
	Internal rhythmic movement	Using one's own organization of time and space
	External rhythmic movement	Moving to an externally produced beat, such as a drum or a sound recording
	Movement and singing	Singing while performing body movements
Later	Movement and playing	Moving to an external beat that they themselves produce (drumming and walking)

What to Look for in Music Development

LISTENING

- ❏ How does the baby respond to popular music with a fast tempo or classical music with a slow tempo?
- ❏ How does the infant's response differ between hearing a sound recording of a lullaby and a lullaby sung in close proximity to her face?
- ❏ Does the infant track the sound as an instrument or voice moves around her?
- ❏ Does the baby respond differently to a familiar or unfamiliar voice outside of her visual field?

SINGING

- ❏ Does the infant match the pitch of a single note sung in close proximity?
- ❏ Does the infant imitate a simple lullaby for brief or long periods?
- ❏ Does the young child sing song fragments or entire songs during play?
- ❏ Does singing to a recording or singing a cappella (without music accompaniment) change the intonation (ability to sing correct pitch) of the child's voice?
- ❏ What is the range of the child's singing? When using a kazoo, does he hum at a higher pitch when prompted?
- ❏ Does the young child sing spontaneously?

MOVING

- ❏ When the sound of recorded music starts or stops, does the young child start or stop playing her drum? Does she start or stop marching?
- ❏ Does the child sing while performing patsch/clap for the entire song chorus?
- ❏ Does the child play the drum slowly and loudly at the same time, or rapidly and softly?
- ❏ When walking with peers in a circle dance, does the child maintain grasp on a hula hoop, parachute, or resistive exercise band?
- ❏ Does the child match the pulse of the music when she plays the woodblock or claves?
- ❏ When the child walks while holding a drum, does she tap the same rhythm as that of her footsteps?

Of Special Interest—The Child Who Is Artistically Gifted

Giftedness, talent, and creativity can be hard to define. According to Csikszentmihalyi (1997), "Talent differs from creativity in that it focuses on an innate ability to do something very well" (p. 27). In other words, someone can have talent yet not be creative. Likewise, he found that the creative adults he researched did not necessarily demonstrate exceptional talent.

First time use of charcoal by girl age 4 years, 10 months.

While talent often refers to superior abilities in the performing arts or sports or in a single school subject, giftedness often refers to strong skills in academic areas (Pariser & Zimmerman, 2004). Winner (1996) designates the following three primary traits of the gifted child:

1. He shows rapid developmental growth in and masters a domain at a young age.
2. He is extremely motivated to learn as much about the domain as possible.
3. He creates in a way uniquely different from others around him.

So, how do you see artistic giftedness in a young child (Nyman, 1995)?

➢ She shows an early interest in art.
➢ Her fine motor skills and observation skills are advanced.
➢ When drawing, her work is developmentally more advanced than that of peers.
➢ Her drawings are more detailed and naturalistic and represent three dimensions because of a keen perception of the world.
➢ She produces a large number of drawings that seem to tell stories.

The child who is artistically gifted still begins with scribbling and "tadpole" drawings, yet quickly moves beyond these, creating symbolic work by age three. Of course, rapid artistic growth moving toward three-dimensional realism is influenced by our Western culture. Although all children begin with scribbling and representational forms, gifted or talented children of other cultures may be more advanced in brushing techniques or a multiple viewpoint perspective (Su, 1995) or may be more advanced in elaborative stories about their drawings.

It is important to identify the artistically gifted child at an early age so that enrichment and advanced programs can be implemented. However, assessing artistic or musical potential can be difficult, as very young children have had limited experience with the arts. General abilities such as linguistic skills, motor development, and socio-emotional maturity may be also be signs of artistic or creative giftedness (Tannenbaum, 1992). Additionally, a child can be more developed in some areas but not in others (for example, he can have advanced language, yet motor skills are at age level). Scales are commercially available for assessing the artistically gifted child.

A list of commercially available tests of giftedness can be found on the accompanying CD-ROM.

Print the Anecdotal Record from the CD-ROM. Highlight (code) the behavioral indicators of creative (music, art, and general creativity) development. Coding can be done best by using highlighters, colored pencils, or thin-tipped markers.

QUESTIONS TO CONSIDER ○ ○ ○

1. What childhood memories do you have of being creative? What memories do you have of creating art, music, or dance? How was it, or how was it not, nurtured?

2. How does society and culture affect a child's growth in art, music, or movement?

3. When do you feel most creative? Is there a time of day or a mindset that is required?

REFERENCES ○ ○ ○

Beattie, D. K. (2000). Creativity in art: The feasibility of assessing current conceptions in the school context. *Assessment in Education, 7*(2), 175–192.

Campbell, P. S., & Scott-Kassner, C. (2005). *Music in childhood: From preschool through the elementary grades* (3rd ed.). Belmont, CA: Thompson Schirmer.

Coleman, K., & Brunk, B. (1995). *Prelude music therapy assessment kit: Special education edition.* Grapevine, TX: Prelude Music Therapy Products.

Csikszentmihalyi, M. (1997). *Creativity: Flow and the psychology of discovery and invention.* New York: Harper Perennial.

Davis, J., & Gardner, H. (1992). Learning and teaching for aesthetic knowing. In B. Reimer & R. Smith (Eds.), *The arts, education, and aesthetic knowing: Ninety-first yearbook of the national society for the study of education, Part II.* Chicago: The University of Chicago Press.

Gardner, H. (1982). *Art, mind, and brain.* New York: Basic Books.

Golomb, C. (2002). *Child art in context: A cultural and comparative perspective.* Washington, D.C.: American Psychological Association.

Gordon, E. E. (1986). A factor analysis of the music aptitude profile, the primary measures of music audiation, and the intermediate measures of music audiation. *Bulletin of the Council for Research in Music Education, 87,* 17–25.

Guilford, J. P. (1967). *The nature of human intelligence.* New York: McGraw-Hill.

Hetland, L., & Winner, E. (2001). The arts and academic achievement: What the evidence shows. Executive summary. *Arts Education Policy Review, 102*(5), 3–6.

Hodges, D. (2002). Musicality from birth to five. *International Foundation for Music Research News, 1*(1). Retrieved August 24, 2004, from http://www.music-research.org/Publications/V01N1_musicality.html

Kellogg (1970). *Analyzing children's art.* Mountain View, CA: Mayfield Publishing Company.

Kim, J. (2000). Children's pitch matching, vocal range, and developmentally appropriate practice. *Journal of Research in Childhood Education, 14*(2), 152–160.

Landy, J. M., & Burridge, K. R. (1999). *Fundamental motor skills and movement activities for young children.* West Nyack, NY: The Center for Applied Research in Education.

Lowenfeld, V., & Brittain, W. L. (1987). *Creative and mental growth* (8th ed.). Upper Saddle River, NJ: Prentice Hall.

Malchiodi, C. A. (1998). *Understanding children's drawings*. New York: Guilford Press.

Nyman, A. L. (1995). Educating the artistically gifted student in early childhood. In C. M. Thompson (Ed.), *The Visual Arts and Early Childhood Learning*. Reston, VA: National Art Education Association.

Pariser, D., & Zimmerman, E. (2004). Learning in the visual arts: Characteristics of gifted and talented individuals. [Electronic version]. In E. W. Eisner & M. D. Day (Eds.), *Handbook of Research and Policy in Art Education*. Mahwah, NJ: National Art Education Association, Lawrence Eribaum Associates.

Rauscher, F. H., Shaw, G. L., & Ky, K. N. (1993). Music and spatial task performance. *Nature, 365*(6447), 611.

Schellenberg, E. G. (2004). Music lessons enhance IQ. *Psychological Science, 15*(8), 511–514.

Sternberg, R. J. (2001). What is the common thread of creativity? *American Psychologist, 56*(4), 360–362.

Su, C. (1995). A cross-cultural study of partial occlusion in children's drawings. In C. M. Thompson (Ed.), *The Visual Arts and Early Childhood Learning*. Reston, VA: National Art Education Association.

Tannenbaum, A. (1992). Early signs of giftedness: Research and commentary. *Journal for the Education of the Gifted, 15*(2), 104–133.

Torrance, E. P. (1966). *Torrance tests of creative thinking*. Princeton, NJ: Personnel Press.

Wallas, G. (1926). *The art of thought*. New York: Harcourt, Brace and Company.

Webster, P. R. (1990). Creativity as creative thinking. *Music Educators Journal, 76*(9), 22–29.

Weikart, P. S. (2003). *Teaching Movement and Dance: A Sequential Approach to Rhythmic Movement* (5th Ed.). Ypsilanti, MI: High/Scope Press.

Winner, E. (1996). *Gifted children: Myths and realities*. New York: Basic Books.

INTERPRETING OBSERVATIONS
Theoretical Perspectives

What children can do with the assistance of others might be in some sense even more indicative of their mental development than what they can do alone.

—Lev Vygotsky, *Mind in Society*

We ought to regard the breaking of a child's spirit as a sin against humanity.

—Erik Erikson, *Identity and the Life Cycle*

The fact is that people are good, if only their fundamental wishes are satisfied, their wish for affection and security. Give people affection and security, and they will give affection and be secure in their feelings and their behavior.

—Abraham Maslow

Creativity is a central source of meaning in our lives . . . most of the things that are interesting, important, and human are the results of creativity . . . [and] when we are involved in it, we feel that we are living more fully than during the rest of life.

—Mihalyi Csikszentmihalyi

Cognitive and Language Theory

CHAPTER OBJECTIVES

- To understand components of cognitive and language theory

- To identify aspects of theory related to the development of children

- To relate developmental theory to specific examples of development

- To analyze a specific child's development as it relates to developmental theory

CHILD STUDY OBJECTIVES

Upon conclusion of this chapter the student will:

- use theory to interpret and understand anecdotal records.

- use theory to interpret and understand checklists.

- use theory to interpret and understand structured play observations.

- use theory to interpret and understand visual documentation.

- use theory to interpret and understand parent questionnaires.

- analyze and synthesize developmental theory to write developmental summaries.

INTRODUCTION TO THEORIES OF CHILD DEVELOPMENT

If you are like most students, studying theory is not even on your "top ten things to do with my day" list. Many people view theory as speculative and unrelated to the reality of how children actually grow and develop. Through the use of observations, interviews, and analysis we gather useful facts about the child, his family, and his development. Data collected through checklists and visual documentation adds to the body of knowledge regarding an individual child. Information such as the average height of a two-year-old, the development of the pincer grasp, and the onset of puberty are all facts. It is the *facts* of development that are collected during an in-depth child study.

Theory is an explanation of how the facts fit together. Theory can help determine which facts are most important for understanding a child. It can help to clarify how relationships among and between facts are significant. Theory is what makes sense out of facts. Without theory, facts remain a clutter of documentation, unconnected and unrelated to how and why children grow up as they do.

ANECDOTAL RECORD 13–1

Child's Name: Vicky

Date: September 22

Time: 10:09 a.m.

Observer: A. Kovacik

Location: Oak School Kindergarten

Six-year-old Vicky complained to the art teacher that Michael had more clay than she did. The teacher assured Vicky that she measured each child's clay on a scale and each child had the same amount. Vicky insisted that Michael had more. The teacher went with Michael and Vicky to the scale where each child weighed the clay. Sure enough the portions were equal. Both children agreed that they were the same. Vicky and Michael went back to their seats. Once again Vicky complained that Michael had more clay. The teacher reminded Vicky that the portions were the same when they were measured. She walked Vicky back to her seat and noticed that Michael had rolled his clay into a long snake while Vicky's clay remained in a ball. The teacher leaned over the table and rolled Vicky's clay into a long snake. "Now are they the same." Vicky smiled and said, "Yes, thank you."

The facts provided by this anecdotal record do very little to explain what motivated Vicky in her quest for equal amounts of clay. Theory helps us look at facts from different

----

Theory.   The analysis of a set of facts in their relation to one another.

perspectives. As you read this chapter, consider Vicky and her clay dilemma. Which theories can help you better understand the facts of this anecdotal record?

PIAGET'S COGNITIVE-DEVELOPMENTAL THEORY

Jean Piaget was intrigued that, when interviewed, children gave the same sort of "wrong answer" to his questions. Not only did children share misconceptions, they also justified their answers in similar ways. Piaget could see "intelligence at work where others could only see childish mistakes" (Peterson & Felton-Collins, 1986). Those mistakes fueled more than sixty years of investigation, as Piaget interviewed, observed, and wrote about children's cognitive development.

Piaget's investigation of children's cognitive development included how children think, know, perceive, remember, recognize, abstract, and generalize. During his investigation Piaget discovered that children who are about the same age think and process information in a similar manner to one another. Additionally, he recognized that a child's thinking is different from that of an adult. Not only does the child process less information than the adult, but that information is processed in a very different way. Another key idea Piaget held was that development progresses through a fixed sequence of stages. He identified four stages of development, termed *sensorimotor, preoperational, concrete operational,* and *formal operational.* Each stage of development differs from the next, but each incorporates the previous stage (see Figure 13-1).

Sensorimotor Stage

During the **sensorimotor stage** of development the child relies on his senses to explore the world. In fact, for a young child, the best way to learn about an object is to taste it. Mouthing is common during this stage, as it helps children "come to know" the world around them. Infants organize their physical actions, sucking, grasping, and hitting, so that they can interact with the surrounding world. Understanding *object permanence,* or learning that things still exist even when they cannot be seen, is an important task of this stage (Peterson & Felton-Collins, 1986.) The following account of a game of peek-aboo is an example of object permanence.

FIGURE 13–1   **Each stage builds on the prior stage—new learning builds on prior learning.**

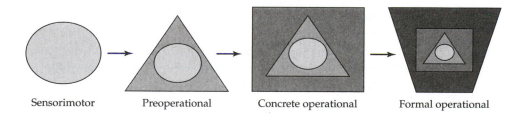

| Sensorimotor | Preoperational | Concrete operational | Formal operational |

Sensorimotor stage.   The first major stage of cognitive development, when the child uses sensory and motor skills to gain knowledge.

ANECDOTAL RECORD 13–2

Child's Name: Marcus

Date: January 10

Time: 10:15 a.m.

Observer: Miss Beth

Location: Samaritan Early Education Center

Eight-month-old Marcus sits with me on the floor during playtime. With both hands, I hold a scarf up in front of Marcus and say, "Where is Marcus? I can't find Marcus." Marcus pulls on the scarf with his right hand and peeks over the top. He laughs. I laugh and say, "There he is! I found Marcus. Peekaboo!" I cover a toy truck located on the floor between us with the scarf. Marcus watches my actions. I ask, "Where did the truck go?" Marcus pulls the scarf off of the truck. He laughs. "There it is. Marcus found the truck! Peekaboo truck, we see you."

Preoperational Stage

During the **preoperational stage,** the child still relies on his senses to gain understanding of the world, but increasingly uses words to represent things and ideas. Thought is **egocentric;** the child views the world from his own perspective and in fact is unaware that other viewpoints exist. The preoperational child reasons and explains events on the basis of intuition or magical thought. The preoperational child begins to understand concepts of past, present, and future. However, children in this stage still have difficulty understanding how steps of a project fit together as a whole. For example, a three-year-old child may actively participate in mixing ingredients for baking bread and when the bread is finished the child may report that it is soft and good to eat because the cook has magic oven mitts.

Like the sensorimotor stage, the preoperational stage includes developmental tasks in which children engage. The preoperational stage spans approximately five years. Therefore, characteristics of the period will not be obvious in the youngest of the group. These developmental tasks include *egocentrism, centration, irreversibility,* and *animism.*

Egocentrism   As mentioned above, egocentrism is quite simply the child's inability to take the perspective of another. Additionally, preoperational children seem to think that others know what it is they are thinking, seeing, or doing. A three-year-old who talks on the telephone with grandma will likely hold up toys and discuss events as if grandma were present in the room. A game of hide-and-seek with young preoperational

....

Preoperational stage.   The second major stage of cognitive development, marked by the ability to use symbols and language.

Egocentric.   A cognitive state where the individual views only his own perspective.

thinkers, where the child stands in clear view of others covering her own eyes and expecting that she cannot be seen, is another demonstration of egocentric thought.

Centration   The task of **centration** refers to the child's ability to concentrate on only one characteristic or attribute of an object at a time. The preoperational child's thinking does not allow him to focus on more than one attribute at a time, making problem solving challenging. For example, a child given wooden beads to sort, some of which are blue and some that are orange, will likely be able to sort them accurately by color. The child may also be able to report which color has greater representation. He may report that there are four blue beads and six orange beads. However, having focused or centered on color, he may not be able to accurately report whether there are more orange beads than wooden beads. The preoperational thinker focuses on appearance and finds it difficult to consider that someone is simultaneously a nurse and a mother. But the preoperational child does engage in classification and seriation tasks. *Classification* and *seriation* are based on how things are related. Classification or sorting focuses on how objects are the same in aspects such as color, shape, or texture, while seriation or ordering focuses on how things differ.

Irreversibility   **Irreversibility** refers to the preoperational child's inability to reverse logical operations. For example, the equation $3 + 2 = 5$ may be understood by a four-year-old, but when asked to produce 3 again he may not produce $5 - 2 = 3$. This inability is often seen in tasks of conservation. *Conservation* refers to the ability to understand that, when unchanged, quantities of objects continue to have the same amount or volume regardless of their shape. Take, for example, a dinner conversation with three-year-old Timothy. He complained that he could not finish the roast beef on his plate because "it is too big." After the meat was cut into small pieces Timothy reported, "Now I can eat it—it is not so much." Preoperational thinkers may understand that the number or amount is the same until the order or arrangement is changed. See Figure 13–2 for an example of this conservation of number.

FIGURE 13–2   Conservation of number.

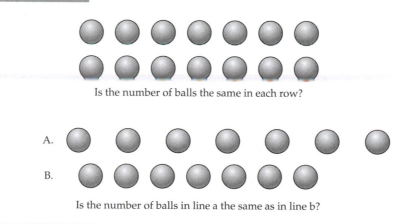

Is the number of balls the same in each row?

A.

B.

Is the number of balls in line a the same as in line b?

Centration.   Piaget's term for the child's ability to deal with more than one aspect of a problem at any one time.

Irreversibility.   The inability of the preoperational child to understand that operations can be reversed.

When in reverse, which train car exits the tunnel first?

Animism   Animism is the child's belief that the world and the objects in it are alive. Ideas of animism change to more scientific understanding as the child grows; however, even adults sometimes display this type of thinking. A child may report that the snowman is cold when left outdoors or that the door is bad for pinching his fingers, much like an adult who kicks his stalled automobile.

Animism.   When the child believes that the world around him is alive.

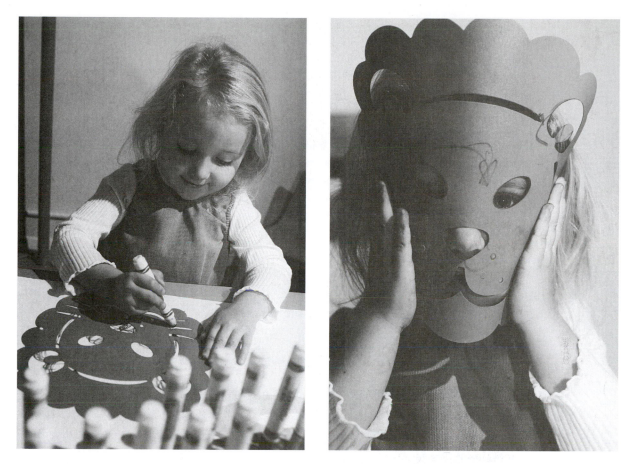

Preoperational children have difficulty distinguishing the person behind the mask. Will other children her age know who she is behind the mask? Will she think she is changed?

Concrete Operational Stage

Much more logical, a child in the **concrete operational stage** is developing an understanding of number and relationships. Problems are considered and solved mentally, although still in terms of concrete objects. The term **concrete** does not necessarily mean that the child needs to see or manipulate a real object (although that is helpful) but that the child needs to perceive the object, either directly or through imagination. **Operations,** or actions carried out mentally rather than physically, are what sets the concrete operational thinker apart from the preoperational thinker. For example, two-year-old Adin pours a pint of milk into his cup, causing it to overflow onto the table and floor. His surprise is expressed in an audible gasp, as the cold milk soaks his shirt and shorts. Nine-year-old Aaron understands that the carton contains more milk than the cup can

....

Concrete operational stage.   The period of cognitive development characterized by the child's ability to internalize actions and rules in thinking.

Concrete.   Capable of being perceived by the senses; not abstract or imaginary.

Operations.   Actions carried out mentally, rather than physically.

accommodate and he either leaves some milk in the carton or uses a larger cup. Aaron is able to internalize or carry out his actions in thought without the need to physically spill milk.

The concrete operational child is beginning to understand conservation and reversibility. She understands that objects or quantities remain constant even when their appearance has changed. She can reverse the order of operations, drastically increasing her mathematical ability. These new skills are the result of her ability to decenter her attention or recognize that two or more dimensions of an event interact to produce a given result. Children enjoy humor that reflects their developmental levels. For example, an interest in riddles appears between ages six and eight. During this time concrete operational thought processes are developing, allowing children to reverse ideas mentally. Jokes containing double meanings (puns) or implied meanings (based on illogical behavior) are also enjoyed in middle childhood (Crain, 2000).

If you understand these jokes, you may be a concrete operational thinker.

- Why wouldn't the canary pay for his date's dinner? He was too cheep.
- What kinds of waves are impossible to swim in? Microwaves.
- Why was the chicken team so bad at baseball? They kept hitting fowl balls.
- Why was the rabbit so unhappy? He was having a bad hare day.

Source: Weitzman, Blank, and Green (2000).

Formal Operational Stage

The child in the **formal operational stage** is able to think in terms of abstractions. The child is able to hypothesize and theorize as he demonstrates new understanding of logical-mathematical and spatial-temporal types of learning. Thinking is more organized and systematic, relying less on trial and error by the young thinker. Although adults possess the ability to engage in formal operations, few of us use these skills because daily life rarely requires them. That said, the algebra student may perform better on measures of formal operations than his parent. Table 13–1 outlines Piaget's four stages of cognitive development.

Observations That Could Be Linked to Piaget's Theory of Development

- ❑ Does the child seek objects or toys that are out of sight?
- ❑ Does the child explore items orally?
- ❑ Does the child attribute life characteristics to inanimate objects?
- ❑ Does the child engage in pretend or representational play?
- ❑ Does the child become upset when events don't match his current level of understanding?

Formal operational stage.   Fourth stage of cognitive development, in which the child is able to organize ideas or hypothetical situations as well as objects.

| TABLE 13-1 | Piaget's Stages of Cognitive Development |

Age Range	Stage	Behavior
0–2 years	Sensorimotor	Children learn through senses and reflexes.
2–6 years	Preoperational	Children use symbolic thinking, including language, to understand the world. Thought is egocentric, causing a child to understand the world from his own perspective.
6–11 years	Concrete operational	Children understand and apply logical operations to interpret experiences logically and rationally.
12–adult	Formal operational	Adolescents and adults think in abstractions and reason analytically.

MONTESSORI'S PHILOSOPHY

Maria Montessori is most known for developing a method of teaching that is very influential in early childhood education. In reality, it is not so much her method of teaching that lives on but rather her philosophy concerning the development of the human spirit. What many people do not realize about Montessori's philosophy, however, is that it developed out of continual observation of children and experimentation with various teaching techniques. As a result of extensive observation and research, Montessori formed several key concepts in the field of child development.

Sensitive Periods

Montessori was the first theorist to talk about *sensitive periods* of development. Sensitive periods are those times during a child's development when the child is driven by some inner force to learn something and to achieve an inner peace or, in other words, reach a state of normalization. Montessori identified several distinct sensitive periods in a child's development.

The first sensitive period of a child's development occurs in the first three years of life. This sensitive period is demonstrated as a strong need for order. Children place and replace items and objects in the proper location. On a practical level this may speak to the young child's insistence on ritual and predictable schedules. Between ages one and two children fix their attention on detail. They notice small spiders and shiny buttons or, when looking at a book, point to an inconspicuous "kitty" pictured on a page. During this time children demonstrate a sensitive period for the use of their hands. They open, shut, fill, dump, grasp, and manipulate. As children grow they become sensitive to touch as they explore objects and textures with closed eyes. Montessori described the sensitive period for walking as a second birth, as the child passes from a helpless to an active being (Crain, 2000). Children are driven by the desire to walk so much that they walk simply to do so, without a specific destination in mind.

As the child begins to walk and gains greater mobility, he enters into a sensitive period for independent skill development. It is during this time that the child insists on independent acts such as dressing, eating, toileting, bathing, playing, etc. It is important, under Montessori theory, for the adult to allow the child to engage in these acts even though the child may experience mild frustration during the task and it may be more time-consuming.

ANECDOTAL RECORD 13–3

Child's Name: Melissa

Date: February 3

Time: 9:15 a.m.

Observer: D. Ahola

Location: Gateway Montessori Classroom

Two-year-old Melissa toddles into her classroom on Monday morning. Mom comes in behind her and immediately walks over to the teacher to talk to her. "I'm sorry we're late," Mom says to the teacher. "I couldn't get her to keep her pants on this morning—she kept taking them off and putting them back on. I would walk away for one minute and her pants would be off again! We'd put them on again and just that fast she'd take them off. I don't know what to do!" The teacher replied with a smile, "Don't worry. I think I know what's happening. We'll work with her today." The teacher had an idea about what was happening and an idea about what to do about it. When the teacher caught up to Melissa she was just outside the bathroom and sure enough she had taken off her pants and was beginning to put them back on again. The teacher said, "Melissa, would you like to try to put on some different pants today?" Melissa nodded her head yes. So the teacher took her over to a quiet area and gave her five more pairs of pants (toddler size). Melissa stayed in the area, putting on and taking off pants for the next hour. After the hour she put on her own pants and came out and said, "I'm ready" and she went to play in the water table.

This is clearly an example of a sensitive period for dressing oneself—another step toward independence. If given enough time and practice, Melissa will work on the skill until she has mastered it or until she is "ready."

Another sensitive period involves the acquisition of language. In the learning of language, children focus on words, meanings, and grammar. When a child is in a sensitive period for learning to read, his focus is on activities that will get him to a level of mastery. At these times it is the job of the educator (or teacher, parent, peer) to give the instruction and resources necessary to reach the goal. Montessori also made it clear that it is imperative to observe the child carefully for the emergence of sensitive periods, so as to teach skills related to the child's interest. So, rather than having a set age at which to teach specific skills, the Montessori teacher watches for the child's timetable to direct instruction. Montessori viewed it as not only useless but harmful to try to teach a child something that he is not sensitive to learning. It is useless because the child will not respond, it is harmful because precious time is being wasted on something that the child is not sensitive to, and besides, what he is sensitive to is quickly fading. "As soon as children find something that interests them they lose their instability and learn to concentrate" (Montessori, 1966).

Observations That Could Be Linked to a Sensitive Period

- ❑ The child gets completely absorbed in something.
- ❑ The child does not want to stop engaging in an activity.
- ❑ Even though the child may have difficulty with something, she keeps trying.
- ❑ The child "plays around" with the skill or concept.
- ❑ After the child engages in the activity or exercise for a period of time, he comes away with a sense of satisfaction and peace.

Absorbent Mind

Infant and young child minds are likened to sponges under Montessori's principle of the absorbent mind. This means that everything that the young mind is exposed to is taken in and absorbed; formal teaching is unnecessary for learning to take place. For example, consider how children learn language. The child does not have to be taught how to speak—she learns it naturally. Therefore, by providing experiences in which the child can engage and observe the natural world she will learn without formal instruction. Montessori considered sensory experience and keen observation key to learning for young children.

Observations That Could Be Linked to the Absorbent Mind

- ❑ Does the child keenly observe?
- ❑ Does the child self-teach?
- ❑ Does the child watch an activity many times before trying it himself and when he does, is he successful?
- ❑ Does the child use new vocabulary after only hearing it once or twice?

Inner Peace

A critical piece of Montessori theory is the development of inner peace. Inner peace develops as the child is free to explore the prepared environment and is free of adult constraints such as time and direction. When the child has gained a sense of inner peace she has reached what Montessori termed *normalization*. When the child attains normalization she can fully explore the environment and absorb all it has to offer.

The Montessori philosophy of education includes ideas about independence, concentration, free choice, and gradual preparation. Montessori educators do not direct or instruct children, but rather provide opportunities for children's independent mastery. The assumption is that if the environment includes the proper materials, those that reflect the child's inner needs, then children will enthusiastically work on their own. To create the right environment, the Montessori educator observes and interviews children. With the correct materials children are free to concentrate on those tasks that are

A child's sense of inner peace develops through listening to the inner voice.

most meaningful. Take, for instance, the following situation, which Maria Montessori experienced herself. A girl was placing different-sized cylinders in the holes of a wooden frame until she had them all in place. She immediately took them out and repeated the task. In fact the girl repeated the sequence 42 times, in spite of Montessori's efforts to distract her. When given tasks that meet inner needs at sensitive periods, the child is tenaciously focused (Crain, 2000).

VYGOTSKY'S SOCIAL-HISTORICAL THEORY

Lev Vygotsky felt that the child's development is influenced by family, community, socioeconomic status, education, and culture. As children and adults interact, they share values and beliefs that influence learning and ultimately development. Speaking one to another helps children understand new concepts and ideas, thus influencing their learning. For Vygotsky, play is the language arena where children discuss, negotiate, pretend, and explore new experiences (Mooney, 2000).

Zone of Proximal Development

Two key ideas put forward by Vygotsky are the zone of proximal development and scaffolding. The **zone of proximal development** is the distance between the most difficult task the child can accomplish unassisted and the most difficult task the child can do

....

Zone of proximal development.   The Vygotskian concept of the range of skills that are within the child's reach but not currently mastered (see Figure 13–3).

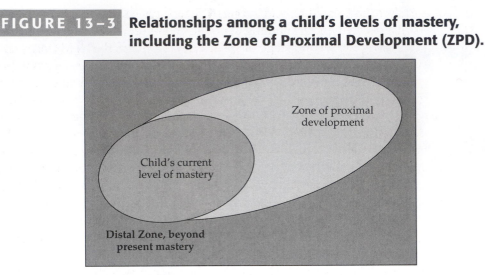

FIGURE 13-3   Relationships among a child's levels of mastery, including the Zone of Proximal Development (ZPD).

with help. For example, a young child who is currently pulling himself up and cruising around the furniture can do so independently, but he needs assistance to walk from one point to another. This assistance comes in the form of an adult holding the child's hands or providing a sturdy push toy. Although there are many gross motor skills that the child has not yet mastered, walking is the next skill that the child will accomplish independently and therefore is in the child's zone of proximal development.

Scaffolding

As the adult supports, or scaffolds, the child's approximations to walking, she offers assistance with the skill until the child walks independently. **Scaffolding** requires careful observation so that adults can determine where children are in their learning process and where they are capable of going, given their individual needs and the context in which they develop.

Stages of Speech Development

Vygotsky's studies led him to believe that language provides the shared experience necessary for building cognitive development. He concluded that speech development proceeds through four stages and is governed by the same mental structures that govern other tasks requiring signs or symbols, such as counting and memorizing with visual cues.

The first stage of speech is called the *primitive* or *natural stage*. This stage represents the time before language is part of conscious thought and spans from birth through the second year. Initially this stage is reflexive and includes sounds such as crying, cooing, and babbling. Soon, however, it expands to include sounds that are social reactions to other

---

Scaffolding.   The process by which a caregiver structures learning experiences to lead the child to the next level of learning.

people, such as laughter and gurgles. The next phase of "thoughtless" speech includes the words that are typically naming in nature and reinforced through conditioning.

During the second stage of speech development, the child learns that words have a symbolic function. The child actively seeks out the words for objects in his environment, greatly increasing his vocabulary. Language and thought begin to merge. At this time the child begins to use tools in a purposeful way toward a desired end.

The third stage, or egocentric speech, emerges out of the child's understanding that the words he says have a relationship to objects in his environment. **Inner speech** makes up a large portion of the language used by the preschool child, particularly during play. This speech takes on the form of a running monologue that accompanies the child's play, whether with others or alone. A child may use speech during play to describe what he is doing, such as, "Now the truck is going up and it is heavy and the people yell, 'Help, help.'" No response is required, since the child is not directing the speech toward any one person. Vygotsky viewed inner speech as an important new tool of thought. Not only does the child think to speak but the speech itself informs and modifies the child's thoughts. To test his ideas about speech, Vygotsky set up problems to arise during the play situations of young children. A pencil might be missing, or paper that was too big or too small was left for the child. It appears that children exhibited much greater levels of inner speech during these times than during times when they did not experience a problem (Thomas, 1992).

At about age seven, egocentric speech becomes less apparent. Vygotsky believed that speech moved to a more internalized mode, that soundless speech is employed as children gain greater skills in manipulating ideas mentally. Throughout the rest of life people use a combination of egocentric and soundless speech as tools of thought. Think about the last time you spoke to yourself while solving a difficult problem.

ANECDOTAL RECORD 13–4

Child's Name: Julia

Date: March 3

Time: 10:30 a.m.

Observer: Mrs. Thomas

Location: ABC Nursery School

Three-year-old Julia gathers a doll and a blanket in the housekeeping area. She takes off her shoes and says, "My shoes are off. Now my feet don't have shoes." Julia positions her doll on her hip and sits on the floor. She says, "I will go to bed with the baby." She sits up and reaches over her body with her right arm as she is holding the doll in her left arm. She pulls the blanket over her body and says, "I cover up. I lay down. I go to sleep."

It appears that Julia's inner speech mirrors her motor behavior.

....

Inner speech.   Private, running monologue used by children to support thought.

Stages in Conceptual Thought Development

Using a set of wooden blocks of various shapes, colors, and sizes, Vygotsky tested how children approached problems. On the bottom surface of each block was written one of four nonsense words. Based on the assumption that conceptual thinking is a function of organizing the environment by abstracting and labeling, Vygotsky outlined three major stages of the development of conceptual thought. Basically, Vygotsky examined how children group things that are the same and different.

In the first stage, thinking is unorganized. The child puts things in groups and labels those groups based on chance. Behaviors include trial and error grouping, random grouping, and blind guessing. Stage two, *thinking in complexes,* occurs when the child organizes objects in a concrete and factual manner rather than in an abstract way. The child may sort by color, shape, or nearness of objects to each other. Children may establish collections of objects, such as generating groups of blocks that all contrast. For example, a spoon, a fork, a knife, a cup, and a plate all make up a place setting. Children may link items to make a chain, or attend to grouping in a manner that puts some items with others based on one attribute. The placing of a trapezoid with triangles because the "points" are the same falls into this category. The third and final level of conceptual thought involves the process of synthesizing and analyzing. Vygotsky considered the beginnings of abstract thought to be the point at which children identified ways in which objects were maximally similar. The next step to abstraction involves selecting items with a single characteristic. The final step occurs when the child accurately synthesizes all the attributes to create a new grouping (Thomas, 1992).

Observations That Could Be Linked to Vygotsky's Theory of Cognitive Development

- ❑ Does the child show approximations toward greater complexity in skills?
- ❑ Does the child use speech to organize thoughts?
- ❑ Does the child engage in egocentric speech during play?
- ❑ Does the child sort objects and materials in an organized manner?

SKINNER'S BEHAVIORIST THEORY

Burrhus Frederic Skinner was an American behaviorist. He was a pioneer of experimental psychology who sought to understand behavior as a function of environmental influences and reinforcement. He is most noted for his ideas on **operant conditioning.** Operant conditioning is the changing or modification of behavior through environmental responses or reinforcement. When the behavior increases, it is assumed to have been reinforced; a decrease in behavior is related to punishment.

For B. F. Skinner, speech, language, and other means of communication were viewed as behaviors. Thus a baby making vocal sounds accidentally hits upon "da, da," elicits a positive response from his father, who reinforces the likelihood that the child

----

Operant conditioning.   The changing or modification of behavior through environmental responses or reinforcement.

will repeat the sound due to the desire to elicit the same response. Furthermore, Skinner made the assertion that the structure of a sentence consists of associations among the words in the sentence. For example, the child understands the words "boy" and "run" and upon hearing them used in a sentence ("The boy is running.") imitates the adult by saying "boy run." The child is said to learn all aspects of language through positive reinforcement. However, since spoken language does not generally represent proper language, it seems unlikely that children learn to speak and use the rules of language in this manner alone (Thomas, 1992).

BANDURA'S SOCIAL LEARNING THEORY

Albert Bandura's ideas regarding the way children learn are closely aligned with behaviorist theory. He does, however, differ on four important points: (1) how children acquire a new behavior, (2) how children learn from models, (3) how consequences influence future actions, and (4) how complex behaviors develop (Thomas, 1992).

How Children Acquire a New Behavior

Although many behaviorists believe that child's behavior is the result of trial and error, or random actions that are learned through reinforcement, Bandura felt that children reproduce actions that they have observed. Bandura's theory focuses on children's learning as the result of watching other people. **Observational learning** has been observed in many cultures. Tribal girls in Guatemala learn to weave from watching an older woman model the process. Bandura referred to this as *no-trial learning*, meaning that the child acquires learning all at once by using observation exclusively. Additionally, Bandura considers another form of imitation called **incidental learning.** This learning occurs when the child has nothing to gain from reproducing the behavior but rather stores the information until a later time when it may be useful. Bandura viewed learning through observation as a cognitive function, since the child forms a mental representation of observations and then creates structures by which the same work can be demonstrated. Table 13–2 outlines the components of observational learning.

How Children Learn from Models

Children learn from models because the observed behavior may prove useful at some future time. In order for children to learn from a model they must engage in the following functions: attend, remember, reproduce, and desire. Children need to attend to the behaviors of the model without being distracted by incidental actions. Once attending, the child has to do something with the new information in order to remember it. Young children use visual cues for memory. The younger the child, the less he understands

----

Observational learning.   Learning that occurs as a function of observing, retaining, and replicating behavior observed in others.

Incidental learning.   Gaining information in an informal manner and storing it for later use.

TABLE 13-2   Components of Observational Learning

Attentional processes	Attention is required to model what has been seen. Governed by the needs and interests of the observer.	Television presents a powerful model for children's imitation.
Retention processes	Children make symbolic associations to remember behaviors for later use. Children use a variety of codes for memory, including visual and verbal. However, children under five rely on visual codes, since verbal codes are not as familiar.	Young children do not yet understand that they cannot remember everything; they do not yet have an understanding of metacognition.
Motor reproduction processes	Reproduction of behavior relies on physical motor ability. Young children may not yet have developed these motor skills.	A child may watch a man play football, but he lacks the coordination to imitate the behavior. With maturation and practice he will eventually demonstrate the skill.
Reinforcement and motivational processes	Not all observed behavior is reproduced by the child. The child reproduces behavior based on individual needs, interests, and rewards.	If a child observes another child who is rewarded for sitting quietly, he will sit quietly also and may or may not continue based on the child's own needs and interests.

Source: Crain (2000).

metacognition, or thinking about thinking. In other words, young children don't know that they will forget information without engaging in a task to remember it. Children engage in motor reproduction as a means of learning. Young children with limited motor skill may not be able to accurately reproduce modeled behavior. Children engage in approximations of the behavior until they are able to reproduce it accurately. Lastly, motivation is a factor in the child's reproduction of modeled behavior. The behavior may not meet the child's current need and therefore is not reproduced (Thomas, 1992).

How Consequences Affect Learning

For Bandura, consequences do not directly reinforce a child's behavior in an immediate fashion but are rather regulators for future behavior. If each time a student raises his hand in class the teacher yells at him for interrupting, other children will likely view the consequence as a deterrent to their own future hand-raising behavior. As children observe others and notice what consequences others experience from their behavior,

....

Metacognition.   Knowledge of one's own thinking processes; knowing what one knows and how one learns.

they determine their own desire to engage in the same behavior. Bandura referred to his concept as **vicarious learning.**

Development of Complex Behavior

Patterns of behavior or complex behavior are acquired in their entirety rather than in a slow, gradual process of reinforcement. After observing a model the child generally reproduces or imitates the entire behavior pattern without reinforcement. However, even complex behaviors, once learned, may not be demonstrated until the child is motivated to do so. For Bandura, modeling is a feature of the socialization process of behavior. Aspects of social behavior considered relevant to social learning theory are aggression, gender roles, prosocial behavior, self-regulation, and *self-efficacy* or self-evaluation.

Observations That Could Be Linked to Bandura's Social Learning Theory

- ❑ Does the child attend to what others are doing?
- ❑ Does the child attempt to remember observed behavior?
- ❑ Does the child imitate the behavior of others?
- ❑ Does the child regulate her own behavior based on the consequences received by others who engage in the same behavior?

GARDNER'S THEORY OF MULTIPLE INTELLIGENCES

Howard Gardner developed the theory of *multiple intelligences.* This theory identifies the different ways that individuals come to know or understand the world around them. While each of us has the potential to learn through all the intelligences, some of them become more dominant than others. Gardner originally identified seven types of intelligences, but recently added more. He also states that there are certainly more types of intelligences that have not yet been uncovered but exist nonetheless. Figure 13–4 lists the recognized intelligences and relevant information.

Observations That Could Be Linked to Gardner's Theory of Multiple Intelligences

- ❑ Does the child have a preferred type of activity (one of the identified intelligences)?
- ❑ In dramatic play situations, what role does the child typically take?
- ❑ Does the child have a specific way of showing how he learns best?
- ❑ If the child is going to produce something that demonstrates his learning, what form does it take (story, picture, creation)?

Resources for assessing multiple intelligences appear on the accompanying CD-ROM.

Vicarious learning.   Learning through observation. Gaining knowledge without actually engaging in the experience physically.

FIGURE 13-4   **Gardner's multiple intelligences.**

1. **Linguistic intelligence (word smart)** refers to the ability to manage language, both written and spoken, effectively. Those individuals who have strengths in linguistic intelligence have the ability to learn languages easily and express themselves poetically.
   - Thinks: in words
   - Loves: reading, writing, telling stories, and playing word games
   - Needs: books, tapes, writing tools, journals, discussions, debates, and stories

2. **Logical-mathematical intelligence (number smart)** consists of high levels of mathematical understanding with an ability to analyze problems logically. Strengths are demonstrated in scientific thinking.
   - Thinks: by reasoning
   - Loves: experimenting, questioning, calculating, and figuring out logic puzzles
   - Needs: items to think about and explore, manipulative toys, puzzles, brain teasers, analogies, and calculators

3. **Musical intelligence (music smart)** involves the ability to understand and perform music. Those with musical intelligence demonstrate the ability to recognize and repeat tones, rhythms, and pitches.
   - Thinks: via rhythm and melodies
   - Loves: singing, whistling, humming, tapping feet, and clapping hands
   - Needs: sing-along time, background music, trips to concerts, and instruments

4. **Bodily-kinesthetic intelligence (body smart)** includes the use of the whole body or parts of the body to solve problems.
   - Thinks: through body sensations
   - Loves: dancing, running, building, gesturing, and touching
   - Needs: role-play, drama, movement, hands-on learning, and building materials

5. **Visual-Spatial intelligence (picture smart)** involves the ability to mentally represent the spatial world. This intelligence includes the ability to use patterns in space visually.
   - Thinks: in images and pictures
   - Loves: designing, drawing, visualizing, and doodling
   - Needs: art, Legos, videos, movies, slides, imagination games, mazes, patterns, puzzles

6. **Naturalist intelligence (nature smart)** consists of the ability to discern details of the natural world and a sensitivity to the natural world, including land, sky, and water.
   - Thinks: by sensitivity to the natural world
   - Loves: observing, experimenting, cultivating, and recognizing patterns
   - Needs: observation notebooks, opportunities to care for animals and plants, binoculars, microscopes, cameras, strolls through the park and woods, and contact with wildlife

7. **Interpersonal intelligence (people smart)** is the ability to understand the intentions and motivation of others. People with interpersonal intelligence work well with others.
   - Thinks: by bouncing ideas off other people
   - Loves: leading, organizing, relating, manipulating, celebrating, and mediating
   - Needs: friends, group games, clubs, and community events

8. **Intrapersonal intelligence (self smart)** refers to the ability to understand oneself, to appreciate one's own feelings, fears, and motivations.
   - Thinks: deeply inside oneself
   - Loves: setting goals, dreaming, being quiet, planning, thinking, and reflecting
   - Needs: secret places, time alone, self-paced projects, choices, and quiet time

ANECDOTAL RECORD 13–5

Child's Name: Peter

Date: May 20

Time: 9:15 a.m.

Observer: Ruby

Location: Campus Child Care

Four-year-old Peter was enrolled in the preschool late in the year. His family had recently moved into the community and Peter was still adjusting to the preschool program. On this morning Peter was working in the writing center when he said to me, "I want to write that the lady slithered down the stairs." Before I responded, with pursed lips and shaking his head Peter said, "No, no, not slithered. Not right. The lady slinked down the stairs—that's it." Admittedly I enjoyed listening to Peter. He spoke with the most refined British accent. I asked if I could keep his story to show it to his mother. Peter agreed and moved on to play. When Peter's mother arrived I shared the story with her. She smiled. I asked, "I notice that you don't have a British accent. Is your husband English?" Peter's mother answered, "No." I persisted, "Is Peter's nanny English?" "No," came the response. "What about a neighbor?" Peter's mother took a hard look at me. "No, nobody we know is from England. Why do you ask?" Astonished, I replied, "Surely you have noticed that Peter speaks with a distinct British accent." "Oh, that. Yes, I know. Last year he spoke like a dolphin."

CHOMSKY'S NATIVIST THEORY OF LANGUAGE

The manner in which a child acquires language has long been debated by linguist and child developmentalist alike. Linguist Noam Chomsky is credited with bringing to the debate the idea that children are born with a capacity for learning language. In other words, a child's brain is hardwired to learn language. Prior to Chomsky's nativist theory, it was widely accepted that language acquisition is largely due to cultural reinforcement or imitation. But imagine how slowly language would develop if every utterance made by a child needed to be directly reinforced. Language is too complex to be mastered through imitation or conditioning alone.

Poverty of the Stimulus

Creating the term **poverty of the stimulus,** Chomsky argued that children are exposed to very little correctly formed language. When people speak, they make mistakes, use slang, and omit ideas understood nonverbally. Yet even very young children learn to

Poverty of the stimulus.   The notion that children are exposed to very little correctly formed spoken language.

speak their native language correctly. Nativist theories hold that children learn through their natural ability to organize language but that such skills are not fully developed without the modeling and reinforcement of others. It is important to note that the child navigates the laws of language without formal instruction.

Language Acquisition Device

Chomsky theorizes that children master language rules and components rapidly, due to an innate ability called the **language acquisition device (LAD).** That is to say, humans are born with a set of rules about language already in our brains, which Chomsky refers to as the universal grammar (Chomsky, Belletti, & Rizzi, 2002). This grammar offers a certain number of sentence structure possibilities. For example seventy-five percent of languages, including English, have subject-verb-object sentence structures. American children may construct sentences such as "I throw the ball." Japanese children use a subject-object-verb structure and may utter "As for me, the ball I throw." Welsh children say, "Throw I the ball," utilizing a verb-subject-object structure. Experience in one's native culture helps the child to unconsciously set the parameters for the language he will use. It is as if the brain is programmed, with all possibilities and language experiences informing the correct selection (Falk, 1997). Consider how children self-correct language by reading the example below.

Researcher Roger Brown (1973) tape-recorded children's spontaneous speech. Here are some tag questions produced by a boy called Adam one day when he was four years old.

Ursula's my sister, isn't she?
I made a mistake, didn't I?
Diandros and me are working, aren't we?
He can't beat me, can he?
He doesn't know what to do, does he?

Interestingly, Adam constructed 32 such questions in a single hour. Children demonstrate the need to practice new capabilities. On each tag question Adam changed the sentence from either a negative statement to a positive statement, or from a positive statement to a negative statement. He did so correctly on all 32 examples. Additionally, in the example of "I made a mistake, didn't I?" he used *didn't* even though it was not in the original statement.

Observations That Could Be Linked to Chomsky's Theory of Language Development

- ❏ Does the child creatively construct sentences?
- ❏ Does the child practice newly acquired grammatical skills repeatedly?
- ❏ Does the child use rules incorrectly, such as "I goed to the store"?
- ❏ Does the child change the order of sentences while still preserving the meaning?

....

Language acquisition device (LAD).   The notion that the learning of language is aided by an innate human ability to speak. The LAD has sets of language rules for all languages.

View the Anecdotal Record on the CD-ROM. Identify possible explanations of development according to cognitive development theory. For example, what could be said about the child's development from Gardner's, Montessori's, or Piaget's theory?

QUESTIONS TO CONSIDER ○ ○ ○

1. What standards are used to distinguish good theory from bad theory?
2. Why do scholars develop different theories rather than agree on an existing theory?
3. In what ways do different theories contribute to the understanding of cultural influences of development?
4. What educational theory do you suppose teachers study in China?

REFERENCES ○ ○ ○

Brown, R. (1973). *A first language: The early stages.* Cambridge, MA: Harvard University Press.

Chomsky, N., Belletti, A., & Rizzi, L. (Eds.). (2002). *On nature and language.* Cambridge, UK: Cambridge University Press.

Crain, W. (2000). *Theories of development: Concepts and applications* (4th ed.). Upper Saddle River, NJ: Prentice Hall.

Falk, Y. N. (1997). *Case typology and case theory.* The Hebrew University of Jerusalem. Retrieved January 13, 2006, from http://pluto.mscc.huji.ac.il/~msyfalk/Case-T&T.pdf

Peterson, R., & Felton-Collins, V. (1986). *The Piaget handbook for teachers and parents: Children in the age of discovery, preschool–third grade.* New York: Teachers College Press.

Montessori, M. (1966). *The Secret of Childhood.* Notre Dame, IN: Fides Publishers.

Mooney, C. G. (2000). *Theories of childhood: An introduction to Dewey, Montessori, Erikson, Piaget, and Vygotsky.* St. Paul, MN: Red Leaf Press.

Thomas, R. M. (1992). *Comparing theories of child development* (3rd ed.). Belmont, CA: Wadsworth.

Weitzman, I., Blank, E., & Green, R. (2000). *Jokelopedia: The biggest, best, silliest, dumbest, joke book ever.* New York: Somerville House Books.

Social, Emotional, and Creativity Theory

CHAPTER OBJECTIVES

- To understand components of social, emotional, and creative theory
- To identify aspects of theory related to the development of children
- To apply theory of development to observed behaviors in children
- To analyze the relationship between specific characteristics of development and developmental theory

CHILD STUDY OBJECTIVES

Upon conclusion of this chapter the student will:

- use theory to interpret and understand anecdotal records.
- use theory to interpret and understand checklists.
- use theory to interpret and understand structured play observations.
- use theory to interpret and understand visual documentation.
- use theory to interpret and understand parent questionnaires.
- analyze and synthesize developmental theory to write developmental summaries.

INTRODUCTION TO THEORIES OF SOCIAL AND EMOTIONAL DEVELOPMENT

In the previous chapter we discussed the various theories on what children might think and how their thinking and language develop. In this chapter we focus on theories of how children feel and how those emotions affect all aspects of development. The following theories address individual differences in processing and demonstrating emotions as well as the social aspect of learning.

As one observes children regularly it becomes apparent that one of the ways in which they process their emotions is through their play, drawings, and interests. For example, why do so many children create toy guns, draw guns, and develop play scripts around guns and fighting? One answer could be that because our culture projects fear of gun violence the child learns to work through the fear by playing with it, and thus takes control of the fear. For another example, a child demonstrating severe separation anxiety may show extraordinary interest in watching other children separate in order to process her own anxiety.

ERIKSON'S PSYCHOSOCIAL THEORY

Erik Erikson's theory focuses on the social and emotional aspects of human development. This stage theory spans development from birth through old age. Within each stage of Erikson's theory, specific tasks are accomplished or a **crisis** (or crises) is overcome, permitting the developing person to pass through one stage to the next. Successful resolution of each stage affects the next stage. Individuals form personality strengths and weakness as they pass through each stage. Erikson theorized that growth involves friction—in other words, children experience conflict as they grow and change into adults. He coined the phrase **identity crisis,** helping us to understand the personality changes occurring in the young adult. During the early years of life, patterns develop that regulate or influence a person's lifelong development (Mooney, 2000). Erikson thought it possible to readdress issues from a previous stage of development. However, true basic components of trust and mistrust are formed early in life and influence later development.

Erikson's Stages of Development

Early childhood is the critical period for the development of trust, autonomy, initiative, and industry, as described in Erikson's first four stages of psychosocial development.

Trust vs. Mistrust   During the first stage of psychosocial development, referred to as *Trust versus Mistrust,* babies interact with their environment in order to get their basic needs meet. They cry when they have a need and adults respond in ways that are culturally relevant. What is most important regarding these interactions is that the caregiver be consistent, predictable, and reliable in his responses to the child. Children learn

....

Crisis.   State of confusion.

Identity crisis.   A psychosocial state or condition of role confusion.

that adults will respond and are therefore trustworthy. Additionally, the child is learning to trust herself to regulate her own actions and reactions. As the adult expresses confidence in the child's abilities, the child begins to trust herself. Positive, calm interactions between adults and children reassure the child that human closeness is good and that there is hope.

ANECDOTAL RECORD 14–1

Child's Name: Jessica

Date: March 14

Time: 11:50 a.m.

Observer: J. Thomas

Location: Sunshine Daycare, Infant Room

Four-month-old Jessica naps each morning between 10:30 a.m. and 12:00 p.m. Her caregiver generally begins warming her bottle at about 11:55 a.m. Jessica awakens in her crib. She opens her eyes and moves her head to the left. She can see her caregiver through the bars in the crib. Jessica makes vocalizations but is not crying. Her caregiver looks over at the crib and says: "Hi, Jess. I see that you are awake. Are you hungry? Do you want to get up?" Jessica kicks her legs and makes more vocalizations. The caregiver approaches the crib and picks Jessica up. She holds Jessica face to face and talks with her as she assesses the infant's mood. This helps the caregiver decide whether Jessica would like her diaper changed first or would prefer her bottle without delay. Jessica engages in this routine with her primary caregiver each day.

Because the caregiver responds consistently to her, Jessica will develop a sense of trust.

Autonomy vs. Shame and Doubt   The second stage, *Autonomy versus Shame and Doubt,* encompasses the child's desire to exercise choice. During this stage the child is experiencing a growing ability to do things for himself. Newly acquired independence supports the child's sense of self and growing autonomy. Toddlers expressing their autonomy may use words such as *me* or *mine*, and the powerful and insistent *no*. They express preferences and explore with their entire bodies, jumping, climbing, and throwing.

In order to moderate children's assertiveness, adults offer guidance and socialization. Thus the conflict between autonomy and shame and doubt is born. Autonomy comes from within as a result of physical maturation. The child can control her own body and master many functions. Shame and doubt are the result of the child's increased understanding of social and cultural expectations (Crain, 2000). A child who falls down might feel ashamed that others might notice the falling behavior and think him clumsy. Doubt stems from the child's understanding that he is not all powerful and that others have power and abilities also. The balance is in a child who can adjust to social regulation but still retains his sense of autonomy. Children who are excessively shamed, ridiculed for attempts at self-mastery, and overly controlled may develop lasting feelings of shame and doubt that interfere with their developing sense of self (Crain, 2000). When a child successfully resolves this crisis, balancing social controls and the expression of self-determination, Erikson says the child has "will."

ANECDOTAL RECORD 14–2

Child's Name: Mitchell

Date: December 10

Time: 5:10 p.m.

Observer: T. Jones

Location: Springfield Community Childcare

At the end of the day two-year-old Mitchell is picked up from the child care center by his mother. Together they take his coat, hat, mittens, and boots out of his cubby. Mitchell's mother holds his coat as he slips his arms into it. She zips it and snaps the top button. She bends over, unties his sneakers, and removes them from his small feet. As she opens the left boot to place it on Mitchell's foot he yells, "No, I do!" Mitchell's mother stops and asks, "Do you want to put your own boots on?" Mitchell repeats, "I can do it," as he takes the boot from his mother. He sits on the floor with a bound and stretches his arm out with the boot held tightly in his hands. After several attempts he successfully forces his foot into the boot. He stands up and stomps his foot on the floor. He bends over and fastens the Velcro closure. Mitchell's mother smiles down at him. "You did it. Do you want to put the other boot on?" she asks, as she holds it out for him to take. "No! You do it," is the reply.

Initiative vs. Guilt   *Initiative versus Guilt* describes the crisis of Erikson's third stage. Children in this stage are set on accomplishments and are ready to make plans, set goals, and persevere toward achievement. Most four- and five-year-olds are at this stage, seeking to acquire a sense of purpose (Mooney, 2000). Children who have successfully passed through the second stage are less impulsive and are ready to learn from teachers and peers. Children can focus on a task and complete it independently, as well as cope without guilt when things go astray. When adults support and encourage children's competence, their confidence grows. When adults do for children what they can do for themselves, or focus on children's mistakes, they grow to feel guilty and discouraged.

Industry vs. Inferiority   During the fourth stage, *Industry versus Inferiority,* children master important cognitive and social skills. Children focus on learning the skills of their culture. American stage-four children go to school and learn reading, writing, and arithmetic. They are industrious in their approach to academic tasks as well as in their play with peers. The crisis in this stage occurs when children feel inferior to others. Inferiority may be the result of an event that reduced the child's impression of her own

TABLE 14-1 Erikson's Stages of Psychosocial Development

Age	Stage	Psychological Strengths	Psychological Weaknesses
0–1 year	Trust vs. Mistrust	Hope, faith	Sensory distortion, withdrawal
2–3 years	Autonomy vs. Shame and Doubt	Will, determination	Impulsivity, compulsion
4–5 years	Initiative vs. Guilt	Purpose, courage	Ruthlessness, inhibition
6–12 years	Industry vs. Inferiority	Competence	Narrow virtuosity, inertia
Adolescence	Identity vs. Role Confusion	Fidelity, loyalty	Fanaticism
Young Adulthood	Intimacy vs. Isolation	Love	Promiscuity, exclusivity
Middle Age	Generativity vs. Stagnation	Care	Rejection
Old Age	Ego Integration vs. Despair	Wisdom	Presumption, despair

worth or it may be the result of unresolved earlier crises. Table 14–1 shows Erikson's stages of psychosocial development, from birth through school age to old age.

ANECDOTAL RECORD 14–3

Child's Name: Kayla

Date: May 5

Time: 9:20 a.m.

Observer: A. Kovacik

Location: Jumping Jack Preschool

During circle time, four-year-old Kayla reported that she was going to work at the easel. She had noticed the new paints displayed on the easel tray when she entered the room. Kayla announced, "I will work at the easel. I will make a picture for my sister. It is her birthday. She likes pink." Kayla approached the easel and covered her clothing with a plastic smock. She dipped the paintbrush into the pink paint and applied a thick layer to the paper that was secured to the easel. Pink paint dripped down the paper and on to the floor. Kayla stopped some of the drips with the paintbrush but others left the floor speckled. Kayla's teacher stayed close to the easel and cleaned each drip with a paper towel as it fell. She smiled at Kayla. After several minutes, Kayla put the paintbrush back into the cup and took her smock off. The teacher asked, "Are you all done?" With a heavy sigh Kayla said, "No, it's not working out. The paint is very drippy. I'll do one at home."

ANECDOTAL RECORD 14–4

Child's Name: Jasmine

Date: October 8

Time: 10:00 a.m.

Observer: A. Kovacik

Location: Woodside Elementary, Second Grade classroom

Second graders at Woodside Elementary don't use books for their arithmetic instruction. Mr. Ray, the second grade teacher, has created a file system of reusable laminated math work pages that the children select independently. Children record their individual progress in folders provided by Mr. Ray that are stored in each child's desk. Eight-year-old Jasmine attended during the morning math lesson led by Mr. Ray. She selected a level 1 math worksheet from the cart and completed it successfully. She recorded her success in her folder and went on to level 2. While working on the level 2 task, Jasmine became confused. She sought help from Mr. Ray, who encouraged her to use the math manipulatives displayed on the counter at the back of the room. Jasmine worked for several minutes with the math cubes and went back to her desk, where she successfully completed the math task. Again she recorded her progress in her folder and said to Mr. Ray, "I am becoming very good at math."

Observations That Could Be Linked to Erikson's Psychosocial Theory

❑ Does the child calm down when an adult responds?

❑ Does the child communicate needs?

❑ Can the caregiver anticipate the child's needs? Does the caregiver read the child's cues?

❑ Does the caregiver respond to the child's needs?

❑ Does the child explore independently?

❑ Does the child use possessive language (*me, mine, I*)?

❑ Does the child express assertiveness (e.g., *"NO"*)?

❑ Does the child show self-confidence?

❑ Does the caregiver allow independent skill development?

❑ Does the child plan activities?

❑ Does the child take risks?

❑ How does the child cope with failure?

❑ How does the child react to adult regulation or intervention?

❑ Does the child engage in goal-directed activity?

❑ Does the child focus attention?

❏ Is the child easily distractible?

❏ Does the child share ideas and works?

❏ Does the child show pride in accomplishments?

❏ Does the child demonstrate belonging?

❏ Does the child persevere?

GREENSPAN'S THEORY OF EMOTIONAL DEVELOPMENT

Stanley Greenspan is best known for his work with children with special needs. From his theories regarding social and emotional development he developed a practice called "Floortime," which is specifically designed to address the social and emotional deficits that some children present. Greenspan stresses that the emotional milestones of development are critical to further development in the areas of cognitive, intellectual, and social development (Greenspan & Wieder, 1998).

Greenspan identifies six emotional milestones that a typically developing child raised in a nurturing environment will reach automatically. It is important to remember that this is a stage theory, so a milestone can only be met if the previous milestone has been mastered. Table 14–2 identifies and describes the emotional milestones in Greenspan's theory.

Emotional Milestone 1: Self-Regulation and Interest in the World

The infant is extremely curious about the world around her. She scans the environment and attends to sensorial input, while learning not to be overwhelmed by it. This milestone is reached when the baby can focus her interests and at the same time calm herself.

Two-month-old Jasmine watches intently as her daddy moves the rattle back and forth in front of her. As the rattle is moving it is making a sound and the face of it is twirling. Jasmine watches for about seven seconds, then looks away and puts her thumb up to her mouth.

Emotional Milestone 2: Intimacy

The infant falls in love with her caregivers in order to reach this milestone. She finds pleasure in her caregivers' presence and she makes eye contact and attempts to snuggle.

While in her mother's arms, four-month-old Julianne focuses on her mother's face and particularly on her eyes while her mother talks to her.

Emotional Milestone 3: Two-Way Communication

By nine months the infant has learned how to draw the caregivers into her world. She realizes she can influence her caregivers and when she shows intention, the caregiver will respond. It is this interchange back and forth that signals the beginnings of communication. Greenspan calls this opening and closing circles. The infant opens the circle with reaching for the caregiver or making a sound; the caregiver responds with a smile, reaching back, or making another sound, thus building on the infant's initiated action. Finally, the infant closes the circle by responding back to the caregiver. The infant

TABLE 14–2   **Greenspan's Emotional Milestones**

Emotional Milestone	Characteristics	Differences in Development
Self-regulation and interest in the world (by three months)	Infant self-regulates in response to stimuli, focus develops, ability to stay calm	The infant may be hypersensitive to sensorial input, such as movement, sound, or visuals; the infant may seem uninterested in the world and/or oblivious to caregivers.
Intimacy (by five months)	Infant seeks out pleasurable relationships with primary caregivers; shows joys when caregivers enter into visual field, smiles at caregivers; baby falls in love with caregivers	If the child is hypersensitive to stimuli, he may avoid intimacy because of added tactile, visual, and auditory input supplied by caregivers.
Two-way communication (by nine months)	Baby shows intention to bring caregiver into circle; smiles at caregiver while looking for response from caregiver; reacts by cooing, reaching to continue interaction; begins to act to produce other reactions	Children with motor or cognitive delays may not have capabilities to engage because of limitations with movements or imitative abilities; underresponsive sensorially
Complex communication (by 18 months)	Child's ability to express herself grows immensely—now she can respond in many different ways: can express herself creatively, can show individuality in responses and ways in which to open circles, can understand complex behavioral patterns of adults	Children with cognitive delays such as mental retardation have difficulty with motor planning, making it difficult to organize complex patterns of behavior and difficult to comprehend complex, multi-step directions; child may move aimlessly or recklessly.
Emotional ideas (by 30 months)	Child begins to put the symbols (words) with feelings and ideas, most often through developing play scenarios; child manipulates ideas in ways that meet her needs; child uses words or other symbols to show interest or delight.	Child with language delays has difficulty matching words with ideas and has difficulty producing words; children with limited experiences due to illness or motoric delays have not developed play themes.
Emotional thinking (by 48 months)	The child builds bridges between ideas in order to play out elaborate themes; can use feelings to explain reasons for something desired; engages in conversation with multiple back-and-forth sequences	Children with cognitive delays may not have developed representational thinking or the ability to use symbols.

quickly learns the many situations in which this process works—she initiates an action and others respond. Unlike the first stages of reflexive action, in this stage the infant has made connections between her actions and others' reactions.

Eight-month-old Rashonda is sitting in her high chair eating her favorite snack of Cheerios. She is just beginning to learn how to hold her new blue sippy cup. Her mother has put in just a little bit of water while the learning process continues. While trying to grasp and lift the cup it falls on the floor. Rashonda watches it hit the ground and follows with an "UH-OH!!" While pointing to the cup, Rashonda is making various sounds. Mother looks over and says, "Uh-oh, your cup fell." Mom picks it up, gives it a quick wash, and places it back on the high chair. As Mom is giving it back, she smiles at Rashonda and says, "Silly girl." Rashonda smiles back and lifts her arms up and down. After Mom turns away Rashonda makes several noises but Mom does not turn back. Rashonda reaches for the cup and it falls on the floor again—this time Rashonda smiles before Mom even turns back around.

Emotional Milestone 4: Complex Communication

By 18 months the toddler has developed more complex emotions and more ways of expressing those emotions. She has expanded her behavioral repertoire as well, and by linking these she can communicate fairly complex thoughts. She can also begin to decipher the complex messages that others are trying to send via their gestures. The toddler no longer has to be the passive recipient of something that is out of sight or out of the caregiver's mind. For instance, the toddler who does not have much spoken language yet can tell a caregiver in several ways that she wants to go outside. She can go to the window and point, or she can take the caregiver by the hand and lead him over to the door to go outside. More complex thoughts, needs, and intentions can now be communicated via gestures that link directly to reactions sought from the caregiver. Greenspan considers this the precursor to speech.

Fifteen-month-old Taylor looks up and sees her caregiver talking on the phone. She picks up the toy phone on the floor and puts it to her ear. She stands and walks to her caregiver and holds out the phone for her and extends her free hand to take the caregiver's phone from her. The caregiver disconnects her phone and hands it to Taylor, who then babbles into the phone.

Emotional Milestone 5: Emotional Ideas

By approximately 30 months the child will begin using words and gestures to express emotions. Whereas prior to this the child would cry or throw a tantrum to show anger, now he expresses the feeling with words. The child who stands, puts his hands on his hips and says, "I'm mad at you" is able to use emotional ideas. The words and gestures have become the symbols for the emotion and the child can put these together consistently. Additionally, it is at this time when children begin to act out their own emotions in dramatic play. The child will work out emotions through the play, almost experimenting with how emotions affect his own behavior and the behavior of others.

Two-and-a-half-year-old Jaime asks Mom for a cookie. Mom says, "Not now honey, it's almost time for dinner." Jaime continues to ask for the cookie and finally Mom, in a very stern voice, says, "No cookie—and if you keep asking me you will not get one later." Jaime goes into the playroom and picks up his teddy bear. Using his best teddy bear voice he says, "I want cookie," pretending the bear said this. To which Jaime in his own voice replies, "Yes, I give you cookie."

Emotional Milestone 6: Emotional Thinking

By age four the child can now link ideas together and play out scenarios in logical order. Whereas in the fifth stage the expression of ideas and emotions is scattered and vulnerable to many distractions, this next emotional milestone requires the child to stick with a theme and link the actions together in some sort of logical order. That is not to say that make-believe and imagination are not involved—but the ideas are linked. This new ability to link emotions and ideas lends itself to understanding time and space concepts. The child can now begin to understand that what he does right now can have an effect on what happens in the future. Again, these concepts play out and are developed primarily during play scenarios.

Four-year-old Dimetri was sitting in the block corner surrounded by blocks. Shauna, his teacher, sat down next to him and asked him about his structure. "Well," he said, "these guys made this house and then they had two more babies, so then they made it bigger. In some more days the aliens came and knocked this part down so now they have to make it again."

Observations That Could Relate to Greenspan's Emotional Milestones

❑ Does the infant show interest in various stimuli/sensations?

❑ Can the infant remain calm and focused?

❑ Can the infant recover from stress?

❑ Does the infant show interest in the primary caregiver?

❑ Does the infant respond to caregiver overtures? Does she respond with pleasure? Does she study the caregiver?

❑ Does the infant become distressed when the caregiver is unresponsive during play?

❑ Does the infant show anger when frustrated?

❑ Does the infant respond to gestures with intentional gestures?

❑ Does the infant initiate interactions?

❑ At what age does the infant demonstrate the emotions of pleasure, excitement, curiosity, anger, and fear?

❑ Does the toddler close circles of communication?

❑ Does the child use words to express emotions?

❑ Does the child express play actions?

❑ Does the child communicate wishes, intentions, and feelings using words, gestures, or touch?

❑ Does the child link several ideas to create play themes?

MASLOW'S HIERARCHICAL THEORY OF DEVELOPMENT

Abraham Maslow developed a theory of personality development based on motivation to fulfill certain needs (Maslow, 1943). Maslow described these needs as being hierarchical in nature, meaning that some needs are more basic or more powerful than others. As these needs are satisfied, other higher needs emerge (Maslow, 1971). Figure 14–1 illustrates the hierarchy of needs.

FIGURE 14–1   **Maslow's hierarchy of needs.**

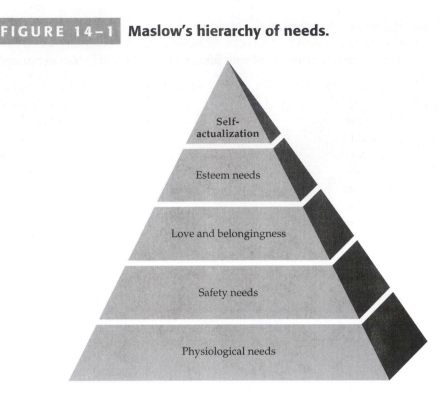

Maslow's hierarchy of needs can be divided into basic needs and growth needs. One must satisfy lower level basic needs before progressing on to meet higher level growth needs. Once these needs have been reasonably satisfied, one may be able to reach the highest level, called self-actualization.

Basic Needs

Basic needs include:

➤ *Physiological Needs.* Food, water, oxygen, etc. Anything the physical organism needs to survive.

➤ *Safety Needs.* If the physiological needs are relatively well gratified, there then emerges a new set of needs, the safety needs: security; stability; dependency; protection; freedom from fear, anxiety, and chaos; and the need for structure, order, law, and limits.

➤ *Belongingness and Love Needs.* If both the physiological and the safety needs are fairly well gratified, there will emerge the love and affection and belongingness needs. The love needs include giving and receiving affection.

➤ *Esteem Needs.* These are first, the desire for strength, achievement, adequacy, mastery, and competence, and second, respect or esteem from other people, status, recognition, attention, importance, dignity, or appreciation.

The basic needs or deficiency needs must be met in order to move on to the growth needs, culminating in self-actualization. If you have significant problems during your development—a period of extreme insecurity or hunger as a child, the loss of a family member through death or divorce, or significant neglect or abuse—you may "fixate" on that set of needs for the rest of your life (Huitt, 2004). Consider the example of this below.

I had been teaching in a toddler room at an inner-city child care facility and one day a brother and sister arrived for the first time at our center. The children were both quiet and still for the majority of the morning. When it came time for lunch, the two children did not want to join the others but stood, holding hands, watching the other children eat. Although I continually tried to gently coax them to eat they did not want to join us. As we began cleaning up and toileting and getting ready for nap, I looked over and saw the two children going through the garbage can and putting the food in the can into their coat pockets. I told them I could give them other food but they refused. I found out later that day about the children's past. Both of them had been left for days on end without anyone taking care of them. When they had been found this time they had been left for four days with no food in the house. They had learned to get food from garbage cans around the building. After about two weeks of continual coaxing and gentle persuasion the children began eating with us—but they never stopped taking food from the garbage.

Growth Needs and Self-Actualization

The growth needs do not involve balance or homeostasis as do the basic deficiency needs. The growth needs involve the continuous desire to fulfill potentials, to "be all that you can be." They are a matter of becoming the most complete person you can. Hence the term, *self-actualization.* Recently, Maslow has identified additional growth needs. One is the cognitive need, or the need to know and understand, and one is the aesthetic need, the need for beauty and order. When these are met, the individual has the potential to experience self-actualization (Maslow & Lowery, 1998).

In order to be truly self-actualizing, your lower needs must be taken care of, at least to a considerable extent. This makes sense: If you are hungry, you are continually looking for food. If you are unsafe, you have to be continuously on guard. If you are isolated and unloved, you have to satisfy that need. If you have a low sense of self-esteem, you have to be defensive or compensate. When lower needs are unmet, you can't fully devote yourself to fulfilling your potential.

It is very difficult to define a self-actualized person, but Maslow described the needs or the motivations of a self-actualizing person as follows. The self-actualizing person strives for:

- Truth
- Goodness
- Beauty
- Uniqueness
- Justice and order
- Simplicity
- Playfulness
- Self-sufficiency
- Meaningfulness

Maslow estimates that only one in ten people become self-actualized and strive for these things, not because they are bad or lazy, but because they must concentrate on basic needs and cannot see their way to these goals.

Observations That Could Be Linked to Maslow's Theory

- ❑ Does the child indicate that all her basic needs are met?
- ❑ What are the child's primary motivations (acceptance, competency)?
- ❑ Does the child freely explore the environment?
- ❑ Does the child appear to be calm or anxious?

CSIKSZENTMIHALYI'S THEORY OF CREATIVITY

Csikszentmihalyi's theory of creativity is similar to Vygotsky's theory of cognitive development in that both rely on the interaction of the individual with society and culture. Csikszentmihalyi's "systems perspective" considers not only the psychology of the creative individual but also the role of cultural domain and the social community. Whereas some theories consider only the individual's ability to create something novel as being the essence of creativity, Csikszentmihalyi believes that three components, the individual, the cultural domain and society, all must mesh together in order for creativity to occur.

The Individual

Csikszentmihalyi studied creative people for twenty years and from it developed a theory called "Flow" (1991). When an individual becomes completely immersed in what he is doing, when he no longer has any concept of time because of his involvement with something, and when he is working for the sake of working rather than for some extrinsic reward, he has reached a state of *flow*. When a person reaches flow, individual creativity can follow.

The state of flow, according to Csikszentmihalyi, is the special state of involved enchantment that lies somewhere between boredom and anxiety. A person in flow state is mentally involved in the challenge. Similar to Vygotsky's notion of "zone of proximal development," there is a space between being too easy and being much too hard, and when an individual feels he is challenged yet can accomplish something, he has the potential to reach flow.

Another characteristic of the flow state is that the individual is motivated by the intrinsic pleasure of the activity, not for some arbitrary reward put forth by another individual or even by society. According to Csikszentmihalyi, creativity is a central source of meaning in our lives (1996).

The Cultural Domain and Society

Csikszentmihalyi characterizes individual creativity as the "little c" and creativity as an interaction between the culture and society as the "big C." In his view, the cultural domain and society judge and either promote a creative endeavor or ignore it. When the

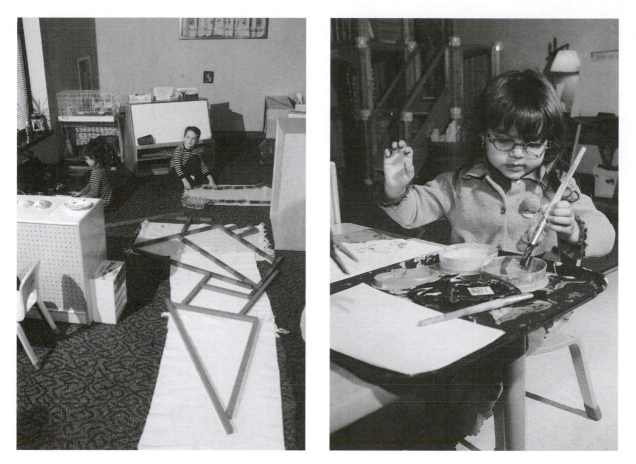

When children become completely engrossed in an activity, they are more likely to demonstrate creativity.

cultural domain and society embrace an individual's creativity, the "big C" occurs and this is truly creativity.

Observations That Could Be Linked to Csikszentmihalyi's Theory

❑ Does the child become involved in activities of his own free will?

❑ Does the child disregard possible interruptions when involved in activities?

❑ What kinds of activities or works does the child engage in to the exclusion of others?

❑ Does the child lose track of time when engaged?

❑ Does the child engage in activities for her own enjoyment or because of external rewards?

❑ Does the child use problem-solving techniques to come up with novel solutions to problems?

 View the Anecdotal Record on the CD-ROM. Identify possible explanations of development according to social/emotional and creative development theory. For example, what could be said about the child's development from Erikson's, Greenspan's, Maslow's, or Csikszentmihalyi's theory?

QUESTIONS TO CONSIDER ○ ○ ○

1. Research shows that creative ability is very high during early childhood but drops markedly during school-age days up to adulthood. Why do you think this is? What kinds of parental and classroom practices foster creative thinking? What kinds of practices discourage creativity?

2. What advice do you think Erikson would give parents regarding the spoiling of a baby?

3. Discuss the components of the early childhood classroom necessary according to Maslow's theory to support development to its furthest potential.

REFERENCES ○ ○ ○

Crain, W. (2000). *Theories of development: Concepts and applications* (4th ed.). Upper Saddle River, NJ: Prentice Hall.

Csikszentmihalyi, M. (1991). *Flow: The psychology of optimal experience*. New York: HarperCollins.

Csikszentmihalyi, M. (1996). *Creativity*. New York: HarperCollins.

Greenspan, S. I., & Wieder, S. (1998). *The child with special needs: Encouraging intellectual and emotional growth*. Reading, MA: Perseus Books.

Huitt, W. (2004). Maslow's hierarchy of needs. *Educational Psychology Interactive.* Valdosta, GA: Valdosta State University. Retrieved July 28, 2005, from http://chiron.valdosta.edu/whuitt/col/regsys/maslow.html

Maslow, A. (1943). A theory of human motivation. *Psychological Review, 50,* 370–396. Retrieved January 17, 2006, from http://psychclassics.yorku.ca/Maslow/motivation.htm

Maslow, A. (1971). *The farther reaches of human nature*. New York: Viking Press.

Maslow, A., & Lowery, R. (Eds.). (1998). *Toward a psychology of being* (3rd ed.). New York: Wiley & Sons.

Mooney, C. G. (2000). *Theories of childhood: An introduction to Dewey, Montessori, Erikson, Piaget, and Vygotsky.* St. Paul, MN: Red Leaf Press.

IV

PUTTING IT ALL TOGETHER

The Key is curiosity, and it is curiosity, not answers that we model. As we seek to know more about a child, we demonstrate the acts of observing, listening, questioning and wondering.

— Vivian Paley

15

Writing the Reports

CHAPTER OBJECTIVES

- To describe qualitative research and its benefits for child study

- To identify multifaceted aspects of human development

- To understand components of ecological theory

- To understand that development in one domain influences development in another

- To describe the influences of family, culture, history, and society on development

CHILD STUDY OBJECTIVES

Upon conclusion of this chapter the student will:

- assess, interpret, and synthesize raw data from the study of a child.

- write comprehensive developmental summaries.

- compile child study data in an organized fashion.

OVERVIEW OF THE SUMMARY REPORTS

This chapter examines the six reports you will generate from the data collected for the child study. Each report is a comprehensive summary of one of the domains of development. The six reports cover

- the physical domain: growth, gross motor, and fine motor development
- the cognitive domain: memory, problem solving, logical thinking, and theory of mind
- the social domain: attachment, social competency, and social play
- the emotional domain: temperament, emotions, and identity
- language and literacy domain: listening, speaking, writing, and reading
- creativity: art, music, and movement

The child study is a form of **qualitative research** that is used to look at an individual child. Increasingly, researchers are using qualitative methods like the child study to understand how children grow and develop (Jessor & Colby, 1996). This shift signifies a sharp contrast to large groups studied with **quantitative research** methods. Many researchers are now using an **ethnographic method.** Much as you have done for the child study, the ethnographer uses methods such as interviews, observations, and narrative and event analysis, conducted in the child's natural environment. The synthesis of data from the anecdotal records, checklists, structured play assessments, visual documentation, parent questionnaires, and background history will reveal the development of the child you have carefully observed and interviewed.

The child study report is much like a story; it presents the concrete details of actual events, and has a plot, character, and often even dialogue (Boehrer, 1990). The case study report is a combination of a description of the child's development and an analysis of that development. Each step of the research or document gathering process is carefully reviewed to give the reader as much context as possible, in order to convey the reasons and support for conclusions regarding the child's development.

The child study may deepen understanding of theories of development, shedding light on the ways various theories emphasize different aspects of development. A detailed explanation of the theoretical positions taken by the writer, including an explanation of how theories drove the inquiry and influenced interpretation or led to selecting documentation such as checklists, assessments, and participants for interview, helps to make evident the connections between the data and the conclusions.

....

Qualitative research.   Seeks to understand development or other social phenomena through descriptive analysis, using interviews and observation within the natural setting.

Quantitative research.   A technique in which scientific numerical data is gathered and statistically analyzed, primarily from large groups, to support the existence of relationships and/or effects.

Ethnographic method.   A qualitative research method often used in cultural anthropology. Observations and interviews are used to study a particular place, group of people or subculture, or event.

Each student researcher addresses the selection of documentation techniques and tools based on individual theoretical orientations. It is important to examine and reflect on the theories driving the research questions. Take, for example, the structured play assessment. To which theory did you ascribe as you wrote and administered this interactive examination of the child's development? Did you recreate the conservation experiments made famous by Jean Piaget or did you opt to examine operant conditioning as a Skinnerian would?

Because child studies are exploratory in nature, most end with implications for further study. The reports generated for the child study should offer insight for additional questions to explore regarding the child's development, make predictions as to the child's future learning needs, and offer curricular suggestions for meeting those needs.

Examples of summary reports are found on the accompanying CD-ROM.

PREPARING TO WRITE THE REPORTS

Consider the interaction of various components of the child's development as you prepare to write the reports. Following are three components that warrant particular attention: characteristics of the unique child, universal developmental milestones, and the child's contextual development (NAEYC, 1998).

The Unique Child

Understanding the child's uniqueness comes from careful observation of his personality, temperament, and preferences. The student researcher uncovers characteristics of the child's uniqueness through anecdotal records, parent interviews, background history, visual documentation, and interaction with the child. It is important to examine the child's uniqueness in an objective manner without using language laden with subjectivity. For example, when describing a child's unique personality one should avoid words like *difficult*, *cranky*, or *moody*. Although such words may describe what you have learned about the child, they are heavy with values and reflect the antithesis of culturally preferred characteristics. It is best to describe observable traits in more specific terms, such as "The child's resting and eating habits are inconsistent and often the child is tired after missing a nap or after having a restless night" or "The child takes toys from other children without asking if he can play with them and hits children when they approach him." It is clear how both types of statements give information regarding the child's personality, but the later examples do so without making judgments. Temperament, personality, sense of self, identity, preferences, and self-esteem should all be considered when writing about the child's uniqueness.

Universal Characteristics

Universal characteristics of the child's development are likely uncovered in the checklists, rating scales, and assessments. Since assessment tools are often standardized, they demonstrate how the child reaches each milestone in relation to how other children the same age reach the same milestone. If it is stated in the child study report that a child demonstrates age-appropriate gross motor ability, it is important to state the standards by which the child was measured. Noting by which standard the child was measured is critical, as some developmental milestones such as toilet learning and theory of mind are directly related to the child's cultural experiences. Child study reports focus on the child's accomplishments; in other words, what the child can do instead of what the child cannot do. Reflecting on the child's performance is an important component. It is not enough to describe what the child can do; rather it is necessary to reflect on why the child engages in such behaviors. For example, a report that notes that the child "seeks objects when partially hidden" might go on to explain that such behavior is an indication of grasping the concept of object permanence, as per the cognitive theory of Jean Piaget.

Context of Development

Viewing the child within the cultural context in which she lives, grows, and develops is the next critical component of the child study reports. Noting in objective terms how the child's family, school, community, culture, and values influence her development offers a contextual window through which development can be better understood and reflected upon. For example, noting that the child is the youngest in a large family of adults who all care for her in a communal home environment and reflecting on how such an experience influences the child's social and emotional development is an example of how examination of the child's contextual development informs the overall understanding of the child.

The diagram pictured in Figure 15–1 illustrates how an individual child's development is unique and universal within the context of the child's family, culture, ethnicity, religion, or society. For example, due to cultural values four-month-old Tye has never been placed on the floor. He is mostly held by an adult or carried close to the body in a sling. Universal development dictates that children roll, sit, creep, and walk within the first year and one-half of life. Tye will follow this universal principle, but due to contextual influences will do so differently than other children not of his culture. In this case cultural context influences developmental universals and is therefore pictured as the outer circle in the diagram.

FIGURE 15–1 **Developmental considerations for the report.**

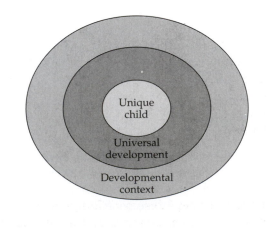

Source: NAEYC (1998)

 **An alternative conceptualization of the understanding of a particular child's development.**

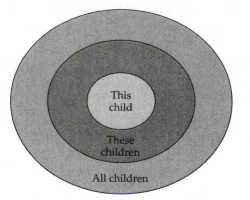

Source: Elizabeth Ann Jenkins. Instructor, Early Childhood Education Department at Orlando Tech., Orange County Public Schools, Orlando, FL.

An Alternative Conceptualization

One might also consider the diagram in Figure 15–2 as a way of understanding development. In the process of understanding a particular child's development, researchers may benefit from the following sequence: the understanding of all children, the understanding of these children, and the understanding of this child in particular.

All Children

The understanding of "all children" refers to universal development governed by principles and sequences apparent all over the world—in every culture, every society, and among all humans. Principles of universal development define development as continuous in nature and that it proceeds from the simple to the complex, from general to specific. Development proceeds from the head downward, and from the center of the body outward. These trends are thought to have no cultural or societal boundaries.

These Children

The understanding of "these children" refers to developmental trends apparent in a particular culture to which an individual child belongs. For example, all American children share some common developmental characteristics, but middle-class American children may have a greater number of developmental characteristics in common, and middle-class American children who live in Detroit and attend ABC Nursery School likely share values, experiences, and customs that influence their behavior.

This Child

Lastly, understanding "this child" indicates that individual development shares some characteristics of contextual and universal development but remains unique. Figure 15–2 visually demonstrates that all children share some common developmental characteristics with these children. These children may, however, have developmental characteristics that are not shared by all children. Similarly, the individual child shares some developmental characteristics with these children but certainly continues to develop in a unique manner.

CULTURAL VARIATION: MOTOR DEVELOPMENT

In a research study of urban Navajo and European-American mothers' responses to children's behavior in the classroom, Guilmet (1979) found differences regarding individual interpretation. In one example the mothers observed a European-American boy engaged in high levels of verbal and physical activity. The Navajo mothers rated the boy poorly, as they viewed the high verbal and physical activity as negative. The European-American mothers rated the boy's behavior as positive. The values and ideals held by both groups of mothers will influence their interactions with their children, therefore having an impact on the children's development.

BRONFENBRENNER'S ECOLOGICAL SYSTEMS THEORY

All development occurs within various contexts: within the family, history, culture, society, and economy. Ecological theorist Urie Bronfenbrenner postulated that development occurs in increasingly complex reciprocal interactions between the individual and the environment. As children grow and develop, interactions become more varied and therefore more complex. Take, for example, the infant, who has a relatively narrow scope of interactions among parents, caregiver, and family. As the child grows, interactions become more complex with influences from family, friends, church, and school. Ultimately the child engages with numerous individuals, as well as groups, cultures, subcultures, and governments, to mention a few. As evidenced in the child study, development is a product of the individual child's characteristics, the environment, and the conditions surrounding a particular developmental dimension. Those environmental factors closest to the child have the greatest influence on the child's development, and more distant factors have a weaker influence. For example, the child's home culture is more influential than the ethnic practices of the child's ancestors (Bronfenbrenner, 1979).

Nested Systems

Bronfenbrenner emphasized that the developing child is involved in a series of environmental systems that interact with one another and with the child to influence development. In other words, the interaction between the child and others is important, but the relationships among environmental systems are also important. This multi-layered ecological system includes the *microsystem, mesosystem, exosystem, macrosystem,* and *chronosystem.* See Figure 15–3 for a diagram showing Bronfenbrenner's nested systems.

FIGURE 15–3 Bronfenbrenner's ecological theory model.

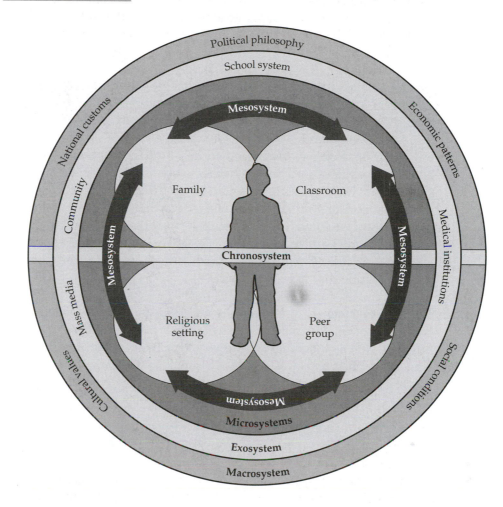

The Microsystem and the Mesosystem The innermost circle of layer of the ecological theory is referred to as the **microsystem** and includes those individuals and experiences that directly influence the child. Experiences of the microsystem may include interactions with the family, child care center, school, and friends. Take, for instance, six-year-old Ben, whose microsystem includes his mother, father, and four-year-old sister. Also included are his teacher, first grade classmates, and after school program provider. He spends time during the week and on weekends with his best friends Mark and Fred, who live in his neighborhood. Four-year-old Natalia, a Russian immigrant, lives with her mother, father, grandmother, young aunt, and cousin. Her microsystem also includes another aunt who cares for her and her cousin while her parents, aunt, and grandmother work at a family-owned bakery. As Natalia gets older and enters school, her relationships will change to include peers and teachers. At age four, her family is the most important part of her microsystem, but just as in Ben's case, peers will become increasingly

Microsystem. In Bronfenbrenner's ecological theory, the context in which the child lives and interacts.

more influential. The **mesosystem** refers to the interrelatedness of components of the microsystem. For example, the child interacts with his family, school, doctor, and peers. The doctor interacts with the family and perhaps even the school. Peers interact with the family and the school.

The Exosystem   The **exosystem** includes those settings that influence the child's development but with which the child has no direct interactions. Included in Ben's exosystem is his mother's job, which requires travel that takes her away from home for weeks at a time. Also included is his father's job, which is stressful and often unrewarding. Additionally, Ben's sister has significant motor delays and often works with a physical therapist. Relatives live near Ben and visit at holidays and during the summer. Natalia's exosystem includes the bakery where members of her family work. It also includes other Russian immigrants who live in the same neighborhood. Both of Natalia's parents attend English as a second language classes in the evening and spend hours practicing on weekends. Natalia's aunt is in regular contact with relatives still living in Russia and writes letters daily. Often Natalia's parents, grandmother, and aunt work long shifts at the bakery, leaving the apartment as early as 4:30 in the morning and returning well past dinner.

The Macrosystem   The **macrosystem** represents the values, ideologies, and laws of the culture or society. Social rules and ideologies distinguish one culture or country from another, as well as different subcultures within a single country. Ben's macrosystem includes the values and ideas shared by his middle-class neighbors, who arrange visits and play dates formally. He is never left without direct supervision, even when playing in his yard or close to home. The socioeconomic status of Ben's family is upper-middle income with significant savings for vacations, college, and retirement. Natalia's macrosystem consists of poor, Russian-speaking immigrant neighbors who share experiences and resources. Her extended family owns one car that is often shared by neighbors. Repairs to the apartment and automobile are done by neighboring skilled Russian immigrants in exchange for baked goods or child care. Natalia plays outdoors daily in all types of weather and roams freely within the apartment complex, where over one-third of the residents speak Russian. Ben and Natalia are exposed to different sets of values and beliefs that influence their development in different ways.

The Chronosystem   The four systems—the micro-, meso-, exo-, and macrosystems—change over time. Bronfenbrenner's term for this change is called the **chronosystem**

Mesosystem.   In Bronfenbrenner's ecological theory, the interrelations that occur among and between the components of the microsystem.

Exosystem.   In Bronfenbrenner's ecological theory, the collection of settings that influence the child's development but with which the child does not directly interact.

Macrosystem.   In Bronfenbrenner's ecological theory, the system that surrounds the microsystem, mesosystem, and exosystem and represents the values, ideologies, and laws of a culture.

Chronosystem.   In Bronfenbrenner's ecological theory, the time-based dimension that can alter the operation of the microsystem, mesosystem, macrosystem, and exosystem.

(Bronfenbrenner, 2004). The chronosystem can change all other ecological levels from the the microsystem to the macrosystem. The child and his environment undergo changes over time. Some changes are the result of the child's maturation or unexpected circumstances, such as illness or an accident. Other changes are due to external factors such as the birth of a sibling, divorce, or a change in school. This moving and changing system influences the child's development, just as the growing and changing child influences the system. This multifaceted system presents challenges as one attempts to study all aspects of development at once. Widely used linear models of studying children and families within their cultures yield results but fail to do so in a systematic manner. The examination of the interrelatedness of all of the aspects and influences of development leads to a more comprehensive understanding of the child and is a critical component in writing child study summary reports.

DESIGNING THE REPORT

When designing the child study report the student must follow three steps:

1. Identify and describe concept development.
2. Relate concept development to theories.
3. Support observations and predictions with documentation.

1. *Identify and describe concept development.* When writing the reports it is necessary to consider a few questions. Think about each aspect of the report as if you were a news reporter, conveying information in a manner that is clear, concise, and interesting. Answer the question: "What did I observe or learn about the child?" These objective, descriptive statements may come from any source of data collection used during the study. For example, you may have noticed that the child uses the pincer grasp to pick up small objects and that this newly developed skill has influenced his interest in finger food. This fine motor skill needs additional exploration, which is answered with *how* questions.

- ❏ How does the child use the pincer grasp?
- ❏ How was the information gained?
- ❏ How does this skill influence other areas of development?
- ❏ Are the child's movements purposeful?
- ❏ What contributed to the development of the skill?

2. *Relate concept development to theories.* The next question to address is to what theory you attribute the behaviors that you have observed or to whom—which theorist. For example, perhaps the three-year-old subject of your child study has been drawing cars with two wheels under the squarish representation of the automobile body and two wheels on what seems to be the automobile roof. When questioned about the placement of the wheels the three-year-old quite obviously states, "Cars have four wheels." You may relate this to ideas about perspective put forth by Piaget.

3. *Support observations and predictions with documentation.* The last question to ask when writing the child study reports is *why*. Why are the observations and theory

you have outlined important to the child's development? All recommendations and predictions should be supported with documentation. The writer reflects on what was
learned about the child, how that relates to theory, and what implications the child study
data has for curricular development. Child studies are a good way to develop plans for
further assessment, instruction, or intervention. With the aid of careful documentation
the developmental summary should explore all of these possibilities, ultimately providing the reader with a comprehensive plan to support the child's further development.

Questions to Consider When Writing the Child Study Domain Reports

- *What* exactly did the child say and do?
- *How* did the child do the things that were observed?
- *Who*—whose theory did you select to support developmental observations?
- *Why*—interpret and reflect on the child's development in context and relate observations
  to cultural influences.

ORGANIZATION

It is helpful to arrange all data, anecdotal records, checklists, structured play experiences,
visual documentation, parent questionnaires, and background history in an organized
manner as you prepare to write the child study reports. Read over the anecdotal records
and make index cards for each record, coded for a specific domain. For example, if all
notes regarding cognitive development are coded yellow, create index cards for each of
the yellow entries. Organizing notes in this manner provides a snapshot of a particular
domain and makes writing reports easier. Reviewing all documentation for a specific domain, making notes regarding the child's development in the domain, and creating an
outline following the *what, how, who,* and *why* questions discussed in the box facilitates
the writing of the child study reports.

The best way to organize large amounts of information is in a neat and easily read-
able outline. Even if you are not a good note taker, outlines can help you to organize your
thoughts. There are two basic types of outlines, a topic outline and a formal outline.

Topic Outline

A topic outline is used when there is an obvious and natural connection between ideas.
A sample might look like this:

1. Introduction
2. Give background history of the child
3. Display an overview of the child study
4. Briefly state the concluding intent
5. Body
6. Describe elements of the child's development

7. Support developmental observations with documentation
8. Relate developmental observations to theory
9. Conclusion
10. Reflect on child's development, including the strengths and weaknesses of the study
11. Provide recommendations for curriculum development or further inquiry

Formal Outline

Formal outlines are organized using numbers and letters to signify the main point and following or subordinate points of an essay. Formal outlines can improve the focus of an essay. There are many ways to organize the ideas of the child study report. Remaining flexible will help to create an interesting and accurate report. An annotated sample of a formal outline follows.

I. Main Idea: Child study overview
   A. Subordinate Idea: Learning about child from history
   B. Subordinate Idea: Learning about child from observation
   C. Subordinate Idea: Learning about child from assessments
      1. Supporting Detail: Checklists
      2. Supporting Detail: Structured play
      3. Supporting Detail: Visual documentation
II. Main Idea: Learning about child from history
   A. Subordinate idea: This child's background
      1. Supporting Detail: Health history
         a. Immunizations
         b. Growth
         c. Accidents
      2. Supporting Detail: Education history
      3. Supporting Detail: Parenting history

Good organization will help in the composition of a comprehensive, informative summary and reflection of the development of a single child. Table 15–1 is an example of a rubric used to evaluate and grade reports covering a child's developmental domains. The table is arranged so that aspects of the five developmental domains—cognitive, language, motor, social, and emotional—are organized to reflect the child's unique development, progress toward developmental universals, and the context in which development occurs. The rubric can be adapted and changed to reflect course content. For example, Arnold Gesell is not listed on the sample rubric but developmental sequences or milestones are often discussed in child development courses and therefore could be included in the student's developmental report. Also, students can select from the rubric developmental concepts they wish to include in the developmental summaries. Developmental concepts listed don't apply to every subject of a child study. For example, the cognitive

TABLE 15–1 Rubric for the Reports Covering Developmental Domains

	Unique	Universal	Context	Score
	(Characteristics unique to the individual child's development in each domain)	*(Characteristics of the child's development that are typical and closely match theoretical suppositions)*	*(Characteristics of the child's development that are influenced by the child's culture, ethnicity, religion, family, education, socioeconomic status, etc.)*	1-10 **possible**
Cognitive	Students should address the following concepts in regard to the child's individual development: Memory ___ Adaptation ___ Assimilation ___ Accommodation ___ Object permanence ___ Goal-directed behavior ___ Play ___ Egocentrism ___ Theory of mind ___ Metacognition ___ Special needs ___	Students should address the following theoretical base in relationship to the individual child's development: Piaget's theory ___ Information processing ___ Visual cliff ___ Vygotsky ___ Gardner ___	Students should address the following concepts in regard to the child's ecological system: Affordances ___ Bronfenbrenner ___ Meaningful learning ___	
Language	Students should address the following concepts in regard to the child's individual development: Means of communication ___ Vocabulary ___ Naming explosion ___ Holophrases ___ Fast mapping ___ Grammar ___ Receptive language ___ Expressive language ___ Code ___ switching ___ Reading ___ Writing ___ Special needs ___	Students should address the following theoretical base in relationship to the individual child's development: Chomsky ___ Skinner ___ Vygotsky ___ Sensitive period ___ Critical period ___	Students should address the following concepts in regard to the child's ecological system: Native language ___ Bilingualism ___ Parental involvement ___ Social economic status ___ Bronfenbrenner ___	

Motor

Students should address the following concepts in regard to the child's individual development:

Body size ___ Sleep patterns ___ Eating habits ___ Chronic illness ___ Special needs ___ Senses ___ Reflexes ___ Perception ___ Gross motor skills ___ Fine motor skills ___ Balance ___ Spatial awareness ___ Temporal awareness ___ Body awareness ___ Activity level ___ Special needs ___

Students should address the following norms in relationship to the individual child's development:

Growth chart norms ___ Typical skills norms ___ Sleep norms ___ Gender variations ___ Assessment report ___

Students should address the following concepts in regard to the child's ecological system:

Health care ___ Nutrition ___ Environmental health issues ___ Sleep arrangements ___ Exposure to toys and materials to enhance motor skills ___ Hereditary/Genetic concerns ___ Cultural expectations ___ Safety ___ Bronfenbrenner ___

Social

Social referencing ___ Self awareness ___ Sense of self ___ Gender identification ___ Peers ___ Friendship ___ Prosocial behaviors ___ Empathy ___ Aggression ___ Moral reasoning ___ Special needs ___

Stage of social play ___ Bandura ___ Freud and gender ___ Behaviorism ___ Kohlberg ___ Gilligan ___

Social referencing ___ Bronfenbrenner ___ Child care ___ Gender roles ___ Expectations of child ___ Media influence ___ Parenting styles ___ Influence of war ___ Morality ___ Values ___ Traditions ___

Emotional

Temperament ___ Attachment ___ Emotional regulation ___ Self expression ___ Special needs ___

Emergence of emotions ___ Stranger wariness ___ Separation anxiety ___ Erikson ___

Ainsworth ___ Bronfenbrenner ___ Family structure ___ Parenting styles ___ Child care ___ Cultural attitudes ___ developmental summary for a four-year-old would not include information regarding object permanence. You may also wish to include creativity as a developmental domain for the grading rubric requiring six reports of the child's development. Each child's development is unique, so evidence of individual development, discussion of universal milestones, and consideration of developmental context will differ from study to study.

The rubric aids in grading the reports and provides specific feedback for the student. Recording the grade directly on the rubric leaves the student's work clean so that he or she can share with the child's family.

QUESTIONS TO CONSIDER ○ ○ ○

1. Think about developmental and learning theories discussed in this text. Which theory do you most support? When reviewing documentation collected for the child study, can you identify any one theory that informed the way you viewed the child? Explain.

2. Consider the family members of the subject of your child study. Do you think that they will agree with your impressions of the child's development? In what ways are the family's ideas about the child likely to agree with your own? In what ways are they likely to differ?

3. Think about all of the documentation that you collected for the child study. What technique provided the most information regarding the child's development? What technique was least helpful? What sort of information did you gain from the anecdotal records, checklists, structured play observation, visual documentation, parent questionnaire, background history? How did these techniques help you to understand the child's development?

REFERENCES ○ ○ ○

Boehrer, J. (1990). Teaching with cases: Learning to question. *New Directions for Teaching and Learning, 42,* 41–57.

Bronfenbrenner, U. (1979). *The ecology of human development: Experiments by nature and design.* Cambridge, MA: Harvard University Press.

Bronfenbrenner, U. (Ed.). (2004). *Making human beings human: Bioecological perspectives on human development.* Thousand Oaks, CA: Sage.

Guilmet, G. M. (1979). Maternal perceptions of urban Navajo and Caucasian children's classroom behavior. *Human Organization, 38,* 87–91.

Jessor, R., & Colby, A. (Eds.). (1996). *Ethnography and human development: Context and meaning in social inquiry.* Chicago: University of Chicago Press.

National Association for the Education of Young Children (NAEYC) (Producer). (1998). *Tools for teaching developmentally appropriate practice: The leading edge in early childhood education* [Videotape]. (Available from the National Association for the Education of Young Children, 1509 16th Street N.W., Washington, DC 20036.)

Preparing and Presenting the Child Study

CHAPTER OBJECTIVES

- To organize and complete the child study
- To reflect on the child study process
- To integrate the child study process into teaching practice

CHILD STUDY OBJECTIVES

Upon conclusion of the chapter the student will:

- organize all child study documents into one unit.

INTRODUCTION TO ORGANIZATION

Congratulations! By now you have completed all the pieces of a valid child study and it is time to prepare it for presentation to parents and consulting professionals (in this case, probably your instructor).

Consider the organization and preparation of the child study to be a very important final step. You have worked very hard on this project and all your efforts deserve recognition. This is a large body of work and in order for it to be accessible and functional the organization is a key to its value. Each individual who looks at this work must be able to compare with developmental milestones and cross-reference the examples that go along with your interpretations. Therefore, making sure that every piece of information is labeled and placed in a logical order is critical.

STEPS IN ORGANIZING THE CHILD STUDY

1. *Gather all the pieces that have been completed.* The pieces of the child study include:

   ➢ Five to eight coded anecdotals

   ➢ Two completed checklists for each domain of development (two for cognitive, two for social, two for emotional, two for creativity, two for fine motor and two for gross motor, and two for language/literacy)

   ➢ One completed structured observation for each domain of development (six in all)

   ➢ As many pieces of visual documentation as you have gathered (pictures of children, work samples, audio recordings, etc.)

   ➢ Completed background history, including the parent interview

   ➢ One report for each domain of development (six in all)

2. *Next, decide how you would like to organize the pieces.* Most people will choose to organize it in one of two ways. The first way is to simply put all the like pieces together—all the anecdotes together in one section, all the checklists together, and so on. The second way requires you to separate all the pieces into the domains of development. So all the cognitive pieces of the study would go together in one section, all the social pieces in a section, and so on. Either way is acceptable. However, if this is to be used with families, separating by developmental domain is the recommended approach.

3. *Gather the necessary materials to put it all together.* Figure 16–1 gives a list of required and suggested materials.

Finally, you can put the whole child study together; it is now ready for you to present to parents or other professionals. Figure 16–2 contains an evaluation checklist for the completed child study.

FIGURE 16–1   Required and suggested materials for presenting the child study.

Materials for Presentation of the Child Study

➤ Binder (required). Some may say that an expandable file is just as good, but getting to the materials and cross-referencing becomes difficult if you have to pull out every piece. Also, make sure to get a binder that is large enough so that when the pages are being turned each one stays on the rings.

➤ Tabs (required). In order for the information to be accessible, each section must be identified. One must have the capability to turn to any section at any time. Each section needs to be labeled. Dividers between the sections are a good idea, as well.

➤ Plastic sheet protectors (optional). In order to keep the documentation protected for future reference or for your own portfolio, plastic sheet protectors are recommended. It may be that the only pieces that go into the protectors are the visual documentation such as drawings, writing, paintings, and pictures, which can otherwise get damaged.

➤ Computer-generated cover sheets and/or section dividers (optional). Some people like to get creative with their child studies. Making an interesting cover or dividers is where this can enter in.

Note: It is not recommended to put the child's picture on the cover. Remember, this is a confidential piece of work and putting the child's picture on the cover openly displays the child.

➤ Tools for putting it together (some are required). To assemble the report you need things like tape, scissors, hole punchers, and a stapler.

FIGURE 16–2   Grading rubric for the child study.   ● ● ●

Areas of Child Study	Your Points/Possible Points
Anecdotals	_____/_____
Tools of Observation	_____/_____
Tests of Observation	_____/_____
Reports on Domains	_____/_____
Background Information	_____/_____
Visual Documentation	_____/_____
Presentation of Paper (organization)	_____/_____
Child Study Due Date: _____	_____/=_____

QUESTIONS TO CONSIDER ○ ○ ○

1. After completing a child study, how might a teacher use it? List at least three ways.

2. Identify ways to modify the child study techniques to use with an entire class.

3. Describe how you might share the child study with colleagues, peers, and parents.

Index

Page numbers followed by a "t" or "f" indicate that the entry is included in a table or figure.

Under-responsive children, 110
Universal characteristics, 289–290
Use-dependent development, 171

V

Validity, 29, 31
Verb tense, 197–198
Verification, 224, 225t
Vestibular system, 110
Vicarious learning, 265
Video recordings, 58f
Violence, 170–171
Vision development, 93
Visual documentation
    advantages, 61–62
    art for at-risk children, 67–68
    developmental significance, 62–65
    forms, 57–58f
    purpose, 59
    Reggio Emilia educational approach, 60–61

    storage, 67
    systematic gathering technique, 65–67
Visual-spatial intelligence, 266t
Vocabulary spurts, 194
Vygotsky, L., 258–262

W

Wait time, 48
Work samples, 57f, 62–66
Writing, children's. *See also* Literacy development
    components, 204–205
    development, 205–210, 217t
    fine motor development, 106, 107t
    overview, 204
    purpose, 204
    work samples, 63–65

Z

Zone of proximal development, 258–260